LINQ TO OBJECTS USING C# 4.0

LINQ to Objects Using C# 4.0

Using and Extending LINQ to Objects and Parallel LINQ (PLINQ)

Troy Magennis

⋏⋏ Addison-Wesley

Upper Saddle River, NJ • Boston • Indianapolis • San Francisco
New York • Toronto • Montreal • London • Munich • Paris • Madrid
Capetown • Sydney • Tokyo • Singapore • Mexico City

Many of the designations used by manufacturers and sellers to distinguish their products are claimed as trademarks. Where those designations appear in this book, and the publisher was aware of a trademark claim, the designations have been printed with initial capital letters or in all capitals.

The author and publisher have taken care in the preparation of this book, but make no expressed or implied warranty of any kind and assume no responsibility for errors or omissions. No liability is assumed for incidental or consequential damages in connection with or arising out of the use of the information or programs contained herein.

The publisher offers excellent discounts on this book when ordered in quantity for bulk purchases or special sales, which may include electronic versions and/or custom covers and content particular to your business, training goals, marketing focus, and branding interests. For more information, please contact:

U.S. Corporate and Government Sales
(800) 382-3419
corpsales@pearsontechgroup.com

For sales outside the United States please contact:

International Sales
international@pearson.com

Visit us on the Web: informit.com/aw

Library of Congress Cataloging-in-Publication Data:

Magennis, Troy, 1970-
 LINQ to objects using C# 4.0 : using and extending LINQ to objects and parallel LINQ (PLINQ) / Troy Magennis.
   p. cm.
 Includes bibliographical references and index.
 ISBN 978-0-321-63700-0 (pbk. : alk. paper) 1. Microsoft LINQ. 2. Query languages (Computer science) 3. C#
(Computer program language) 4. Microsoft .NET Framework. I. Title.
 QA76.73.L228M345 2010
 006.7'882—dc22
                    2009049530

Pearson Education, Inc.
Rights and Contracts Department
501 Boylston Street, Suite 900
Boston, MA 02116
Fax (617) 671 3447

ISBN-13: 978-0-321-63700-0
ISBN-10: 0-321-63700-3

Text printed in the United States on recycled paper at RR Donnelly in Crawfordsville, Indiana.

First printing March 2010

To my wife, Janet Doherty, for allowing me to spend those extra hours tapping away on the keyboard; thank you for your support and love.

CONTENTS

FOREWORD

I have worked in the software industry for more than 15 years, the last four years as CIO of Sabre Holdings and the prior four as CTO of Travelocity. At Sabre, on top of our large online presence through Travelocity, we transact $70 billion in annual gross travel sales through our network and serve over 200 airline customers worldwide. On a given day, we will process over 700 million transactions and handle 32,000 transactions per second at peak. Working with massive streams of data is what we do, and finding better ways to work with this data and improve throughput is my role as CIO.

Troy is our VP over Architecture at Travelocity, where I have the pleasure of watching his influence on a daily basis. His perspective on current and future problems and depth of detail are observed in his architectural decisions, and you will find this capability very evident in this book on the subject of LINQ and PLINQ.

Developer productivity is a critical aspect for every IT solution-based business, and Troy emphasizes this in every chapter of his book. Languages and language features are a means to an end, and language features like LINQ offer key advances in developer productivity. By simplifying all types of data manipulation by adding SQL-style querying within the core .NET development languages, developers can focus on solving business problems rather than learning a new query language for every data source type. Beyond developer productivity, the evolution in technology from individual processor speed improvements to multi-core processors opened up a big hole in run-time productivity as much of today's software lacks investment in parallelism required to better utilize these new processors. Microsoft's investment in Parallel LINQ addresses this hole, enabling much higher utilization of today's hardware platforms.

Open-standards and open-frameworks are essential in the software industry. I'm pleased to see that Microsoft has approached C# and LINQ in an open and inclusive way, by handing C# over as an ECMA/ISO standard, allowing everyone to develop new LINQ data-sources and to extend the LINQ query language operators to suit their needs. This approach showcases the traits of many successful open-source initiatives and demonstrates the competitive advantages openness offers.

Decreasing the ramp-up speed for developers to write and exploit the virtues of many-core processors is extremely important in today's world and will have a very big impact in technology companies that operate at the scale of Sabre. Exposing common concurrent patterns at a language level offers the best way to allow current applications to scale safely and efficiently as core-count increases. While it was always possible for a small percentage of developers to reliably code concurrency through OpenMP or hand-rolled multi-threading frameworks, parallel LINQ allows developers to take advantage of many-core scalability with far fewer concerns (thread synchronization, data segmentation, merging results, for example). This approach will allow companies to scale this capability across a much higher percentage of developers without losing focus on quality. So roll up your sleeves and enjoy the read!

—Barry Vandevier
Chief Information Officer, Sabre Holdings

PREFACE

LINQ to Objects Using C# 4.0 takes a different approach to the subject of Language Integrated Query (LINQ). This book focuses on the LINQ syntax and working with in-memory collections rather than focusing on replacing other database technologies. The beauty of LINQ is that once you master the syntax and concepts behind how to compose clever queries, the underlying data source is mostly irrelevant. That's not to say that technologies such as LINQ to SQL, LINQ to XML, and LINQ to Entities are un-important; they are just not covered in this book.

Much of the material for this book was written during late 2006 when Language Integrated Query (LINQ) was in its earliest preview period. I was lucky enough to have a window of time to learn a new technology when LINQ came along. It became clear that beyond the clever data access abilities being demonstrated (DLINQ at the time, LINQ to SQL eventually), LINQ to Objects would have the most impact on the day-to-day developers' life. Working with in-memory collections of data is one of the more common tasks performed, and looking through code in my previous projects made it clear just how complex my for-loops and nested if-condition statements had evolved. LINQ and the language enhancements being proposed were going to change the look and feel of the way we programmed, and from where I was sitting that was fantastic.

The initial exploration was published on the HookedOnLINQ.com Wiki (120 odd pages at that time), and the traffic grew over the next year or two to a healthy level. Material could have been pulled together for a publication at that time (and been first to market with a book on this subject, something my Addison-Wesley editor will probably never forgive me for), but I felt knowing the syntax and the raw operators wasn't a book worth reading. It was critical to know how LINQ works in the real world and how to use it on real projects before I put that material into ink. The first round of books for any new programming technology often go slightly deeper than the online-documentation, and I wanted to wait and see how the LINQ story unfolded in real-world applications and write the first book of the second-generation—the book that isn't just reference, but has integrity that only real-world application can ingrain.

The LINQ story is a lot deeper and has wider impact than most people realize at first glance of any TechEd session recording or user-group presentation. The ability to store and pass code as a data structure and to control when and how that code is executed builds a powerful platform for working with all matter of data sources. The few LINQ providers shipped by Microsoft are just the start, and many more are being built by the community through the extension points provided. After mastering the LINQ syntax and understanding the operators' use (and how to avoid misuse), any developer can work more effectively and write cleaner code. This is the purpose of this book: to assist the reader in beginning the journey, to introduce how to use LINQ for more real-world examples and to dive a little deeper than most books on the subject, to explore the performance benefits of one solution over another, and to deeply look at how to create custom operators for any specific purpose.

I hope you agree after reading this book that it does offer an insight into how to use LINQ to Objects on real projects and that the examples go a step further in explaining the patterns that make LINQ an integral part of day-to-day programming from this day forward.

Who Should Read This Book

The audience for this book is primarily developers who write their applications in C# and want to understand how to employ and extend the features of LINQ to Objects. LINQ to Objects is a wide set of technology pieces that work in tandem to make working with in-memory data sources easier and more powerful. This book covers both the initial C# 3.0 implementation of LINQ and the updates in C# 4.0. If you are accustomed to the LINQ syntax, this book goes deeper than most LINQ reference publication and delves into areas of performance and how to write custom LINQ operators (either as sequential algorithms or using parallel algorithms to improve performance).

If you are a beginning C# developer (or new to C# 3.0 or 4.0), this book introduces the code changes and syntax so that you can quickly master working with objects and collections of objects using LINQ. I've tried to strike a balance and not jump directly into examples before covering the basics. You obviously should know how to build a LINQ query statement before you start to write your own custom sequential or parallel operators to determine the number of mountain peaks around the world that are taller than 8,000 meters (26,000 feet approximately). But you will get to that in the latter chapters.

Overview of the Book

LINQ to Objects Using C# 4.0 starts by introducing the intention and benefits LINQ offers developers in general. Chapter 1, "Introducing LINQ," talks to the motivation and basic concepts LINQ introduces to the world of writing .NET applications. Specifically, this chapter introduces before and after code makeovers to demonstrate LINQ's ability to simplify coding problems. This is the first and only chapter that talks about LINQ to SQL and LINQ to XML and does this to demonstrate how multiple LINQ data sources can be used from the one query syntax and how this powerful concept will change application development. This chapter concludes by listing the wider benefits of embracing LINQ and attempts to build the big picture view of what LINQ actually is, a more complex task than it might first seem.

Chapter 2, "Introducing LINQ to Objects," begins exploring the underlying enabling language features that are necessary to understand how the LINQ language syntax compiles. A fast-paced, brief overview of LINQ's features wraps up this chapter; it doesn't cover any of them in depth but just touches on the syntax and capabilities that are covered at length in future chapters.

Chapter 3, "Writing Basic Queries," introduces reading and writing LINQ queries in C# and covers the basics of choosing what data to project, in what format to select that data, and in what order the final result should be placed. By the end of this chapter, each reader should be able to read the intention behind most queries and be able to write simple queries that filter, project, and order data from in-memory collections.

Chapter 4, "Grouping and Joining Data," covers the more advanced features of grouping data in a collection and combining multiple data sources. These partitioning and relational style queries can be structured and built in many ways, and this chapter describes in depth when and why to use one grouping or joining syntax over another.

Chapter 5, "Standard Query Operators," lists the many additional standard operators that can be used in a LINQ query. LINQ has over 50 operators, and this chapter covers the operators that go beyond those covered in the previous chapters.

Chapter 6, "Working with Set Data," explores working with set-based operators. There are multiple ways of performing set operations over in-memory collections, and this chapter explores the merits and pitfalls of both.

Chapter 7, "Extending LINQ to Objects," discusses the art of building custom operators. The examples covered in this chapter demonstrate how to build any of the four main types of operators and includes the common coding and error-handling patterns to employ in order to closely match the built-in operators Microsoft supplies.

Chapter 8, "C# 4.0 Features," is where the additional C# 4.0 language features are introduced with particular attention to how they extend the LINQ to Objects story. This chapter demonstrates how to use the dynamic language features to make LINQ queries more fluent to read and write and how to combine LINQ with COM-Interop in order to use other applications as data sources (for example, Microsoft Excel).

Chapter 9, "Parallel LINQ to Objects," closely examines the motivation and art of building application code that can support multi-core processor machines. Not all queries will see a performance improvement, and this chapter discusses the expectations and likely improvement most queries will see. This chapter concludes with an example of writing a custom parallel operator to demonstrate the thinking process that goes into correctly coding parallel extensions in addition to those provided.

Conventions

There is significant code listed in this book. It is an unavoidable fact for books about programming language features that they must demonstrate those features with code samples. It was always my intention to show lots of examples, and every chapter has dozens of code listings. To help ease the burden, I followed some common typography conventions to make them more readable. References to classes, variables, and other code entities are distinguished in a `monospace` font. Short code listings that are to be read inline with the surrounding text are also presented in a `monospace` font, but on their own lines, and they sometimes contain code comments (lines beginning with `//` characters) for clarity.

```
// With line-breaks added for clarity
var result = nums
            .Where(n => n < 5)

            .OrderBy (n => n);
```

Longer listings for examples that are too big to be inline with the text or samples I specifically wanted to provide in the sample download project are shown using a similar `monospace` font, but they are denoted by a listing number and a short description, as in the following example, Listing 3-2.

Listing 3-2   Simple query using the Query Expression syntax

```
List<Contact> contacts = Contact.SampleData();

var q = from c in contacts
        where c.State == "WA"
        orderby c.LastName, c.FirstName
        select c;

foreach (Contact c in q)
    Console.WriteLine("{0} {1}",
        c.FirstName, c.LastName);
```

Each example should be simple and consistent. For simplicity, most examples write their results out to the Console window. To capture these results in this book, they are listed in the same font and format as code listings, but identified with an output number, as shown in Output 3-1.

Output 3-1

```
Stewart Kagel
Chance Lard
Armando Valdes
```

Sample data for the queries is listed in tables, for example, Table 2-2. Each column maps to an object property of a similar legal name for queries to operate on.

Words in **bold** in normal text are defined in the Glossary, and only the first occurrence of the word gets this treatment. When a `bold monospace` font in code is used, it is to draw your attention to a particular key point being explained at that time and is most often used when an example evolves over multiple iterations.

Sample Download Code and Updates

All of the samples listed in the book and further reference material can be found at the companion website, the HookedOnLINQ.com reference wiki and website at http://hookedonlinq.com/LINQBook.ashx.

Some examples required a large sample data source and the Geonames database of worldwide geographic place names and data. These data files can be downloaded from http://www.geonames.org/ and specifically the http://download.geonames.org/export/dump/allCountries.zip file. This file should be downloaded and placed in the same folder as the executable sample application is running from to successfully run those specific samples that parse and query this source.

Choice of Language

I chose to write the samples in this book using the C# language because including both C# and VB.Net example code would have bloated the number of pages beyond what would be acceptable. There is no specific reason why the examples couldn't have been in any other .NET language that supports LINQ.

System Requirements

This book was written with the code base of .NET 4 and Visual Studio 2010 over the course of various beta versions and several community technical previews. The code presented in this book runs with Beta 2. If the release copy of Visual Studio 2010 and .NET 4 changes between this book publication and release, errata and updated code examples will be posted on the companion website at http://hookedonlinq.com/LINQBook.ashx.

To run the samples available from the book's companion website, you will need to have Visual Studio 2010 installed on your machine. If you don't have access to a commercial copy of Visual Studio 2010, Microsoft has a freely downloadable version (Visual Studio 2010 Express Edition), which is capable of running all examples shown in this book. You can download this edition from http://www.microsoft.com/express/.

ACKNOWLEDGMENTS

It takes a team to develop this type of book, and I want our team members to know how appreciated their time, ideas, and effort have been. This team effort is what sets blogging apart from publishing, and I fully acknowledge the team at Addison-Wesley, in particular my editors Joan Murray and Olivia Basegio for their patience and wisdom.

To my technical reviewers, Nick Paldino, Derik Whittaker, Steve Danielson, Peter Ritchie, and Tanzim Saqib—thank you for your insights and suggestions to improve accuracy and clarity. Each of you had major impact on the text and code examples contained in this book.

Some material throughout this book, at least in spirit, was obtained by reading the many blog postings from Microsoft staff and skilled individuals from our industry. In particular I'd like to thank the various contributors to the Parallel FX team blog (http://blogs.msdn.com/pfxteam/), notably Igor Ostrovsky (strongly influenced my approach to aggregations), Ed Essey (helped me understand the different partitioning schemes used in PLINQ), and Stephen Toub. Stephen Toub also has my sincere thanks for giving feedback on the Parallel LINQ chapter during its development (Chapter 9), which dramatically improved the content accuracy and depth.

I would also like to acknowledge founders and contributors to Geonames.org (http://geonames.org), whose massive set of geographic data is available for free download under creative commons attribution license. This data is used in Chapter 9 to test PLINQ performance on large data sets.

Editing isn't easy, and I'd like to acknowledge the patience and great work of Anne Goebel and Chrissy White in making my words flow from post-tech review to production. I know there are countless other staff who touched this book in its final stages of production, and although I don't know your names, thank you.

Finally, I'd like to acknowledge readers like you for investing your time to gain a deeper understanding of LINQ to Objects. I hope after reading it you agree that this book offers valuable insights on how to use LINQ to Objects in real projects and that the examples go that step further in explaining the patterns that make LINQ an integral part of day-to-day programming from this day forward. Thank you.

ABOUT THE AUTHOR

Troy Magennis is a Microsoft Visual C# MVP, an award given to industry participants who dedicate time and effort to educating others about the virtues of technology choices and industry application.

A keen traveler, Troy currently works for Travelocity, which manages the travel and leisure websites travelocity.com, lastminute.com, and zuji. As vice president of Architecture, he leads a talented team of architects spread across four continents committed to being the traveler's companion.

Technology has always been a passion for Troy. After cutting his teeth on early 8-bit personal computers (Vic20s, Commodore 64s), he moved into electronics engineering, which later led to positions in software application development and architecture for some of the most prominent corporations in automotive, banking, and online commerce.

Troy's first exposure to LINQ was in 2006 when he took a sabbatical to learn it and became hooked, ultimately leading him to publish the popular HookedOnLINQ website.

CHAPTER 1

INTRODUCING LINQ

Goals of this chapter:

- Define "Language Integrated Query" (LINQ) and why it was built.
- Define the various components that make up LINQ.
- Demonstrate how LINQ improves existing code.

This chapter introduces LINQ—from Microsoft's design goals to how it improves the code we write for data access-based applications. By the end of this chapter, you will understand why LINQ was built, what components makeup the LINQ family, and LINQ's advantages over previous technologies. And you get a chance to see the LINQ syntax at work while reviewing some before and after code makeovers.

Although this book is primarily about LINQ to Objects, it is important to have an understanding of the full scope and goals of all LINQ technologies in order to make better design and coding decisions.

What Is LINQ?

Language Integrated Query, or LINQ for short (pronounced "link"), is a set of **Microsoft .NET Framework** language enhancements and libraries built by Microsoft to make working with data (for example, a collection of in-memory objects, rows from a database table, or elements in an XML file) simpler and more intuitive. LINQ provides a layer of programming abstraction between .NET languages and an ever-growing number of underlying data sources.

Why is this so inviting to developers? In general, although there are many existing programming interfaces to access and manipulate different sources of data, many of these interfaces use a specific language or syntax of their own. If applications access and manipulate data (as most do), LINQ allows developers to query data using similar **C#** (or **Visual**

Basic.NET [VB.NET]) language syntax independent of the source of that data. This means that whereas today different languages are used when querying data from different sources (**Transact-SQL** for **Microsoft SQL Server** development, **XPath** or **XQuery** for XML data, and code nested for/if statements when querying in-memory collections), LINQ allows you to use C# (or VB.Net) in a consistent type-safe and compile-time syntax checked way.

One of Microsoft's first public whitepapers on the LINQ technology, "LINQ Project Overview"[1] authored by Don Box and Anders Hejlsberg, set the scene as to the problem the way they see it and how they planned to solve that problem with LINQ.

> After two decades, the industry has reached a stable point in the evolution of object-oriented (OO) programming technologies. Programmers now take for granted features like classes, objects, and methods. In looking at the current and next generation of technologies, it has become apparent that the next big challenge in programming technology is to reduce the complexity of accessing and integrating information that is not natively defined using OO technology. The two most common sources of non-OO information are relational databases and XML.

> Rather than add relational or XML-specific features to our programming languages and runtime, with the LINQ project we have taken a more general approach and are adding general purpose query facilities to the .NET Framework that apply to all sources of information, not just relational or XML data. This facility is called .NET Language Integrated Query (LINQ).

> We use the term language integrated query to indicate that query is an integrated feature of the developer's primary programming languages (e.g., C#, Visual Basic). Language integrated query allows query expressions to benefit from the rich metadata, compile-time syntax checking, static typing and IntelliSense that was previously available only to imperative code. Language integrated query also allows a single general-purpose declarative query facility to be applied to all in-memory information, not just information from external sources.

A single sentence pitch describing the principles of LINQ is simply: LINQ normalizes language and syntax for writing queries against many sources, allowing developers to avoid having to learn and master many different **domain-specific languages (DSLs)** and development environments to retrieve and manipulate data from different sources.

LINQ has simple goals on the surface, but it has massive impact on the way programs are written now and how they will be written in the future. A foundational piece of LINQ technology (although not directly used when executing LINQ to Object queries) is a feature that can turn C# and VB.Net code into a data-structure. This intermediate data-structure called an expression tree, although not covered in this book, allows code to be converted into a data structure that can be processed at runtime and be used to generate statements for a specific domain query language, such as pure SQL statements for example. This layer of abstraction between developer coding language, and a domain-specific query language and execution runtime, allows an almost limitless ability for LINQ to expand as new sources of data emerge or new ways to optimize access to existing data sources come into reality.

The (Almost) Current LINQ Story

The current LINQ family of technologies and concepts allows an extensible set of operators that work over structured data, independent of how that data is stored or retrieved. The generalized architecture of the technology also allows the LINQ concepts to be expanded to almost any data domain or technology.

The loosely coupled product names that form the marketed LINQ family can distract from the true story. Each specific flavor of LINQ carries out its own underlying query mechanism and features that often aren't LINQ-specific, but they all eventually build and converge into a standard C# or VB.Net programming query interface for data—hence, these products get the LINQ moniker. The following list of Microsoft-specific products and technologies form the basis of what features currently constitute LINQ. This list doesn't even begin to cover the community efforts contributing to the overall LINQ story and is intended to just broadly outline the current scope:

- LINQ Language Compiler Enhancements
  - C# 3.0 and C# 4.0; New language constructs in C# to support writing queries (these often build on groundwork laid in C# 2.0, namely generics, iterators, and anonymous methods)
  - VB.Net 9; New language constructs in VB.Net to support writing queries
  - A mechanism for storing code as a data structure and a way to convert user code into this data structure (called an *expression tree*)

- A mechanism for passing the data structure containing user code to a query implementation engine (like LINQ to SQL, which converts code expressions into Transact SQL, Microsoft SQL Server's native language)
- LINQ to Objects
  - A set of standard query operators for working with in-memory data (normally any collection implementing the `IEnumerable<T>` interface) using LINQ language syntax
- LINQ to XML
  - A new API for creating, importing, and working with XML data
  - A set of query operators for working with XML data using LINQ language syntax
- LINQ to Entities (part of the Entity Framework)
  - A mechanism for connecting to any **ADO.Net**-enabled data source to support the Entity Framework features
  - A set of query operators for querying any ADO.Net Entity Framework-enabled data source
- LINQ to SQL (Microsoft has chosen to focus on the LINQ to Entities API predominately going forward; this API will be maintained but not expanded in features with any vigor.)
  - A set of query operators for working the SQL Server data using LINQ language syntax
  - A mechanism that SQL data can be retrieved from SQL Server and represented as in-memory data
  - An in-memory data change tracking mechanism to support adding, deleting, and updating records safely in a SQL database
  - A class library for creating, deleting, and manipulating databases in SQL Server
- Parallel Extensions to .NET and Parallel LINQ (PLINQ)
  - A library to assist in writing multi-threaded applications that utilize all processor cores available, called the Task Parallel Library (TPL)
  - Implementations of the standard query operators that fully utilize concurrent operations across multiple cores, called Parallel LINQ
- LINQ to Datasets
  - Query language over typed and untyped DataSets
  - A mechanism for using LINQ in current DataSet-based applications without rewriting using LINQ to SQL
  - A set of extensions to the DataRow and DataTable that allow to and from LINQ sequence support (for full details see http://msdn.microsoft.com/en-us/library/bb387004.aspx)

This list may be out of date and incomplete by the time you read this book. Microsoft has exposed many extension points, and both Microsoft and third parties are adding to the LINQ story all the time. These same extension points form the basis of Microsoft's specific implementations; LINQ to SQL for instance is built upon the same interface that is available for any developer to extend upon. This openness ensures that the open-source community, Microsoft, and even its competitors have equal footing to embrace LINQ and its essence—the one query language to rule them all.

LINQ Code Makeover—Before and After Code Examples

The following examples demonstrate the approach to a coding problem both with and without using LINQ. These examples offer insight into how current coding practices are changed with the introduction of language-supported query constructs. The intention of these examples is to help you understand how LINQ will change the approach to working with data from different sources, and although you may not fully understand the LINQ syntax at this time, the following chapters cover this gap in understanding.

LINQ to Objects—Grouping and Sorting Contact Records

The first scenario to examine is one in which a set of customer records in a `List<Contact>` collection are grouped by their State (states ordered alphabetically), and each contact ordered alphabetically by the contact's last name.

C# 2.0 Approach

Listing 1-1 shows the code required to sort and group an in-memory collection of the type `Contact`. It makes use of the new features of C# 2.0, being inline **Delegates** and Generic types. Its approach is to first sort the collection by the `LastName` property using a comparison delegate, and then it groups the collection by `State` property in a `SortedDictionary` collection.

NOTE   All of the code displayed in the listings in this book is available for download from http://hookedonlinq.com/LINQBook.ashx. The example application is fully self-contained and allows each example to be run and browsed while you read along with the book.

Listing 1-1   C# 2.0 code for grouping and sorting contact records—see Output 1-1

```csharp
List<Contact> contacts = Contact.SampleData();

// sort by last name
contacts.Sort(
    delegate(Contact c1, Contact c2)
    {
        if (c1 != null && c2 != null)
            return string.Compare(
                c1.LastName, c2.LastName);

        return 0;
    }
);

// sort and group by state (using a sorted dictionary)
SortedDictionary<string, List<Contact>> groups =
    new SortedDictionary<string, List<Contact>>();

foreach (Contact c in contacts)
{
    if (groups.ContainsKey(c.State))
    {
        groups[c.State].Add(c);
    }
    else
    {
        List<Contact> list = new List<Contact>();
        list.Add(c);
        groups.Add(c.State, list);
    }
}

// write out the results
foreach (KeyValuePair<string, List<Contact>>
    group in groups)
{
    Console.WriteLine("State: " + group.Key);
    foreach (Contact c in group.Value)
        Console.WriteLine(" {0} {1}",
            c.FirstName, c.LastName);
}
```

LINQ Approach

LINQ to Objects, the LINQ features designed to add query functionality over in-memory collections, makes this scenario very easy to implement. Although the syntax is foreign at the moment (all will be explained in subsequent chapters), the code in Listing 1-2 is much shorter, and the coding gymnastics of sorting and grouping far less extreme.

Listing 1-2   C# 3.0 LINQ to objects code for grouping and sorting contact records—see Output 1-1

```
List<Contact> contacts = Contact.SampleData();

// perform the LINQ query
var query = from c in contacts
            orderby c.State, c.LastName
            group c by c.State;

// write out the results
foreach (var group in query)
{
    Console.WriteLine("State: " + group.Key);
    foreach (Contact c in group)
        Console.WriteLine(" {0} {1}",
            c.FirstName, c.LastName);
}
```

The Result

The outputs for both solutions are identical and shown in Output 1-1. The advantages of using LINQ in this scenario are clearly seen in code readability and far less code. In the traditional pre-LINQ code, it was necessary to explicitly choose how data was sorted and grouped; there was substantial "how to do something" code. LINQ does away with the "how" code, requiring the minimalist "what to do" code.

Output 1-1   The console output for the code in Listings 1-1 and 1-2

```
State: AK
 Adam Gauwain
State: CA
```

```
 Jeffery Deane
 Barney Gottshall
State: FL
 Collin Zeeman
State: OR
 Ariel Hazelgrove
State: TX
 Mack Kamph
 Blaine Reifsteck
State: WA
 Stewart Kagel
 Chance Lard
 Armando Valdes
```

LINQ to Objects—Summarizing Data from Two Collections and Writing XML

The second scenario to examine summarizes incoming calls from a `List<CallLog>` collection. The contact names for a given phone number is looked up by joining to a second collection of `List<Contact>`, which is sorted by last name and then first name. Each contact that has made at least one incoming call will be written to an XML document, including their number of calls, the total duration of those calls, and the average duration of the calls.

C# 2.0 Approach

Listing 1-3 shows the hefty code required to fulfill the aforementioned scenario. It starts by grouping incoming calls into a `Dictionary` keyed by the phone number. Contacts are sorted by last name, then first name, and this list is looped through writing out call statistics looked up by phone number from the groups created earlier. XML is written out using the `XmlTextWriter` class (in this case, to a string so that it can be written to the console), which creates a well structured, nicely indented XML file.

Listing 1-3   C# 2.0 code for summarizing data, joining to a second collection, and writing out XML—see Output 1-2

```
List<Contact> contacts = Contact.SampleData();
List<CallLog> callLog = CallLog.SampleData();
```

```
// group incoming calls by phone number
Dictionary<string, List<CallLog>> callGroups
    = new Dictionary<string, List<CallLog>>();

foreach (CallLog call in callLog)
{
    if (callGroups.ContainsKey(call.Number))
    {
        if (call.Incoming == true)
            callGroups[call.Number].Add(call);
    }
    else
    {
        if (call.Incoming == true)
        {
            List<CallLog> list = new List<CallLog>();
            list.Add(call);
            callGroups.Add(call.Number, list);
        }
    }
}

// sort contacts by last name, then first name
contacts.Sort(
    delegate(Contact c1, Contact c2)
    {
        // compare last names
        int result = c1.LastName.CompareTo(c2.LastName);

        // if last names match, compare first names
        if (result == 0)
            result = c1.FirstName.CompareTo(c2.FirstName);

        return result;
    });

// prepare and write XML document
using (StringWriter writer = new StringWriter())
{
    using (XmlTextWriter doc = new XmlTextWriter(writer))
    {
        // prepare XML header items
        doc.Formatting = Formatting.Indented;
        doc.WriteComment("Summarized Incoming Call Stats");
        doc.WriteStartElement("contacts");
```

```
// join calls with contacts data
foreach (Contact con in contacts)
{
    if (callGroups.ContainsKey(con.Phone))
    {
        List<CallLog> calls = callGroups[con.Phone];

        // calculate the total call duration and average
        long sum = 0;
        foreach (CallLog call in calls)
            sum += call.Duration;

        double avg = (double)sum / (double)calls.Count;

        // write XML record for this contact
        doc.WriteStartElement("contact");

        doc.WriteElementString("lastName",
            con.LastName);
        doc.WriteElementString("firstName",
            con.FirstName);
        doc.WriteElementString("count",
            calls.Count.ToString());
        doc.WriteElementString("totalDuration",
            sum.ToString());
        doc.WriteElementString("averageDuration",
            avg.ToString());

        doc.WriteEndElement();
    }
}
doc.WriteEndElement();
doc.Flush();
doc.Close();
}

Console.WriteLine(writer.ToString());
}
```

LINQ Approach

LINQ to Objects and the new XML programming interface included in C# 3.0 (LINQ to XML, but this example uses the generation side of this API rather than the query side) allows grouping, joining, and calculating the numerical average and sum into two statements. Listing 1-4 shows the LINQ code that performs the scenario described. LINQ excels at grouping and joining data, and when combined with the XML generation capabilities of LINQ to XML, it creates code that is far smaller in line count and more comprehensible in intention.

Listing 1-4   C# 3.0 LINQ to Objects code for summarizing data, joining to a second collection, and writing out XML—see Output 1-2

```
List<Contact> contacts = Contact.SampleData();
List<CallLog> callLog = CallLog.SampleData();

var q = from call in callLog
        where call.Incoming == true
        group call by call.Number into g
        join contact in contacts on
             g.Key equals contact.Phone
        orderby contact.LastName, contact.FirstName
        select new XElement("contact",
                    new XElement("lastName",
                       contact.LastName),
                    new XElement("firstName",
                       contact.FirstName),
                    new XElement("count",
                        g.Count()),
                    new XElement("totalDuration",
                        g.Sum(c => c.Duration)),
                    new XElement("averageDuration",
                       g.Average(c => c.Duration))
                       );

// create the XML document and add the items in query q
XDocument doc = new XDocument(
    new XComment("Summarized Incoming Call Stats"),
    new XElement("contacts", q)
);

Console.WriteLine(doc.ToString());
```

The Result

The outputs for both of these solutions are identical and shown in Output 1-2. The advantage of using LINQ syntax when working with data from multiple collections, grouping, and aggregating results and writing those to XML can clearly be seen given the reduction of code and the improved comprehensibility.

Output 1-2   The console output for the code in Listings 1-3 and 1-4

```
<!--Summarized Incoming Call Stats-->
<contacts>
  <contact>
    <lastName>Gottshall</lastName>
    <firstName>Barney</firstName>
    <count>4</count>
    <totalDuration>31</totalDuration>
    <averageDuration>7.75</averageDuration>
  </contact>
  ... (records cut for brevity)
  <contact>
    <lastName>Valdes</lastName>
    <firstName>Armando</firstName>
    <count>2</count>
    <totalDuration>20</totalDuration>
    <averageDuration>10</averageDuration>
  </contact>
</contacts>
```

Benefits of LINQ

LINQ appeals to different people for different reasons. Some benefits might not be completely obvious with the current state of the many LINQ elements that have shipped. The extensibility designed into the LINQ libraries and compilers will ensure that LINQ will grow over time, remaining a current and important technology to understand for many years to come.

Single Query Language to Remember

This is the prime advantage LINQ offers developers day to day. Once you learn the set of Standard Query Operators that LINQ makes available in either C# or VB, only minor changes are required to access any LINQ-enabled data source.

Compile-Time Name and Type Checking

LINQ queries are fully name and type-checked at compile-time, reducing (or eliminating) runtime error surprises. Many domain languages like T-SQL embed the query text within string literals. These strings are beyond the compiler for checking, and errors are often only found at runtime (hopefully during testing). Many type errors and mistyped field names will now be found by the compiler and fixed at that time.

Easier to Read Code

The examples shown in this chapter show how code to carry out common tasks with data is simplified, even if unfamiliar with LINQ syntax at the moment. The removal of complex looping, sorting, grouping, and conditional code down to a single query statement means fewer logic errors and simpler debugging.

It is possible to misuse any programming language construct. LINQ queries offer far greater ability to write human- (and compiler-) comprehensible code when working with structured data sources if that is the author's intention.

Over Fifty Standard Query Operators

The built-in set of Standard Query Operators make easy work of grouping, sorting, joining, aggregating, filtering, or selecting data. Table 1-1 lists the set of operators available in the .NET Framework 4 release (these operators are covered in upcoming chapters of this book; for now I just want to show you the range and depth of operators).

Table 1-1 Standard Query Operators in the .NET Framework 4 Release

Operator Type	Standard Query Operator Name
Aggregation	Aggregate, Average, Count, LongCount, Max, Min, Sum
Conversion	AsEnumerable, Cast, OfType, ToArray, ToDictionary, ToList, ToLookup
Element	DefaultIfEmpty, ElementAt, ElementAtOrDefault, First, FirstOrDefault, Last, LastOrDefault, Single, SingleOrDefault

Table 1-1   Standard Query Operators in the .NET Framework 4 Release

Operator Type	Standard Query Operator Name
Equality	`SequenceEqual`
Generation	`Empty, Range, Repeat`
Grouping	`GroupBy, ToLookup`
Joining	`GroupJoin, Join`
Merging	`Zip`
Ordering	`OrderBy, ThenBy, OrderByDescending, ThenByDescending, Reverse`
Projection	`Select, SelectMany`
Partitioning	`Skip, SkipWhile, Take, TakeWhile`
Quantifiers	`All, Any, Contains`
Restriction	`Distinct, Where`
Set	`Concat, Except, Intersect, Union`

Many of the standard Query operators are identical to those found in database query languages, which makes sense; if you were going to design what features a query language should have, looking at the current implementations that have been refined over 30 years is a good starting point. However, some of the operators introduce new approaches to working with data, simplifying what would have been complex traditional code into a single statement.

Open and Extensible Architecture

LINQ has been designed with extensibility in mind. Not only can new operators be added when a need arises, but entire new data sources can be added to the LINQ framework (caveat: operator implementation often needs to consider data source, and this can be complex—my point is that it's possible, and for LINQ to Objects, actually pretty simple).

Not only are the LINQ extension points exposed, Microsoft had implemented their specific providers using these same extension points. This will ensure that any provider, whether it be from open-source community projects to competitive data-access platforms, will compete on a level playing field.

Expressing Code as Data

Although not completely relevant to the LINQ to Objects story at this time, the ability to express LINQ queries as a data-structure opens new opportunities as to how that query might be optimized and executed at runtime. Beyond the basic features of LINQ providers that turn your C# and VB.Net code into a specific domain query language, the full advantage of code built using data or changed at runtime hasn't been fully leveraged at this time. One concept being explored by Microsoft is the ability to build and compile snippets of code at runtime; this code might be used to apply custom business rules, for instance. When code is represented as data, it can be checked and modified depending on its security implications or how well it might operate concurrently based on the actual environment that code is executed in (whether that be your laptop or a massive multi-core server).

Summary

Defining LINQ is a difficult task. LINQ is a conglomerate of loosely labeled technologies released in tandem with the .NET Framework 3.5 and further expanded in .NET Framework 4. The other complexity of answering the question of "What is LINQ?" is that it's a moving target. LINQ is built using an open and extensible architecture, and new operators and data sources can be added by anyone.

One point is clear: LINQ will change the approach to writing data-driven applications. Code will be simpler, often faster, and easier to read. There is no inherent downside to using the LINQ features; it is simply the next installment of how the C# and VB.Net languages are being improved to support tomorrow's coding challenges.

The next chapter looks more closely at how to construct basic LINQ queries in C#, a prerequisite to understanding the more advanced features covered in later chapters.

References

1. Box, Don and Hejlsberg, Anders. 2006. LINQ Project Overview, May. Downloaded from http://download.microsoft.com/download/5/8/6/5868081c-68aa-40de-9a45-a3803d8134b8/LINQ_Project_Overview.doc.

CHAPTER 2

INTRODUCING LINQ TO OBJECTS

Goals of this chapter:

- Define the capabilities of LINQ to Objects.
- Define the C# language enhancements that make LINQ possible.
- Introduce the main features of LINQ to Objects through a brief overview.

LINQ to Objects allows us to query in-memory collections and any type that implements the `IEnumerable<T>` interface. This chapter gives you a first real look at the language enhancements that support the LINQ story and introduces you to the main features of LINQ to Objects with a short overview. By the end of this chapter, the query syntax should be more familiar to you, and then the following chapters bring you deeper into the query syntax and features.

LINQ Enabling C# 3.0 Language Enhancements

Many new language C# language constructs were added in version 3.0 to improve the general coding experience for developers. Almost all the C# features added relate in some way to the realization of an integrated query syntax within called LINQ.

The features added in support of the LINQ syntax fall into two categories. The first is a set of compiler syntax additions that are shorthand for common constructs, and the second are features that alter the way method names are resolved during compilation. All these features, however, combine to allow a fluent query experience when working with structured data sources.

To understand how LINQ to Object queries compile, it is necessary to have some understanding of the new language features. Although this chapter will only give you a brief overview, the following chapters will use all these features in more advanced ways.

NOTE There are a number of other new language features added in both C# 3.0 and C# 4.0 that don't specifically add to the LINQ story covered in this introduction. The C# 4.0 features are covered in Chapter 8. C# 4.0 does require the .NET Framework 4 to be installed on machines executing the compiled code.

Extension Methods

Extension methods allow us to introduce additional methods to any type without inheriting or changing the source code behind that type. Methods introduced to a given type using extension methods can be called on an instance of that type in the same way ordinary instance methods are called (using the dot notation on an instance variable of a type).

Extension methods are built as static methods inside a static class. The first argument in the method has the `this` modifier, which tells the compiler that the following type is to be extended. Any following arguments are treated as normal, other than the second argument becomes the first and so on (the argument prefixed by the `this` modifier is skipped).

The rules for defining an extension method are

1. The extension method needs to be defined in a nongeneric static class
2. The static class must be at the root level of a namespace (that is, not nested within another class)
3. The extension method must be a static method (which is enforced by the compiler due to the class also having to be marked static)
4. The first argument of the extension method must be prefixed with the `this` modifier; this is the type being extended

To demonstrate the mechanics of declaring an extension method, the following code extends the `System.String` type, adding a method called `CreateHyperlink`. Once this code is compiled into a project, any class file that has a `using MyNamespace;` declaration can simply call this method on any string instance in the following fashion:

```
string name = "Hooked on LINQ";
string link = name.CreateHyperlink(
    "http://www.hookedonlinq.com");
```

```
namespace MyNamespace
{
    public static class MyStringExtensions
    {
        // extension method added to the String type,
        // single string argument: url.
        public static string CreateHyperlink(
            this string text,
            string url)
        {
            return String.Format(
                "<a href='{0}'>{1}</a>", url, text);
        }
    }
}
```

Listing 2-1 demonstrates how to create an extension method that returns the SHA1 Hash value for a string (with and without extra arguments). The output of this code can be seen in Output 2-1.

Listing 2-1   Adding a `GetSHA1Hash` method to the `String` type as an example extension method—see Output 2-1

```
public static class MyStringExtensions
{
    // extension method added to the String type,
    // with no additional arguments
    public static string GetSHA1Hash(
        this string text)
    {
        if (string.IsNullOrEmpty(text))
            return null;

        SHA1Managed sha1 = new SHA1Managed();

        byte[] bytes = sha1.ComputeHash(
            new UnicodeEncoding().GetBytes(text));

        return Convert.ToBase64String(bytes);
    }
}
```

```
// SHA1 Hashing a string.
// GetSHA1Hash is introduced via extension method
string password = "ClearTextPassword";
string hashedPassword = password.GetSHA1Hash();

// write the results to the Console window
Console.WriteLine("- SHA1 Hashing a string -");
Console.WriteLine("Original: " + password);
Console.WriteLine("Hashed: " + hashedPassword);
```

Output 2-1

```
- SHA1 Hashing a string -
Original: ClearTextPassword
Hashed: DVuwKeBX7bqPMDefYLOGLiNVYmM=
```

Extension methods declared in a namespace are available to call from any file that includes a `using` clause for that namespace. For instance, to make the LINQ to Objects extension methods available to your code, include the `using System.Linq;` clause at the top of the class code file.

The compiler will automatically give precedence to any instance methods defined for a type, meaning that it will use a method defined in a class if it exists before it looks for an extension method that satisfies the method name and signature.

When making the choice on whether to extend a class using object-oriented principles of inheritance or extension methods, early drafts of the "Microsoft C# 3.0 Language Specification"[1] had the following advice (although the warning was removed in the final specification,[2] it is still good advice in my opinion):

> Extension methods are less discoverable and more limited in functionality than instance methods. For those reasons, it is recommended that extension methods be used sparingly and only in situations where instance methods are not feasible or possible.

The set of standard query operators that form the inbuilt query functionality for LINQ to Objects are made entirely using extension methods that extend any type that implements `IEnumerable<T>` and in some rare cases `IEnumerable`. (Most .NET collection classes and arrays implement `IEnumerable<T>`; hence, the Standard Query Operators are introduced to most of the built-in collection classes.) Although LINQ to Objects would be possible without extension methods, Microsoft would have had to add these operators to each collection type individually, and custom collections of our own type wouldn't benefit without intervention. Extension methods allow LINQ to apply equally to the built-in collection types, and any custom collection type, with the only requirement being the custom collection must implement `IEnumerable<T>`. The current Microsoft-supplied extension methods and how to create new extension methods are covered in detail throughout this book. Understanding extension methods and how the built-in standard Query operators work will lead to a deeper understanding of how LINQ to Objects is built.

Object Initializers

C# 3.0 introduced an object initialization shortcut syntax that allows a single C# statement to both construct a new instance of a type and assign property values in one statement. While it is good programming practice to use constructor arguments for all critical data in order to ensure that a new type is stable and ready for use immediately after it is initialized (not allow objects to be instantiated into an invalid state), Object Initializers reduce the need to have a specific parameterized constructor for every variation of noncritical data argument set needed over time.

Listing 2-2 demonstrates the before and after examples of Object Initializers. Any public field or property can be assigned in the initialization statement by assigning that property name to a value; multiple assignments can be made by separating the expressions with a comma. The C# compiler behind the scenes calls the default constructor of the object and then calls the individual assignment statements as if you had previously assigned properties in subsequent statements manually. (See the C# 3.0 Language Specification in endnote 2 for a more precise description of how this initialization actually occurs.)

Listing 2-2   Object Initializer syntax—before and after

```
// old initialization syntax => multiple statements
Contact contactOld = new Contact();
contactOld.LastName = "Magennis";
contactOld.DateOfBirth = new DateTime(1973, 12, 09);

// new initialization syntax => single statement
Contact contactNew = new Contact
{
    LastName = "Magennis",
    DateOfBirth = new DateTime(1973, 12, 09)
};
```

Although it seems to be a trivial (albeit useful) improvement in syntax in the general form, it is essential when you begin to write LINQ queries and need to construct object instances as part of their result set by setting property values on-the-fly. This is one of the more common scenarios when working with LINQ, and without this feature you would need to define a specific constructor for every set of properties you would like to initialize with a query.

Collection Initializers

With similar ambitions as the Object Initializer syntax, collection initialization was given similar functionality to improve the common construct and then add pattern. The collection must implement System.Collections.IEnumerable and have an appropriate overload for an Add method to support the new initialization syntax. Listing 2-3 demonstrates the use of the new collection initialization syntax and shows the before and after equivalent code patterns. It also demonstrates how to combine collection initialization with Object Initialization, which helps keep the code cleaner and generally easier to read.

Listing 2-3   Collection initialization syntax—before and after

```
// old initialization syntax => multiple statements
List<string> stringsOld = new List<string>();
stringsOld.Add("string 1");
stringsOld.Add("string 2");

// new initialization syntax => single statement
List<string> stringsNew = new List<string> {
    "string 1",
    "string 2" };

// combining object and collection initialization
// create a list of contacts and add two records.
List<Contact> list = new List<Contact> {
    new Contact {
        LastName = "Magennis",
        DateOfBirth = new DateTime(1973,12,09)
    },
    new Contact {
        LastName = "Doherty",
        DateOfBirth = new DateTime(1978,1,05)
    }
};
```

Implicitly Typed Local Variables

When a local variable is defined with the keyword `var` instead of a concrete type, the declared type of the new variable is inferred from the initialization expression. This removes the need to duplicate the type name when it can be inferred by the initial value assignment or initialization expression. Variables initialized using the `var` keyword are strongly-typed; the variable is simply assigned a compile-time type of the initialization value expression. Listing 2-4 demonstrates the use of implicit typing of local variables.

Listing 2-4   Local variable declaration, implicitly typed examples

```
// implicitly typed local variable declarations
var anInt = 1;
var aString = "Testing";
var listContact = new List<Contact>();
var intArray = new int[] { 0, 1, 2, 3, 4 };

// the above are identical to the following declarations
int anIntOld = 1;
string aStringOld = "Testing";
List<Contact> listContactOld = new List<Contact>();
int[] intArrayOld = new int[] { 0, 1, 2, 3, 4 };

// list is defined as type: List<Contact>,
// it shows how object and collection
// initialization work with the var style init.
var list = new List<Contact> {
    new Contact {
        LastName = "Magennis",
        DateOfBirth = new DateTime(1973,12,09)
    },
    new Contact {
        LastName = "Doherty",
        DateOfBirth = new DateTime(1978,1,05)
    }
};
```

To use Implicitly Typed Local Variables, the declaration must follow these rules:

1. No user defined local type called var can exist; otherwise, that type is used.
2. The variable declaration must have an initialization expression (that is, an equal sign followed by an expression, which can be a constant).
3. The initialize expression (the expression to the right side of the equal sign), must have a compile-time type.
4. The declaration cannot include multiple declarations (for example, var x = 10, y = 42;).
5. The variable cannot refer to itself.

Although the usefulness of declaring a variable in this way seems minor, it is a necessary feature for declaring some types that have no other legal way of being declared (Anonymous Types, for instance).

Anonymous Types

Anonymous types are compile-time generated types where the public properties are inferred from the object initialization expression at compile-time. These types can then be used locally within a method as temporary data storage classes, avoiding having to build a specific data class for any and every set of properties. The new class inherits directly from System.Object and for all practical purposes has no name (none that can be referenced from code anyway). What run-time type do you assign anonymous types? They have to be declared using the implicitly typed local variable construct (var) mentioned earlier.

An anonymous type is defined by omitting the type name after a new statement and providing a valid Object Initializer expression that contains one or more assignments. Listing 2-5 demonstrates how to create an anonymous type and how it can be used in subsequent code, the output of which is shown in Output 2-2.

Listing 2-5 Declaring and using anonymous types—see Output 2-2

```
// simple anonymous type declaration
Console.WriteLine("- Simple Anonymous Type -");
var item = new { Name = "Car", Price = 9989.00 };

Console.WriteLine("Type: {0}, Name: {1}, Price: {2}",
    item.GetType().ToString(), item.Name, item.Price);
```

```
// declaring and working with array of anonymous types
Console.WriteLine();
Console.WriteLine("- Iterating Anonymous Types Array -");
var list = new[] {
    new { LastName = "Magennis",
          DateOfBirth = new DateTime(1973,12,09)
    },
    new { LastName = "Doherty",
          DateOfBirth = new DateTime(1978,1,05)
    }
};

foreach (var x in list)
    Console.WriteLine("{0} ({1})",
        x.LastName, x.DateOfBirth);

// compiler optimization - from the C# specification:
// within the same program, two anonymous object
// initializers that specify a sequence of properties of
// the same names and compile-time types in the same order
// will produce instances of the same anonymous type.
var p1 = new { Name = "Lawnmower", Price = 495.00 };
var p2 = new { Name = "Shovel", Price = 26.95 };
p1 = p2; // valid: the same anonymous type.
```

Output 2-2

```
- Simple Anonymous Type -
Type: <>f__AnonymousType0`2[System.String,System.Double],
Name: Car,
Price: 9989

- Iterating Anonymous Types Array -
Magennis (12/9/1973 12:00:00 AM)
Doherty (1/5/1978 12:00:00 AM)
```

The importance of anonymous types becomes evident when writing queries that build collections using a subset of properties from an existing type (known as a *projection*). Imagine if when working with a relational database you couldn't define the column list to be used as the return of an SQL query. The same issue occurs with LINQ; without anonymous types, you would need to define a concrete type for each and every return result set that altered the columns of interest. Optional parameters added in C# 4.0 (covered in Chapter 4, "Grouping and Joining Data") make this somewhat easier, but anonymous types should be considered when results are needed temporarily.

Beyond their usefulness of supporting LINQ, anonymous types allow temporary data structures to be created during processing of that data. It was often necessary to build a plain, old class with nothing more than property declarations to support holding data; anonymous types fulfill this need perfectly. Although it is possible to pass anonymous types beyond the method that declared them by declaring an argument type as `Object`, this is highly discouraged. When using anonymous types outside of LINQ query functionality, keep the scoping to the method they are declared, otherwise define a concrete type or struct.

Lambda Expressions

Lambda expressions build upon the anonymous methods feature added in C# 2.0. Anonymous methods added the ability to inline the code by using the `delegate` keyword, which avoids the need to declare a delegate method in a separate body of code. C# 3.0 introduces the lambda operator `=>`, which can be used to create delegates or expression trees in an even briefer syntax.

NOTE   Delegate is a fancy term for a type-safe reference (pointer) to a function or method. For example, when you need to call code when someone clicks a button, you actually attach a Delegate to the event. The Delegate is the actual method implementing the code elsewhere. However, having to locate Delegate code separately (such as within a concrete method) was a pain, and in C# 2.0 the ability to inline that code was added. In C# 3.0, lambda expressions clean the syntax of writing that in-line code even more.

This C# 2.0 syntax for an anonymous method is

```
delegate (type parameter) {
     [ method body] return [expression]; }
```

The same delegate using the C# 3.0 lambda expression syntax is

```
[parameter] => [expression]
```

Lambda expressions are used when passing method-based arguments to any of the LINQ standard Query operators, like Where for instance. A before and after example of how a Where clause would need to be formatted with and without the new syntax would be

```
// C# 2.0 anonymous method syntax
source.Where(delegate(Contact c) { return c.State == "WA"; });

// C# 3.0 lambda expression syntax
source.Where(c => c.State == "WA");
```

Lambda expressions build upon the original anonymous method syntax by improving compile time type inference (the compiler works out the types of the arguments in most cases, eliminating the need to specify the input argument parameter types) and simplifying the syntax by eliminating the delegate keyword and the return statement for Expression bodies.

NOTE   Lambda expressions are generally single-expression delegates (only contain a single expression) when used with LINQ due to their limitation of not being convertible to expression trees. Anonymous methods can have multiple expressions and span multiple lines.

Some more general forms of lambda expressions taking input arguments and specifying explicit types when necessary (the compiler often can infer the type without assistance) are

```
() => [expression]
([parameter]) => [expression]
([param type][param]) => [expression]
(parameter1, parameter2) => [expression]
([param type][param1, [param type][param2) => [expression]
```

Surrounding parentheses for lambdas with a single parameter is optional. Lambda expressions infer the parameter type and return types in most cases, but if the compiler cannot determine the types, you must explicitly type them by adding a type before the parameter identifier.

```
n => n < 5
(int n) => n < 5            (explicit parameter typing)
n => n % 2 == 1             (true for odd numbers)
(n, index) => n < index     (multiple parameters)
```

Lambda expressions will become second nature when you begin writing LINQ code; for now, just get comfortable with the fact that a lambda expression is simply a nicer way of passing code to another function to execute. Listing 2-6 demonstrates some before and after shots of inlining code as a delegate.

Listing 2-6 Anonymous method (C# 2.0) and Lambda Expression (C# 3.0) examples

```
// connecting code to a buttons click event
//    anonymous method -
Button button = new Button();
button.Click += delegate(object sender, EventArgs args)
{
    MessageBox.Show("Clicked");
};

//    lambda expression -
button.Click += (object sender, EventArgs args) =>
    MessageBox.Show("Clicked");

var data = Contact.SampleData().ToList();

// passing code to a ForEach method on a List<T>
//    anonymous method -
data.ForEach(delegate(Contact c)
    { c.LastName = c.LastName.ToUpper(); });

//    lambda expression -
data.ForEach(c => c.LastName = c.LastName.ToUpper());

data.ForEach( c => Console.WriteLine("{0}, {1}",
    c.LastName, c.FirstName) );

// passing code to an extension method
//    anonymous method -
var q1 = data
        .Where(
            delegate(Contact c){return c.State == "WA";});

//    lambda expression -var q2 = data
        .Where(c => c.State == "WA");
```

Query Expressions

Query expressions is the feature where all of the previous new language constructs merge, and their pivotal role in LINQ can be seen. The following is a brief overview; future chapters cover how to write query expressions in detail, but for now focus on how the language enhancements combine into a query language integrated into C#.

Query expressions are a language syntax enhancement only; the query expression is mapped into a series of extension method calls and then into a series of static method calls by the compiler (for LINQ to Objects, other LINQ providers such as LINQ to SQL do not operate this way—they build to expression trees and are beyond the scope of this book). The advantage of the query expression syntax however, is its clarity and how familiar it appears to anyone who has worked in other query languages. Both query syntax styles and their benefits and tradeoffs are covered in Chapter 3, "Writing Basic Queries," and throughout the rest of the book.

Listing 2-7 shows two functionally identical LINQ queries; the first query1 uses the query expression language syntax, and query2 uses pure extension method calls to compose the query. query1 makes use of anonymous types (line 7), Object Initialization (line 9 and 10), and implicitly typed local variables (line 5). The code shown in query2 is similar to how the compiler converts the query expression syntax into extension method calls, and free-form expressions throughout the query into lambda expressions. This step is transparent and automatic during compilation and is shown here to give you a glimpse into how LINQ query syntax is decomposed into more traditional code constructs. Lambda expressions can be seen where expressions were used (lines 15 and 16), and you can also see extension methods taking the place of the keywords where and select (lines 15 and 16).

Listing 2-7 Example query expression showing the new language constructs in unison

```
1   // note: Person.SampleData() returns a populated
2   // List<Person> sample data collection.
3
4   // LINQ Query Expression Syntax
5   var query1 = from c in Person.SampleData()
6                where c.State == "WA"
7                select new
8                {
9                    Name = c.FirstName + " " + c.LastName,
10                   State = c.State
```

```
11                   };
12
13  // LINQ Extension Method Syntax, identical to above
14  var query2 = Person.SampleData()
15               .Where(c => c.State == "WA")
16               .Select(c => new
17               {
18                   Name = c.FirstName + " " + c.LastName,
19                   State = c.State
20               });
21
22  foreach (var item in query1)
23      Console.WriteLine("{0}, ({1})", item.Name, item.State);
```

A full explanation of the query expression syntax is forthcoming in Chapter 3; for now, the goal is to demonstrate how the language features build the foundation for a solid query language system, as the name suggests—Language Integrated Query.

LINQ to Objects Five-Minute Overview

LINQ to Objects allows .NET developers to write "queries" over collections of objects. Microsoft provides a large set of query operators out of the box, and these operators offer a similar depth of functionality to what is expected from any SQL language working with a relational database.

Traditionally, working with collections of objects meant writing a lot of looping code using `for` loops or `foreach` loops to iterate through a collection, carrying out filtering using `if` statements, while performing other computations like keeping a running sum of a total property.

LINQ frees you from having to write looping code; it allows you to write queries that filter a list or calculate aggregate functions on elements in an in-memory collection, among many other capabilities. You can write queries against any collection type that implements an interface called `IEnumerable<T>`, which most built-in collection classes available in the .NET Framework class libraries certainly do, including simple arrays.

To understand the basic query syntax, Listings 2-8 and 2-9 demonstrate simple LINQ to Object queries, with their respective console output shown in Outputs 2-3 and 2-4.

Listing 2-8   Simple LINQ query over an array of integers—see Output 2-3

```
int[] nums = new int[] { 0, 4, 2, 6, 3, 8, 3, 1 };

var result = from n in nums
             where n < 5
             orderby n
             select n;

foreach (int i in result)
    Console.WriteLine(i);
```

Output 2-3

```
0
1
2
3
3
4
```

Listing 2-9   Simple LINQ that calculates the sum of all values in an integer array—see Output 2-4

```
int[] nums = new int[] { 0, 4, 2, 6, 3, 8, 3, 1 };
int result = nums.Sum();
Console.WriteLine(result);
```

Output 2-4

```
27
```

LINQ to Objects extends any type that inherits from `IEnumerable<T>` (using extension methods as described earlier), introducing a set of query operations similar to those in an SQL language. All basic collection types and arrays built into the .NET Base Class Libraries implement the

`IEnumerable<T>` interface, so with one set of extension methods, Microsoft has added query ability to all collections. Table 1-1 in the previous chapter listed the built-in standard Query operators. Each operator is covered in detail later in this book (Chapters 3 to 6). Most of the operators should be familiar if you have ever worked with a relational database, writing queries in SQL. One important distinction between writing SQL queries and LINQ queries is that the operator order is reversed. If you are used to `Select-From-Where-OrderBy`, it might take some time to overcome the muscle memory and move to `From-Where-OrderBy-Select`. The keyword order difference is for a good reason, and although initially the VB.Net team implemented LINQ in the SQL order, they moved to the C# keyword ordering after realizing the benefits of **Intellisense** support. Specifying the collection first (with the `from` clause) allows Visual Studio to pop up the public fields and properties in a very powerful tooltip when entering the `where` and `select` clauses, as shown in Figure 2-1. If `select` came first, no pop-up assistance can be offered because the editor won't yet know what object type will be used throughout the query.

FIGURE 2-1 By specifying the **from** clause first, the editor can offer a field list when specifying the **select** clause. This would not be possible if the **select** clause came first.

To demonstrate some of LINQ's query capabilities, the rest of this overview works with the sample data shown in Tables 2-1 and 2-2. The examples in this chapter and subsequent chapters query this data in various ways to explore LINQ to Objects in detail.

Table 2-1 Sample Contact Data Used Throughout the Rest of This Book

First Name	Last Name	D.O.B.	Phone	State
Barney	Gottshall	19-Oct-1945	885 983 8858	CA
Armando	Valdes	9-Dec-1973	848 553 8487	WA
Adam	Gauwain	3-Oct-1959	115 999 1154	AK
Jeffery	Deane	16-Dec-1950	677 602 6774	CA
Collin	Zeeman	10-Feb-1935	603 303 6030	FL
Stewart	Kagel	20-Feb-1950	546 607 5462	WA
Chance	Lard	21-Oct-1951	278 918 2789	WA
Blaine	Reifsteck	18-May-1946	715 920 7157	TX
Mack	Kamph	17-Sep-1977	364 202 3644	TX
Ariel	Hazelgrove	23-May-1922	165 737 1656	OR

Table 2-2 Sample Call Log Data Used Throughout the Rest of This Book

Number	Duration (mins)	Incoming	Date	Time
885 983 8858	2	TRUE	7-Aug-2006	8:12
165 737 1656	15	TRUE	7-Aug-2006	9:23
364 202 3644	1	FALSE	7-Aug-2006	10:5
603 303 6030	2	FALSE	7-Aug-2006	10:35
546 607 5462	4	TRUE	7-Aug-2006	11:15
885 983 8858	15	FALSE	7-Aug-2006	13:12
885 983 8858	3	TRUE	7-Aug-2006	13:47
546 607 5462	1	FALSE	7-Aug-2006	20:34
546 607 5462	3	FALSE	8-Aug-2006	10:10
603 303 6030	23	FALSE	8-Aug-2006	10:40

Table 2-2 Sample Call Log Data Used Throughout the Rest of This Book

Number	Duration (mins)	Incoming	Date	Time
848 553 8487	3	FALSE	8-Aug-2006	14:0
848 553 8487	7	TRUE	8-Aug-2006	14:37
278 918 2789	6	TRUE	8-Aug-2006	15:23
364 202 3644	20	TRUE	8-Aug-2006	17:12

The `Contact` and `CallLog` types used throughout this book are simple types declared in the following way:

```
public class Contact
{
    public string FirstName { get; set; }
    public string LastName { get; set; }
    public string Email { get; set; }
    public string Phone { get; set; }
    public DateTime DateOfBirth { get; set; }
    public string State { get; set; }
}

public class CallLog
{
    public string Number { get; set; }
    public int Duration { get; set; }
    public bool Incoming { get; set; }
    public DateTime When { get; set; }
}
```

The example shown in Listing 2-10 demonstrates how to retrieve a list of contacts who are less than 35 years of age, sorted in descending order by age. This query builds a list of formatted strings as the result set as shown in Output 2-5 (although any type concretely defined or anonymous can be returned from a `select` expression).

Listing 2-10   Query returning a list of formatted strings based on data from a query over a collection of Contacts records—see Output 2-5

```
List<Contact> contacts = Contact.SampleData();

var q = from c in contacts
        where c.DateOfBirth.AddYears(35) > DateTime.Now
        orderby c.DateOfBirth descending
        select string.Format("{0} {1} b.{2}",
                    c.FirstName,
                    c.LastName,
                    c.DateOfBirth.ToString("dd-MMM-yyyy")
                );

foreach (string s in q)
    Console.WriteLine(s);
```

Output 2-5

```
Mack Kamph b.17-Sep-1977
Armando Valdes b.09-Dec-1973
```

In addition to filtering items in a collection and projecting the results into a new form, LINQ offers the ability to group the collection items in any form you need. Listing 2-11 and Output 2-6 demonstrate the simplest form of grouping, using the `group by` construct to create a sub-collection of elements from the original collection.

Listing 2-11   Query groups Contact records into sub-collections based on their State—see Output 2-6

```
List<Contact> contacts = Contact.SampleData();

var q = from c in contacts
        group c by c.State;
```

```
foreach (var group in q)
{
    Console.WriteLine("State: " + group.Key);
    foreach (Contact c in group)
        Console.WriteLine("  {0} {1}",
            c.FirstName,
            c.LastName);
}
```

Output 2-6

```
State: CA
  Barney Gottshall
  Jeffery Deane
State: WA
  Armando Valdes
  Stewart Kagel
  Chance Lard
State: AK
  Adam Gauwain
State: FL
  Collin Zeeman
State: TX
  Blaine Reifsteck
  Mack Kamph
State: OR
  Ariel Hazelgrove
```

A key aspect of accessing relational data is the concept of joining to related data. Relational database systems (such as Microsoft SQL Server) have powerful join capabilities built in to allow queries to be written against normalized data, which is a fancy term for "not repeating data" by separating data across multiple tables and linking by a common value. LINQ allows you to join multiple object collections together using syntax similar to SQL, as shown in Listing 2-12 and Output 2-7, which joins the call log data from Table 2-2 with the Contact data from Table 2-1. In this example, the telephone number is used as common matching criteria, and a temporary anonymous type is used to hold the combined result before writing to the console window.

Listing 2-12 Query joins two collections based on the phone number—see Output 2-7. Notice the use of the temporary anonymous type.

```
List<Contact> contacts = Contact.SampleData();
List<CallLog> callLog = CallLog.SampleData();

var q = from call in callLog
        join contact in contacts on
            call.Number equals contact.Phone
        select new  {
            contact.FirstName,
            contact.LastName,
            call.When,
            call.Duration
        };

foreach (var c in q)
    Console.WriteLine(
        "{0} - {1} {2} ({3}min)",
        c.When.ToString("ddMMM HH:m"), c.FirstName,
        c.LastName, c.Duration);
```

Output 2-7

```
07Aug 08:12 - Barney Gottshall (2min)
07Aug 09:23 - Ariel Hazelgrove (15min)
07Aug 10:5 - Mack Kamph (1min)
...
08Jul 14:37 - Armando Valdes (13min)
08May 15:23 - Chance Lard (16min)
08Jun 17:12 - Mack Kamph (24min)
```

To demonstrate the full power of LINQ to Objects query functionality, the query shown in Listing 2-13 summarizes the data from two in-memory collections by using joins, groups, and also aggregate operators in the select clause. The final output of this query is shown in Output 2-8.

Listing 2-13   Incoming call log summary shows filtering, ordering, grouping, joining, and selection using aggregate values—see Output 2-8

```
List<Contact> contacts = Contact.SampleData();
List<CallLog> callLog = CallLog.SampleData();

var q = from call in callLog
        where call.Incoming == true
        group call by call.Number into g
        join contact in contacts on
            g.Key equals contact.Phone
        orderby contact.FirstName, contact.LastName
        select new {
            contact.FirstName,
            contact.LastName,
            Count = g.Count(),
            Avg = g.Average(c => c.Duration),
            Total = g.Sum(c => c.Duration)
        };

foreach (var call in q)
    Console.WriteLine(
        "{0} {1} - Calls:{2}, Time:{3}mins, Avg:{4}mins",
        call.FirstName, call.LastName,
        call.Count, call.Total, Math.Round(call.Avg, 2));
```

Output 2-8

```
Ariel Hazelgrove - Calls:2, Time:27mins, Avg:13.5mins
Armando Valdes - Calls:2, Time:20mins, Avg:10mins
Barney Gottshall - Calls:4, Time:31mins, Avg:7.75mins
Chance Lard - Calls:2, Time:22mins, Avg:11mins
Mack Kamph - Calls:2, Time:44mins, Avg:22mins
Stewart Kagel - Calls:2, Time:13mins, Avg:6.5mins
```

Summary

This concludes our introduction to the language enhancements supporting LINQ and our five-minute overview of LINQ to Objects. The intention of this overview was to give you enough familiarity with LINQ to Objects and the language syntax to delve deeper into writing LINQ queries, which the following chapters encourage.

References

1. C# Version 3.0 Specification 3.0, September 2005. This draft version of the C# specification has advice on when to use Extension Methods, http://download.microsoft.com/download/9/5/0/9503e33e-fde6-4aed-b5d0-ffe749822f1b/csharp%203.0%20specification.doc.

2. C# Language Specification Version 3.0, Microsoft 2007, http://download.microsoft.com/download/3/8/8/388e7205-bc10-4226-b2a8-75351c669b09/CSharp%20Language%20Specification.doc.

CHAPTER 3

WRITING BASIC QUERIES

Goals of this chapter:

- Understand the LINQ syntax options.
- Introduce how to write basic queries.
- Demonstrate how to filter, project, and order data using LINQ queries.

The main goal of this chapter is to introduce the basics of writing queries. These basics include the syntax options available for writing queries, how to filter data, how to order data, and how to return the exact result set you want. By the end of this chapter, you will understand how to write the most common query elements and, in the following chapter, you will expand this understanding into the more advanced query features of grouping and joining with other sources.

Query Syntax Style Options

Most previous examples in this book have used the query expression syntax, but there are two styles for writing LINQ queries. Not all operators are available through the query expression syntax built into the C# compiler, and to use the remaining operators (or to call your own operators), the extension method query syntax or a combination of the two is necessary. You will continually need to know both styles of query syntax in order to read, write, and understand code written using LINQ.

- **Extension method format** (also known as the dot notation syntax)—The extension method format is simply where multiple extension methods are cascaded together, each returning an `IEnumerable<T>` result to allow the next extension method to flow on from the previous result and so on (known as a *fluid interface*).

```
int[] nums = new int[] {0,4,2,6,3,8,3,1};

var result1 = nums.Where(n => n < 5).OrderBy (n => n);

// or with line-breaks added for clarity
var result2 = nums
            .Where(n => n < 5)
            .OrderBy (n => n);
```

- **Query Expression format** (preferred, especially for joins and groups)—Although not all standard query operators are supported by the query expression syntax, the benefit to the clarity of code when they are is very high. The query expression syntax is much gentler than the extension method syntax in that it simplifies the syntax by removing lambda expressions and by introducing a familiar SQL-like representation.

```
int[] nums = new int[] {0,4,2,6,3,8,3,1};


var result = from n in nums
             where n < 5
             orderby n
             select n;
```

- **Query Dot syntax** (a combination of the two formats)—This format combines a query expression syntax query surrounded by parentheses, followed by more operators using the Dot Notation syntax. As long as the query expression returns an IEnumerable<T>, it can be followed by an extension method chain.

```
int[] nums = new int[] {0,4,2,6,3,8,3,1};


var result = (from n in nums
             where n < 5
             orderby n
             select n).Distinct();
```

WHICH QUERY SYNTAX TO USE? Personal preference will dictate this, but the goal is to use the syntax that is easiest to read and that will help developers who come after you to understand your intentions. With this in mind, don't unnecessarily mix the syntax styles in one query; mixing the styles makes the query harder to read by forcing the reader to count brackets and determine which part of a query the extension method syntax applies to. If you do mix styles, keep them together; for example, use the query expression at the start surrounded by parentheses, then the extension methods at the end for the necessary operators (as shown in all examples in this book when mixing was needed).

My preference (because of my SQL background perhaps) is to use the query expression syntax wherever possible and then revert to using the extension method syntax when using an operator not supported by query expressions (the Distinct operator, for instance), but I always add these operators at the end of the query. I'll sometimes use all expression method syntax but never when the query has a Join or GroupBy operator.

Each query syntax has its own merits and pitfalls, which the following sections cover in detail.

Query Expression Syntax

The query expression syntax provided in C# 3.0 and later versions makes queries clearer and more concise. The compiler converts the query expression into extension method syntax during compilation, so the choice of which syntax to use is based solely on code readability.

Figure 3-1 shows the basic form of query expressions built into C# 3.0.

IEnumerable<T>|T   *query-expression-identifier* **=**

   from   *identifier*   **in**   *expression*

   let$_{opt}$ *identifier* = *expression*

   where$_{opt}$ *boolean-expression*

   join$_{opt}$ *type*$_{opt}$ *identifier*   **in**   *expression*   **on**

       expression   **equals**   *expression*   **into**$_{opt}$ *identifier*

   orderby$_{opt}$ *ordering-clause(s)*   **ascending | descending** $_{opt}$

   group$_{opt}$ *expression*   **by**   *expression*   **into** $_{opt}$ *identifier*

   select   *expression*   **into**$_{opt}$ *identifier*

Figure 3-1   The basic query expression syntax form. The C# 3.0 Language Specification outlines exactly how this form is translated into extension methods for compilation.

> **NOTE** The fact that the order of the keywords is different in SQL is unfortunate for those who are SQL masters; however, one very compelling reason for the difference was to improve the developer experience. The From-Where-Select order allows the editing environment (Visual Studio in this case) to provide full Intellisense support when writing the query. The moment you write the `from` clause, the properties of that element appear as you then write the `where` clause. This wouldn't be the case (and isn't in SQL Server's query editing tools) if the C# designers followed the more familiar Select-From-Where keyword ordering.

Most of the query expression syntax needs no explanation for developers experienced with other query syntax, like SQL. Although the order is different than in traditional query languages, each keyword name gives a strong indication as to its function, the exception being the `let` and `into` clauses, which are described next.

Let—Create a Local Variable

Queries can often be written with less code duplication by creating a local variable to hold the value of an intermediate calculation or the result of a subquery. The `let` keyword enables you to keep the result of an expression (a value or a subquery) in scope throughout the rest of the query expression being written. Once assigned, the variable cannot be reassigned with another value.

In the following code, a local variable is assigned, called `average`, that holds the average value for the entire source sequence, calculated once but used in the Select projection on each element:

```
var variance = from element in source
               let average = source.Average()
               select Math.Pow((element - average), 2);
```

The `let` keyword is implemented purely by the compiler, which creates an anonymous type that contains both the original range variable (`element` in the previous example) and the new `let` variable. The previous query maps directly to the following (compiler translated) extension method query:

```
var variance =
    source.Select (
        element =>
            new
```

```
        {
            element = element,
            average = source.Average ()
        }
    )
    .Select (temp0 =>
            Math.Pow (
                ((double)temp0.element - temp0.average)
                , 2));
```

Each additional `let` variable introduced will cause the current anonymous type to be cascaded within another anonymous type containing itself and the additional variable—and so on. However, all of this magic is transparent when writing a query expression.

Into—Query Continuation

The `group`, `join`, and `select` query expression keywords allow the resulting sequence to be captured into a local variable and then used in the rest of the query. The `into` keyword allows a query to be continued by using the result stored into the local variable at any point after its definition.

The most common point `into` is employed is when capturing the result of a group operation, which along with the built-in join features is covered extensively in Chapter 4, "Grouping and Joining Data." As a quick preview, the following example groups all elements of the same value and stores the result in a variable called `groups`; by using the `into` keyword (in combination with the `group` keyword), the `groups` variable can participate and be accessed in the remaining query statement.

```
var groupings = from element in source
            group element by element into groups
            select new {
                Key = groups.Key,
                Count = groups.Count()
};
```

Comparing the Query Syntax Options

Listing 3-1 uses extension method syntax, and Listing 3-2 uses query expression syntax, but they are functionally equivalent, with both generating the identical result shown in Output 3-1. The clarity of the code in the query expression syntax stems from the removal of the lambda expression semantics and the SQL style operator semantics. Both syntax styles are functionally identical, and for simple queries (like this example), the benefit of code clarity is minimal.

Listing 3-1   Query gets all contacts in the state of "WA" ordered by last name and then first name using extension method query syntax—see Output 3-1

```
List<Contact> contacts = Contact.SampleData();

var q = contacts.Where(c => c.State == "WA")
                .OrderBy(c => c.LastName)
                .ThenBy(c => c.FirstName);

foreach (Contact c in q)
    Console.WriteLine("{0} {1}",
        c.FirstName, c.LastName);
```

Listing 3-2   The same query as in Listing 3-1 except using query expression syntax—see Output 3-1

```
List<Contact> contacts = Contact.SampleData();

var q = from c in contacts
        where c.State == "WA"
        orderby c.LastName, c.FirstName
        select c;

foreach (Contact c in q)
    Console.WriteLine("{0} {1}",
        c.FirstName, c.LastName);
```

Output 3-1

```
Stewart Kagel
Chance Lard
Armando Valdes
```

There are extensive code readability advantages to using the query expression syntax over the extension method syntax when your query contains join and/or group functionality. Although not all joining and grouping functionality is natively available to you when using the query expression syntax, the majority of queries you write will not require those extra features. Listing 3-3 demonstrates the rather clumsy extension method syntax for Join (clumsy in the fact that it is not clear what each argument means in the GroupBy extension method just by reading the code). The functionally equivalent query expression syntax for this same query is shown in Listing 3-4. Both queries produce the identical result, as shown in Output 3-2.

If it is not clear already, my personal preference is to use the query expression syntax whenever a Join or GroupBy operation is required in a query. When a standard query operator isn't supported by the query expression syntax (as is the case for the .Take method for example), you parenthesize the query and use extension method syntax from that point forward as Listing 3-4 demonstrates.

Listing 3-3 Joins become particularly complex in extension method syntax. This query returns the first five call-log details ordered by most recent—see Output 3-2

```
List<Contact> contacts = Contact.SampleData();
List<CallLog> callLog = CallLog.SampleData();

var q = callLog.Join(contacts,
                call => call.Number,
                contact => contact.Phone,
                (call, contact) => new
                {
                    contact.FirstName,
                    contact.LastName,
                    call.When,
                    call.Duration
                })
            .OrderByDescending(call => call.When)
            .Take(5);

foreach (var call in q)
    Console.WriteLine("{0} - {1} {2} ({3}min)",
        call.When.ToString("ddMMM HH:m"),
        call.FirstName, call.LastName, call.Duration);
```

Listing 3-4   Query expression syntax of the query identical to that shown in Listing 3-3—
see Output 3-2

```
List<Contact> contacts = Contact.SampleData();
List<CallLog> callLog = CallLog.SampleData();

var q = (from call in callLog
        join contact in contacts on
            call.Number equals contact.Phone
        orderby call.When descending
        select new
        {
            contact.FirstName,
            contact.LastName,
            call.When,
            call.Duration
        }).Take(5);

foreach (var call in q)
    Console.WriteLine("{0} - {1} {2} ({3}min)",
        call.When.ToString("ddMMM HH:m"),
        call.FirstName, call.LastName, call.Duration);
```

Output 3-2

```
07Aug 11:15 - Stewart Kagel (4min)
07Aug 10:35 - Collin Zeeman (2min)
07Aug 10:5 - Mack Kamph (1min)
07Aug 09:23 - Ariel Hazelgrove (15min)
07Aug 08:12 - Barney Gottshall (2min)
```

EXTENSION METHOD DEVELOPER TIPS

- Express the most limiting query method first; this reduces the workload of the successive operators.
- Split each operator onto a different line (including the period joiner). This allows you to comment out individual operators when debugging.
- Be consistent—within an application use the same style throughout.
- To make it easier to read queries, don't be afraid to split up the query into multiple parts and indent to show hierarchy.

QUERY EXPRESSION DEVELOPER TIPS

- If you need to mix extension methods with query expressions, put them at the end.
- Keep each part of the query expression on a separate line to allow you to individually comment out individual clauses for debugging.

How to Filter the Results (Where Clause)

One of the main tasks of a LINQ query is to restrict the results from a larger collection based on some criteria. This is achieved using the Where operator, which tests each element within a source collection and returns only those elements that return a true result when tested against a given predicate expression. A *predicate* is simply an expression that takes an element of the same type of the items in the source collection and returns true or false. This predicate is passed to the Where clause using a lambda expression.

The extension method for the Where operator is surprisingly simple; it iterates the source collection using a foreach loop, testing each element as it goes, returning those that pass. Here is a close facsimile of the actual code in the System.Linq library:

```
public delegate TResult Func<T1, TResult>(T1 arg1);

public static IEnumerable<T> Where<T>(
        this IEnumerable<T> source,
        Func<T, bool> predicate) {

    foreach (T element in source) {
        if (predicate(element))
            yield return element;
    }
}
```

The LINQ to Objects Where operator seems pretty basic on the surface, but its implementation is simple due to the powerful yield return statement that first appeared in the .NET Framework 2.0 to make building collection iterators easier. Any code implementing the built-in enumeration pattern (as codified by any collection that implements the interface

`IEnumerable`) natively supports callers asking for the next item in a collection—at which time the next item for return is computed (supported by the `foreach` keyword as an example). Any collection implementing the `IEnumerable<T>` pattern (which also implements `IEnumerable`) will be extended by the `Where` operator, which will return a single element at a time when asked, as long as that element satisfies the predicate expression (returns `true`).

Filter predicate expressions are passed to the extension method using a lambda expression (for a recap on what a lambda expression is see Chapter 2, "Introducing LINQ to Objects"), although if the query expression syntax is used, the filter predicate takes an even cleaner form. Both of these predicate expression styles are explained and covered in detail in the following sections.

Where Filter Using a Lambda Expression

When forming a predicate for the `Where` operator, the predicate takes an input element of the same type as the elements in the source collection and returns true or false (a Boolean value). To demonstrate using a simple `Where` clause predicate, consider the following code:

```
string[] animals = new string[] { "Koala", "Kangaroo",
    "Spider", "Wombat", "Snake", "Emu", "Shark",
    "Sting-Ray", "Jellyfish" };

var q = animals.Where(
    a => a.StartsWith("S") && a.Length > 5);

foreach (string s in q)
    Console.WriteLine(s);
```

In this code, each string value from the animals array is passed to the `Where` extension method in a range variable called `a`. Each string in `a` is evaluated against the predicate function, and only those strings that pass (return true) are returned in the query results. For this example, only two strings pass the test and are written to the console window. They are

```
Spider
```

```
Sting-Ray
```

The C# compiler behind the scenes converts the lambda expression into a standard anonymous method call (the following code is functionally equivalent):

```
var q = animals.Where(
    delegate(string a) {
        return a.StartsWith("S") && a.Length > 5; });
```

What Is Deferred Execution?

The `Where` clause will only begin testing the predicate when somebody (you through a `foreach` statement or one of the other standard query operators that have an internal `foreach` statement) tries to iterate through the results; until then, the iterator framework just remembers exactly where it was the last time it was asked for an element. This is called deferred execution, and it allows you some predictability and control over when and how a query is executed. If you want results immediately you can call `ToList()`, `ToArray()` or one of the other standard operators that cause immediate actualization of the results to another form; otherwise, the query will begin evaluation only when you begin iterating over it.

Where Filter Query Expressions (Preferred)

The query expression `where` clause syntax drops the explicit range variable definition and the lambda expression operator (`=>`), making it more concise and more familiar to the SQL-style clauses that many developers understand. It is the preferred syntax for these reasons. Rewriting the previous example using query expression syntax demonstrates these differences, as follows:

```
string[] animals = new string[] { "Koala", "Kangaroo",
    "Spider", "Wombat", "Snake", "Emu", "Shark",
    "Sting-Ray", "Jellyfish" };

var q = from a in animals
        where a.StartsWith("S") && a.Length > 5
        select a;

foreach (string s in q)
    Console.WriteLine(s);
```

Using an External Method for Evaluation

Although you can write queries and inline the code for the filter predicate, you don't have to. If the predicate is lengthy and might be used in more than one query expression, you should consider putting it in its own method body (good practice for any duplicated code). Rewriting the previous examples using an external predicate function shows the technique:

```
string[] animals = new string[] { "Koala", "Kangaroo",
    "Spider", "Wombat", "Snake", "Emu", "Shark",
    "Sting-Ray", "Jellyfish" };

var q = from a in animals
        where MyPredicate(a)
        select a;

foreach (string s in q)
    Console.WriteLine(s);

public bool MyPredicate(string a)
{
    if (a.StartsWith("S") && a.Length > 5)
        return true;
    else
        return false;
}
```

To further demonstrate this technique with a slightly more complex scenario, the code shown in Listing 3-5 creates a predicate method that encapsulates the logic for determining "a deadly animal." By encapsulating this logic in one method, it doesn't have to be duplicated in multiple places in an application.

Listing 3-5 **Where** clause using external method—see Output 3-3

```
string[] animals = new string[] { "Koala", "Kangaroo",
    "Spider", "Wombat", "Snake", "Emu", "Shark",
    "Sting-Ray", "Jellyfish" };

var q = from a in animals
        where IsAnimalDeadly(a)
        select a;
```

```
foreach (string s in q)
    Console.WriteLine("A {0} can be deadly.", s);


public static bool IsAnimalDeadly(string s)
{
    string[] deadly = new string[] {"Spider", "Snake",
        "Shark", "Sting-Ray", "Jellyfish"};

    return deadly.Contains(s);
}
```

Output 3-3

```
A Spider can be deadly.
A Snake can be deadly.
A Shark can be deadly.
A Sting-Ray can be deadly.
A Jellyfish can be deadly.
```

Filtering by Index Position

The standard query operators expose a variation of the `Where` operator that surfaces the index position of each collection element as it progresses. The zero-based index position can be passed into a lambda expression predicate by assigning a variable name as the second argument (after the element range variable). To surface the index position, a lambda expression must be used, and this can only be achieved using the extension method syntax. Listing 3-6 demonstrates the simplest usage, in this case simply returning the first and only even-index positioned elements from the source collection, as shown in Output 3-4.

Listing 3-6 The index position can be used as part of the **where** clause predicate expression when using lambda expressions—see Output 3-4

```
string[] animals = new string[] { "Koala", "Kangaroo",
    "Spider", "Wombat", "Snake", "Emu", "Shark",
    "Sting-Ray", "Jellyfish" };

// get the first then every other animal (index is odd)
var q = animals.Where((a, index) => index % 2 == 0);
```

```
foreach (string s in q)
    Console.WriteLine(s);
```

Output 3-4

```
Koala
Spider
Snake
Shark
Jellyfish
```

How to Change the Return Type (Select Projection)

When you write queries against a database system in SQL, specifying a set of columns to return is second nature. The goal is to limit the columns returned to only those necessary for the query in order to improve performance and limit network traffic (the less data transferred, the better). This is achieved by listing the column names after the select clause in the following format. In most cases, only the columns of interest are returned using the SQL syntax form:

```
Select * from Contacts

Select ContactId, FirstName, LastName from Contacts
```

The first query will return every column (and row) of the contacts table; the second will return only the three columns explicitly listed (for every row), saving server and network resources. The point is that the SQL language syntax allows a different set of rows that does not match any existing database table, view, or schema to be the structure used in returning data. Select projections in LINQ query expressions allow us to achieve the same task. If only few property values are needed in the result set, those properties or fields are the only ones returned.

LINQ selection projections allow varied and powerful control over how and what data shape is returned from a query expression.

The different ways a select projection can return results are

- As a single result value or element
- In an `IEnumerable<T>` where `T` is of the same type as the source items
- In an `IEnumerable<T>` where `T` is any existing type constructed in the select projection
- In an `IEnumerable<T>` where `T` is an anonymous type created in the select projection
- In an `IEnumberable<IGrouping<TKey, TElement>>`, which is a collection of grouped objects that share a common key

Each projection style has its use, and each style is explained by example in the following sections.

HOW MUCH DATA ARE YOU PROJECTING IN A SELECT PROJECTION?   As with all good data-access paradigms, the goal should be to return the fewest properties as possible when defining a query result shape. This reduces the memory footprint and makes the result set easier to code against because there are fewer properties to wade through.

Return a Single Result Value or Element

Some of the standard query operators return a single value as the result, or a single element from the source collection; these operators are listed in Table 3-1. Each of these operators end any cascading of results into another query, and instead return a single result value or source element.

Table 3-1   Sample Set of Operators that Return a Specific Result Value Type (covered in Chapters 5 and 6)

Return Type	Standard Query Operator
Numeric	`Aggregate, Average, Max, Min, Sum, Count, LongCount`
Boolean	`All, Any, Contains, SequenceEqual`
Type <T>	`ElementAt, ElementAtOrDefault, First, FirstOrDefault, Last, LastOrDefault, Single, SingleOrDefault, DefaultIfEmpty`

As an example, the following simple query returns the last element in the integer array, writing the number 2 to the Console window:

```
int[] nums = new int[] { 5, 3, 4, 2 };
int last = nums.Last();
ConsoleWriteLine(last);
```

Return the Same Type as the Source— IEnumerable<TSource>

The most basic projection type returns a filtered and ordered subset of the original source items. This projection is achieved by specifying the range variable as the argument after the select keyword. The following example returns an IEnumerable<Contact>, with the type Contact being inferred from the element type of the source collection:

```
List<Contact> contacts = Contact.SampleData();

IEnumerable<Contact> q = from c in contacts
                         select c;
```

A more appropriate query would filter the results and order them in some convenient fashion. You are still returning a collection of the same type, but the number of elements and their order will be different.

```
List<Contact> contacts = Contact.SampleData();

IEnumerable<Contact> q = from c in contacts
                         where c.State == "WA"
                         orderby c.LastName,
                                 c.FirstName ascending
                         select c;
```

Return a Different Type Than the Source— IEnumerable<TAny>

Any type can be projected as part of the select clause, not just the source type. The target type can be any available type that could otherwise be manually constructed with a plain `new` statement from the scope of code being written.

If the type being constructed has a parameterized constructor containing all of the parameters you specifically need, then you simply call that constructor. If no constructor matches the parameter's needed for this projection, either create one or consider using the C# 3.0 type initializer syntax (as covered in Chapter 2). The benefit of using the new type initializer semantics is that it frees you from having to define a specific constructor each time a new projection signature is needed to cater for different query shapes. Listing 3-7 demonstrates how to project an `IEnumerable<ContactName>` using both constructor semantics.

NOTE   Resist the temptation to overuse the type initializer syntax. It requires that all properties being initialized through this syntax be read and write (have a getter and setter). If a property should be read-only, don't make it read/write just for this feature. Consider making those constructor parameters optional using the C# 4.0 Optional Parameter syntax described in Chapter 8, "C# 4.0 Features."

Listing 3-7   Projecting to a collection of a new type—constructed using either a specific constructor or by using type initializer syntax

```
List<Contact> contacts = Contact.SampleData();

// using a parameterized constructor
IEnumerable<ContactName> q1 =
    from c in contacts
    select new ContactName(
            c.LastName + ", " + c.FirstName,
            (DateTime.Now - c.DateOfBirth).Days / 365);

// using Type Initializer semantics
// note: The type requires a parameterless constructor
IEnumerable<ContactName> q2 =
  from c in contacts
  select new ContactName
  {
      FullName = c.LastName + ", " + c.FirstName,
      YearsOfAge =
```

```
            (DateTime.Now - c.DateOfBirth).Days / 365
    };

// ContactName class definition
public class ContactName
{
    public string FullName { get; set; }
    public int YearsOfAge { get; set; }

    // constructor needed for
    // object initialization example
    public ContactName() {
    }

    // constructor required for
    // type projection example
    public ContactName(string name, int age)
    {
        this.FullName = name;
        this.YearsOfAge = age;
    }
}
```

Return an Anonymous Type— IEnumerable<TAnonymous>

Anonymous types is a new language feature introduced in C# 3.0 where the compiler creates a type on-the-fly based on the object initialization expression (the expression on the right side of the initial = sign). Discussed in detail in Chapter 2, this new type is given an uncallable name by the compiler, and without the var keyword (implicitly typed local variables), there would be no way to compile the query. The following query demonstrates projecting to an IEnumerable<T> collection where T is an anonymous type:

```
List<Contact> contacts = Contact.SampleData();

var q = from c in contacts
        select new
        {
```

```
                    FullName = c.LastName + ", " + c.FirstName,
                    YearsOfAge =
                        (DateTime.Now - c.DateOfBirth).Days / 365
        };
```

The anonymous type created in the previous example is composed of two properties, `FullName` and `YearsOfAge`.

Anonymous types free us from having to write and maintain a specific type definition for every different return result collection needed. The only drawback is that these types are method-scoped and cannot be used outside of the method they are declared by (unless passed as a `System.Object` type, but this is not recommended because property access to this object subsequently will need to use reflection).

Return a Set of Grouped Objects— IEnumerable<IGrouping<TKey,TElement>>

It is possible for LINQ to Objects to group results that share common source values or any given characteristic that can be equated with an expression using the `group by` query expression keyword or the `GroupBy` extension method. This topic is covered in great detail in Chapter 4.

How to Return Elements When the Result Is a Sequence (Select Many)

The `SelectMany` standard query operator flattens out any `IEnumerable<T>` result elements, returning each element individually from those enumerable sources before moving onto the next element in the result sequence. In contrast, the `Select` extension method would stop at the first level and return the `IEnumerable<T>` element itself.

Listing 3-8 demonstrates how `SelectMany` differs from `Select`, with each variation aiming to retrieve each individual word within a set of phrase strings. To retrieve the words in Option 1, a sub `for` loop is required, but `SelectMany` automatically performs this subiteration of the original result collection, as shown in Option 2. Option 3 demonstrates that the same result can be achieved using multiple `from` statements in a query expression (which maps the query to use `SelectMany` operator behind the scenes). The Console output is shown in Output 3-5.

Listing 3-8 `Select` versus `SelectMany`—`SelectMany` drills into an `IEnumerable` result, returning its elements—see Output 3-5

```
string[] sentence = new string[] { "The quick brown",
    "fox jumps over", "the lazy dog."};

Console.WriteLine("option 1:"); Console.WriteLine("--------");

// option 1: Select returns three string[]'s with
// three strings in each.
IEnumerable<string[]> words1 =
    sentence.Select(w => w.Split(' '));

// to get each word, we have to use two foreach loops
foreach (string[] segment in words1)
    foreach (string word in segment)
        Console.WriteLine(word);

Console.WriteLine();
Console.WriteLine("option 2:"); Console.WriteLine("--------");

// option 2: SelectMany returns nine strings
// (sub-iterates the Select result)
IEnumerable<string> words2 =
    sentence.SelectMany(segment => segment.Split(' '));

// with SelectMany we have every string individually
foreach (var word in words2)
    Console.WriteLine(word);

// option 3: identical to Opt 2 above written using
// the Query Expression syntax (multiple froms)
IEnumerable<string> words3 =
    from segment in sentence
    from word in segment.Split(' ')
    select word;
```

Output 3-5

```
option 1:
--------
The
quick
brown
```

```
fox
jumps
over
the
lazy
dog.

option 2:
--------
The
quick
brown
fox
jumps
over
the
lazy
dog.
```

How does the `SelectMany` extension method work? It creates a nested `foreach` loop over the original result, returning each subelement using `yield return` statements. A close facsimile of the code behind `SelectMany` takes the following form:

```
static IEnumerable<S> SelectManyIterator<T, S>(
    this IEnumerable<T> source,
    Func<T, IEnumerable<S>> selector)
{
    foreach (T element in source)
    {
        foreach (S subElement in selector(element))
        {
            yield return subElement;
        }
    }
}
```

How to Get the Index Position of the Results

`Select` and `SelectMany` expose an overload that surfaces the index position (starting at zero) for each returned element in the Select projection. It is surfaced as an overloaded parameter argument of the selector lambda expression and is only accessible using the extension method query syntax. Listing 3-9 demonstrates how to access and use the index position value in a Select projection. As shown in Output 3-6, this example simply adds a ranking number for each select result string.

Listing 3-9   A zero-based index number is exposed by the `Select` and `SelectMany` operators—see Output 3-6

```
List<CallLog> callLog = CallLog.SampleData();

var q = callLog.GroupBy(g => g.Number)
            .OrderByDescending(g => g.Count())
            .Select((g, index) => new
            {
                number = g.Key,
                rank = index + 1,
                count = g.Count()
            });

foreach (var c in q)
    Console.WriteLine(
        "Rank {0} - {1}, called {2} times.",
        c.rank, c.number, c.count);
```

Output 3-6

```
Rank 1 - 885 983 8858, called 6 times.
Rank 2 - 546 607 5462, called 6 times.
Rank 3 - 364 202 3644, called 4 times.
Rank 4 - 603 303 6030, called 4 times.
Rank 5 - 848 553 8487, called 4 times.
Rank 6 - 165 737 1656, called 2 times.
Rank 7 - 278 918 2789, called 2 times.
```

How to Remove Duplicate Results

The `Distinct` standard query operator performs the role of returning only unique instances in a sequence. The operator internally keeps track of the elements it has returned and skips the second and subsequent duplicate elements as it returns resulting elements. This operator is covered in more detail in Chapter 6, "Working with Set Data," when its use in set operations is explored.

The Distinct operator is not supported in the query expression syntax, so it is often appended to the end of a query using extension method syntax. To demonstrate how it is used, the following code removes duplicate strings. The Console output from this code is

```
Peter
Paul
Mary
Janet
```

```
string[] names = new string[] { "Peter", "Paul",
    "Mary", "Peter", "Paul", "Mary", "Janet" };

var q = (from s in names
        where s.Length > 3
        select s).Distinct();

foreach (var name in q)
    Console.WriteLine(name);
```

How to Sort the Results

LINQ to Objects has comprehensive support for ordering and sorting results. Whether you need to sort in ascending order, descending order using different property values in any sequence, or all the way to writing a specific ordering algorithm of your own, LINQ's sorting features can accommodate the full range of ordering requirements.

Basic Sorting Syntax

The resulting collection of results from a query can be sorted in any desired fashion, considering culture and case sensitivity. When querying using extension method syntax, the OrderBy, OrderByDescending, ThenBy, and ThenByDescending standard query operators manage this process. The OrderBy and ThenBy operators sort in an ascending order (for example, a to z), and the OrderByDescending and ThenByDescending operators sort in descending order (z to a). Only the first sorting extension can use the OrderBy operators, and each subsequent sorting expression must use the

ThenBy operators, of which there can be zero or many depending on how much control you want over the subsorting when multiple elements share equal order after the previous expressions.

The following samples demonstrate sorting a source sequence first by the [w] key, then in descending order by the [x] key, and then in ascending order by the [y] key:

```
[source].OrderBy([w])
        .ThenByDescending([x])
        .ThenBy([y]);
```

When using the query expression syntax, each sorting key and the optional direction keyword needs to be separated by a comma character. If the descending or ascending direction keywords are not specified, LINQ assumes ascending order.

```
from [v] in [source]
orderBy [w], [x] descending, [y]
select [z];
```

The result from ordering a collection will be an IOrderedEnumerable<T>, which implements IEnumerable<T> to allow further query operations to be cascaded end-to-end.

The ordering extension methods are implemented using a basic but efficient Quicksort algorithm (see http://en.wikipedia.org/wiki/Quicksort for further explanation of how this algorithm works). The implementation LINQ to Objects uses is a sorting type called *unstable*, which simply means that elements that compare to equal key values may not retain their relative positions to the source collections (although this is simply solved by cascading the result into a ThenBy or ThenByDescending operator). The algorithm is fairly fast, and it lends itself to parallelization, which is certainly leveraged by Microsoft's investment in Parallel LINQ.

What Is Parallelization?

Parallelization refers to improving performance of applications by fully leveraging multiple processors and multiple-cores on those processors running code. Parallelization is covered in detail in Chapter 9, "Parallel LINQ to Objects," which also demonstrates how LINQ queries can fully benefit from multicore and multiprocessor hardware improvements.

Reversing the Order of a Result Sequence (Reverse)

Another ordering extension method that reverses an entire sequence is the `Reverse` operator. It is simply called in the form: `[source].Reverse();`. An important point to note when using the `Reverse` operator is that it doesn't test the equality of the elements or carry out any sorting; it simply returns elements starting from the last element, back to the first element. The order returned will be the exact reciprocal of the order that would have been returned from the result sequence. The following example demonstrates the `Reverse` operator, returning `T A C` in the Console window:

```
string[] letters = new string[] { "C", "A", "T" };
var q = letters.Reverse();
foreach (string s in q)
    Console.Write(" " + s);
```

Case Insensitive and Cultural-specific String Ordering

Any standard query operator that involves sorting has an overload that allows a specific comparer function to be supplied (when written using extension method syntax). The .NET class libraries contain a handy helper class called `StringComparer`, which has a set of predefined static comparers ready for use. The comparers allow us to alter string sorting behavior, controlling case-sensitivity and current culture (the language setting for the current thread). Table 3-2 lists the static Comparer instances that can be used in any `OrderBy` or `ThenBy` ascending or descending query operator. (In addition, see the "Custom EqualityComparers When Using LINQ Set Operators" section in Chapter 6, which is specifically about the built-in string comparers and custom comparers.)

Table 3-2 The Built-in **`StringComparer`** Functions to Control String Case Sensitivity and Culture-aware String Ordering

Comparer	Description
CurrentCulture	Performs a case-sensitive string comparison using the word comparison rules of the current culture.
CurrentCultureIgnoreCase	Performs case-insensitive string comparisons using the word comparison rules of the current culture.

Table 3-2 The Built-in `StringComparer` Functions to Control String Case Sensitivity and Culture-aware String Ordering

Comparer	Description
InvariantCulture	Performs a case-sensitive string comparison using the word comparison rules of the invariant culture.
InvariantCultureIgnoreCase	Performs a case-insensitive string comparison using the word comparison rules of the invariant culture.
Ordinal	Performs a case-sensitive ordinal string comparison.
OrdinalIgnoreCase	Performs a case-insensitive ordinal string comparison.

Listing 3-10 demonstrates the syntax and effect of using the built-in string comparer instances offered by the .NET Framework. The Console output is shown in Output 3-7, where the default case-sensitive result can be forced to case-insensitive.

Listing 3-10 Case and culture sensitive/insensitive ordering using `StringComparer` functions—see Output 3-7

```
string[] words = new string[] {
    "jAnet", "JAnet", "janet", "Janet" };

var cs = words.OrderBy(w => w);
var ci = words.OrderBy(w => w,
    StringComparer.CurrentCultureIgnoreCase);

Console.WriteLine("Original:");
foreach (string s in words)
    Console.WriteLine(" " + s);

Console.WriteLine("Case Sensitive (default):");
foreach (string s in cs)
    Console.WriteLine(" " + s);

Console.WriteLine("Case Insensitive:");
foreach (string s in ci)
    Console.WriteLine(" " + s);
```

Output 3-7

```
Original:
 jAnet
 JAnet
 janet
 Janet
Case Sensitive (default):
 janet
 jAnet
 Janet
 JAnet
Case Insensitive:
 jAnet
 JAnet
 janet
 Janet
```

Specifying Your Own Custom Sort Comparison Function

To support any sorting order that might be required, custom sort comparison classes are easy to specify. A custom compare class is a class based on a standard .NET Interface called `IComparer<T>`, which exposes a single method: `Compare`. This interface is not specifically for LINQ; it is the basis for all .NET Framework classes that require sorting (or custom sorting) capabilities.

Comparer functions work by returning an integer result, indicating the relationship between a pair of instance types. If the two types are deemed equal, the function returns zero. If the first instance is less than the second instance, a negative value is returned, or if the first instance is larger than the second instance, the function returns a positive value. How you equate the integer result value is entirely up to you.

To demonstrate a custom `IComparer<T>`, Listing 3-11 demonstrates a comparison function that simply shuffles (in a random fashion) the input source. The algorithm simply makes a random choice as to whether two elements are less than or greater than each other. Output 3-8 shows the Console output from a simple sort of a source of strings in an array, although this result will be different (potentially) each time this code is executed.

Listing 3-11   Ordering using our custom `IComparer<T>` implementation to shuffle the results—see Output 3-8

```
public class RandomShuffleStringSort<T> : IComparer<T>
{
    internal Random random = new Random();

    public int Compare(T x, T y)
    {
        // get a random number: 0 or 1
        int i = random.Next(2);

        if (i == 0)
            return -1;
        else
            return 1;
    }
}

string[] strings = new string[] { "1-one", "2-two",
    "3-three", "4-four", "5-five" };

var normal = strings.OrderBy(s => s);
var custom = strings.OrderBy(s => s,
    new RandomShuffleStringSort<string>());

Console.WriteLine("Normal Sort Order:");
foreach (string s in normal) {
    Console.WriteLine(" " + s);
}

Console.WriteLine("Custom Sort Order:");
foreach (string s1 in custom) {
    Console.WriteLine(" " + s1);
}
```

Output 3-8

```
Normal Sort Order:
 1-one
 2-two
 3-three
 4-four
 5-five
```

```
Custom Sort Order:
 1-one
 2-two
 5-five
 4-four
 3-three
```

A common scenario that has always caused me trouble is where straight alphabetical sorting doesn't properly represent alpha-numeric strings. The most common example is alphabetic sorting strings such as `File1`, `File10`, `File2`. Naturally, the desired sorting order would be `File1`, `File2`, `File10`, but that's not alphabetical. A custom `IComparer` that will sort the alphabetic part and then the numeric part separately is needed to achieve this common scenario. This is called *natural sorting*.

Listing 3-12 and Output 3-9 demonstrate a custom sort class that correctly orders alpha strings that end with numbers. Anywhere this sort order is required, the class name can be passed into any of the `OrderBy` or `ThenBy` extension methods in the following way:

```
string[] partNumbers = new string[] { "SCW10", "SCW1",
    "SCW2", "SCW11", "NUT10", "NUT1", "NUT2", "NUT11" };

var custom = partNumbers.OrderBy(s => s,
    new AlphaNumberSort());
```

The code in Listing 3-12 first checks if either input string is null or empty. If either string is empty, it calls and returns the result from the default comparer (no specific alpha-numeric string to check). Having determined that there are two actual strings to compare, the numeric trailing section of each string is extracted into the variables `numericX` and `numericY`. If either string doesn't have a trailing numeric section, the result of the default comparer is returned (if no trailing numeric section exists for one of the strings, then a straight string compare is adequate). If both strings have a trailing numeric section, the alpha part of the strings is compared. If the strings are different, the result of the default comparer is returned (if the strings are different, the numeric part of the string is irrelevant). If both alpha parts are the same, the numeric values in `numericX` and `numericY` are compared, and that result is returned. The final result is that all strings are sorted alphabetically, and where the string part is the same between elements, the numeric section controls the final order.

Listing 3-12   Sorting using a custom comparer. This comparer properly sorts strings that end with a number—see Output 3-9

```
public class AlphaNumberSort : IComparer<string>
{
    public int Compare(string a, string b)
    {
        StringComparer sc =
            StringComparer.CurrentCultureIgnoreCase;

        // if either input is null or empty,
        // do a straight string comparison
        if (string.IsNullOrEmpty(a) ||
            string.IsNullOrEmpty(b))
                return sc.Compare(a, b);

        // find the last numeric sections
        string numericX = FindTrailingNumber(a);
        string numericY = FindTrailingNumber(b);

        // if there is a numeric end to both strings,
        // we need to investigate further
        if (numericX != string.Empty &&
            numericY != string.Empty)
        {
            // first, compare the string prefix only
            int stringPartCompareResult =
                sc.Compare(
                    a.Remove(a.Length - numericX.Length),
                    b.Remove(b.Length - numericY.Length));

            // the strings prefix are different,
            // return the comparison result for the strings
            if (stringPartCompareResult != 0)
                return stringPartCompareResult;

            // the strings prefix is the same,
            // need to test the numeric sections as well
            double nX = double.Parse(numericX);
            double nY = double.Parse(numericY);
            return nX.CompareTo(nY);
        }
        else
            return sc.Compare(a, b);
    }
```

```
    private static string FindTrailingNumber(string s)
    {
        string numeric = string.Empty;
        for (int i = s.Length - 1; i > -1; i--)
        {
            if (char.IsNumber(s[i]))
                numeric = s[i] + numeric;
            else
                break;
        }
        return numeric;
    }
}

string[] partNumbers = new string[] { "SCW10", "SCW1",
    "SCW2", "SCW11", "NUT10", "NUT1", "NUT2", "NUT11" };

var normal = partNumbers.OrderBy(s => s);
var custom = partNumbers.OrderBy(s => s,
    new AlphaNumberSort());

Console.WriteLine("Normal Sort Order:");
foreach (string s in normal)
    Console.WriteLine(" " + s);

Console.WriteLine("Custom Sort Order:");
foreach (string s in custom)
    Console.WriteLine(" " + s);
```

Output 3-9

```
Normal Sort Order:
NUT1
NUT10
NUT11
NUT2
SCW1
SCW10
SCW11
SCW2
```

```
Custom Sort Order:
  NUT1
  NUT2
  NUT10
  NUT11
  SCW1
  SCW2
  SCW10
  SCW11
```

NOTE To achieve the same result in most Windows operating systems (not Windows 2000, but ME, XP, 2003, Vista, and Windows 7) and without guarantee that it won't change over time (it bears the following warning "Note Behavior of this function, and therefore the results it returns, can change from release to release. It should not be used for canonical sorting applications"), Microsoft has an API that it uses to sort files in Explorer (and presumably other places).

```csharp
internal static class Shlwapi
{
    // http://msdn.microsoft.com/
    // en-us/library/bb759947(VS.85).aspx
    [DllImport("shlwapi.dll",
                CharSet = CharSet.Unicode)]
    public static extern int StrCmpLogicalW(
        string a,
        string b);
}


public sealed class
    NaturalStringComparer: IComparer<string>
{
    public int Compare(string a, string b)
    {
        return Shlwapi.StrCmpLogicalW(a, b);
    }
}
```

Summary

This chapter has covered the essential query functionality of filtering, ordering, and projecting the results into any resulting form you might require. Once you have understood and mastered these basic query essentials, you can confidently experiment with the more advanced query features offered by the other 40-odd standard query operators and begin writing your own operators if necessary.

CHAPTER 4

GROUPING AND JOINING DATA

Goals of this chapter:

- Define the capabilities of LINQ joining and grouping features.
- Demonstrate grouping and joining data sources.
- Discuss the best practices and pitfalls to avoid when grouping and joining data sources.

The main goal of this chapter is to define the capabilities of LINQ to Objects' extensive grouping and joining features. Best practices and the most likely pitfalls to be avoided when grouping and joining data sources are discussed. By the end of this chapter you will be well-versed in how to write queries that group input data into subcollections and how to join data in one collection with matching data from another.

How to Group Elements

Grouping in LINQ enables you to return partitioned sets of data from a collection based on a given key value. An example might be to group all `Contact` records by the `State` property. In LINQ this query can be simply written

```
var q = from c in contacts
        group c by c.State;
```

Or if you prefer the extension method query syntax

```
var q = contacts.GroupBy(c => c.State);
```

The result from a LINQ grouping operation is an enumerable sequence of groups (themselves sequences), with each group having a distinct key value. The key value is determined by the "key selection" expression, which is an expression that equates the key value for each element (c.State in the previous example). All source elements that equate to an equal key value using the key selection expression will be partitioned into the same group.

The GroupBy extension method operator has many overloads; the simplest has just a single key selection argument. The remaining overloads of this operator allow specific control of how element equality is evaluated, the select projection to use for the resulting groups, and what select projection is used for generating each element in any resulting group.

The following GroupBy extension method signature shows all of the possible arguments:

```
public static IEnumerable<TResult>
    GroupBy<TSource, TKey, TElement, TResult>
(
    this IEnumerable<TSource> source,
    Func<TSource, TKey> keySelector,
    Func<TSource, TElement>
        elementSelector,
    Func<TKey, IEnumerable<TElement>, TResult>
        resultSelector,
    IEqualityComparer<TKey> compare
)
```

Independent from how the GroupBy projects the results, the resulting sequence exposes groups that have a common Key property value. The members of these groupings can themselves be enumerated to obtain the individual group elements.

RESULT SEQUENCE ORDERING   The key order by default is the order each key value first appears in the source collection. If you want an alternative key order, sort the source collection first using the normal ordering operators.

Working with Groups

The return collection from a GroupBy or group x by y query is

```
IEnumerable<IGrouping<TKey, TElement>>
```

`IGrouping` interface inherits from `IEnumerable<TElement>` (making itself enumerable) and exposes a `Key` property that indicates the unique result that formed this grouping. This interface has the following form:

```
public interface IGrouping<TKey, TElmt> : IEnumerable<TElmt>
{
    TKey Key { get; }
}
```

LINQ to Objects returns by default an internal concrete class implementation of `IGrouping<Tkey, TElement>`, called `Grouping`. It is exposed via the `IGrouping` interface through the extension method signatures so that Microsoft can develop this over time. The only property you should rely on is the `Key` property. Most methods on the underlying `Grouping` collection type throw a `NotSupportedException` and should be avoided.

Enumerating over the result of a `GroupBy` extension method or `group x by y` query expression yields one `IGrouping<TKey, TElement>` element per unique key. Each group instance has the mandatory `Key` property, and each group can be iterated to get the elements in that group.

The normal pattern for working with groups once they are generated is to use a nested `foreach` loop; the first enumerates the groups, and then an inner loop iterates the elements. The general pattern is

```
foreach (var group in q)
{
    // Group specific code here
    Console.WriteLine("Group key: {0}", group.Key);

    foreach (var element in group)
    {
        // Element specific code here
        Console.WriteLine(" - {0}", element);
    }
}
```

Specifying a Key to Group By

During evaluation, all elements that share common key values as evaluated by the `keySelector` expression will be grouped. Value equality is determined using the default `Equals` operator, although this behavior can be overridden by specifying a custom equality comparison function, as seen shortly.

The `keySelector` expression can be any expression that evaluates a consistent return result for the desired grouping scheme. It is often a single field value from the source collection, but it can be as complex as needed. Listing 4-1 demonstrates how to group using the first three characters of a set of strings (the final groupings are shown in Output 4-1).

Listing 4-1   Elements that share the same return key value from the key selector function will be grouped—see Output 4-1

```
string[] partNumbers = new string[] { "SCW10", "SCW1",
    "SCW2", "SCW11", "NUT10", "NUT1", "NUT2", "NUT11" };

var q = from pn in partNumbers
        group pn by pn.Substring(0,3);

foreach (var group in q) {
    Console.WriteLine("Group key: {0}", group.Key);
    foreach (var part in group) {
        Console.WriteLine("  - {0}", part);
    }
}
```

Output 4-1

```
Group key: SCW
  - SCW10
  - SCW1
  - SCW2
  - SCW11
Group key: NUT
  - NUT10
  - NUT1
  - NUT2
  - NUT11
```

Handling Null Values in keySelector Expressions

Some care when writing the key selector is required for handling null values in the source data. The code shown in Listing 4-1 will fail if any of the part-number strings are null in value the moment the `Substring` method is attempted. Null values are safely handled in general, but if the range variable is processed within the key selector function, the normal null handling rules apply. Thus it is necessary to confirm an element isn't null before attempting to access properties or call methods on these range variables.

The following code throws a `NullReferenceException` when the query `q` is first accessed for iteration:

```
string[] partNumbers = new string[] { "SCW10", null,
    "SCW2", "SCW11", null, "NUT1", "NUT2", null };

// beware - nulls in source data can break your group
// expression. This grouping will fail.
var q = from pn in partNumbers
        group pn by pn.Substring(0, 3);
```

To protect against this circumstance, check the key selection expression for null values and throw all those elements into a group of your choosing to keep the exception from being thrown and to allow the null grouping to be orderly processed, as the following code demonstrates:

```
string[] partNumbers = new string[] { "SCW10", null,
    "SCW2", "SCW11", null, "NUT1", "NUT2", null };

// Advice - Guard against null values in key selection
var q = from pn in partNumbers
        group pn by
            pn == null ? "(null)" : pn.Substring(0,3);
```

The ternary operator (?) and the null-coalescing operator (??) offer a convenient syntax for handling potential null values in the `keySelector` expression. Listing 4-2 demonstrates their use in protecting against a null property value. In this case both operators handle the `state` property being null and groups these elements under the key value string of `(null)`.

USING THE TERNARY (?) AND NULL COALESCING (??)

OPERATORS   The ternary operator shortens the common `if (condition) then` `(true expression) else (false expression)` pattern of code to `(condition)` `? (true expression) : (false expression)`. This is especially useful when handling null values within query expressions where a full if-then-else statement is not valid syntax.

The null-coalescing operator is used to define a default value if the variable it follows has a null value, that is, X = (variable) ?? (default if null). Listing 4-2 demonstrates this usage.

Listing 4-2   Example of using the null-coalescing operator and the ternary operator to protect `keySelector` expressions from null values

```
// Guard against null data using
// ternary (? as shown)
var q1 = from c in Contact.SampleData()
        group c by
            c.State == null ? "(null)" : c.State;

// Guard against null data using
// the null coalescing operator (??).
var q2 = from c in Contact.SampleData()
        group c by
            c.State ?? "(null)";
```

Grouping by Composite Keys (More Than One Value)

To group using more than one value as the key (often referred to as a composite key), you specify the grouping selector clause as an anonymous type (anonymous types are introduced in Chapter 2, "Introducing LINQ to Objects"). Any number of key values can be specified in this anonymous type, and any element that contains identical values will dutifully be co-located in a group.

Listing 4-3 demonstrates the simplicity of specifying multiple key values in the group by expression. In this case, the LastName and the State fields are used for grouping, placing all contacts with the same last name from the same state in a group. The Console output from this example is shown in Output 4-2.

Listing 4-3   Anonymous types can be used to group by more than one value (composite key) — see Output 4-2

```
/* this sample uses the same data as we saw in Table 2-2,
   but i've added 2 Gottshall's (one from the same state
   and another out of that state), and 2 Gauwain's -
```

```
      Firstname      Lastname     State
      ------------------------------------
      Barney         Gottshall    CA
      Mandy          Gottshall    CA    *added
      Bernadette     Gottshall    WA    *added
      Armando        Valdes       WA
      Adam           Gauwain      AK
      Chris          Gauwain      AK    *added
      Anthony        Gauwain      CA    *added
      Jeffery        Deane        CA
      Collin         Zeeman       FL
      Stewart        Kagel        WA
      Chance         Lard         WA
      Blaine         Reifsteck    TX
      Mack           Kamph        TX
      Ariel          Hazelgrove   OR
*/

var q = from c in Contact.SampleData()
        group c by new { c.LastName, c.State };

foreach (var grp in q)
{
    Console.WriteLine("Group - {0}, {1} - count = {2}",
        grp.Key.LastName,
        grp.Key.State,
        grp.Count());
}
```

Output 4-2

```
Group - Gottshall, CA - count = 2
Group - Gottshall, WA - count = 1
Group - Valdes, WA - count = 1
Group - Gauwain, AK - count = 2
Group - Gauwain, CA - count = 1
Group - Deane, CA - count = 1
Group - Zeeman, FL - count = 1
Group - Kagel, WA - count = 1
Group - Lard, WA - count = 1
Group - Reifsteck, TX - count = 1
Group - Kamph, TX - count = 1
Group - Hazelgrove, OR - count = 1
```

It is not essential to use an anonymous type as the grouping key selector to achieve multiple-property groups. A named type containing all of the properties participating in the key can be used for the same purpose, although the method is more complex because the type being constructed in the projection needs a custom override of the methods GetHashCode and Equals to force comparison by property values rather than reference equality. Listing 4-4 demonstrates the mechanics of creating a class that supports composite keys using the fields LastName and State. The results are identical to that shown in Output 4-2.

NOTE Writing good GetHashCode implementations is beyond the scope of this book. I've used a simple implementation in this example—for more details see the MSDN article for recommendations of how to override the GetHashCode implementation available at http://msdn.microsoft.com/en-us/library/system. object.gethashcode.aspx.

Listing 4-4   Creating a composite join key using a normal class type

```
public class LastNameState
{
    public string LastName { get; set; }
    public string State { get; set; }

    // follow the MSDN guidelines -
    // http://msdn.microsoft.com/en-us/library/
    //                     ms173147(VS.80).aspx
    public override bool Equals(object obj)
    {
        if (this != obj)
        {
            LastNameState item = obj as LastNameState;
            if (item == null) return false;
            if (State != item.State) return false;
            if (LastName != item.LastName) return false;
        }

        return true;
    }
```

```
// follow the MSDN guidelines -
// http://msdn.microsoft.com/en-us/library/
//           system.object.gethashcode.aspx
public override int GetHashCode()
{
    int result = State != null ? State.GetHashCode() : 1;
    result = result ^
          (LastName != null ? LastName.GetHashCode() : 2);

    return result;
}
}

var q = from c in Contact.SampleData()
      group c by new LastNameState {
          LastName = c.LastName, State = c.State };
```

Specifying Your Own Key Comparison Function

The default behavior of grouping is to equate key equality using the normal equals comparison for the type being tested. This may not always suit your needs, and it is possible to override this behavior and specify your own grouping function. To implement a custom comparer, you build a class that implements the interface IEqualityComparer<T> and pass this class as an argument into the GroupBy extension method.

The IEqualityComparer<T> interface definition has the following definition:

```
public interface IEqualityComparer<T>
{
    public bool Equals(T x, T y)
    public int GetHashCode(T obj)
}
```

The Equals method is used to indicate that one instance of an object has the same equality to another instance of an object. Overriding this method allows specific logic to determine object equality based on the data within those objects, rather than instances being the same object instance. (That is, even though two objects were constructed at different times and are two different objects as far as the compiler is concerned, we want them to be deemed equal based on their specific combination of internal values or algorithm.)

The GetHashCode method is intended for use in hashing algorithms and data structures such as a hash table. The implementation of this method returns an integer value based on at least one value contained in the instance of an object. The resulting hash code can be used by other data structures as a unique value (but not guaranteed unique). It is intended as a quick way of segmenting instances in a collection or as a short-cut check for value equality (although a further check needs to be carried out for you to be certain of object value equality). The algorithm that computes the hash code should return the same integer value when two instances of an object have the same values (in the data fields being checked), and it should be fast, given that this method will be called many times during the grouping evaluation process.

The following example demonstrates one possible use of a custom equality comparer function in implementing a simple Soundex comparison routine (see http://en.wikipedia.org/wiki/Soundex for a full definition of the Soundex algorithm) that will group phonetically similar names. The code for the SoundexEqualityComparer is shown in Listing 4-5. Soundex is an age-old algorithm that computes a reliable four character string value based on the phonetics of a given word; an example would be "Katie" is phonetically identical to "Katy."

The approach for building the Soundex equality operator is to

1. Code the Soundex algorithm to return a four-character string result representing phonetic sounding given a string input. The form of the Soundex code is a single character, followed by three numerical digits, for example A123 or V456.

2. Implement the GetHashCode for a given string. This will call the Soundex method and then convert the Soundex code to an integer value. It builds the integer by using the ASCII value of the character, multiplying it by 1000 and then adding the three digit suffix of the Soundex code to this number, for example A123 would become, (65 x 1000) + 123 = 65123.

3. Implement the Equals method by calling GetHashCode on both input arguments x and y and then comparing the return integer results. Return true if the hash codes match (GetHashCode can be used in this implementation of overloading the Equals operator because it is known that the Soundex algorithm implementation returns a unique value—this is not the case with other GetHashCode implementations).

Care must be taken for null values and empty strings in deciding what behavior you want. I decided that I wanted null or empty string entries to be in one group, but this null handling logic should be considered for each specific implementation. (Maybe an empty string should be in a different group than null entries; it really depends on the specific situation.)

Listing 4-5 The custom **SoundexEqualityComparer** allows phonetically similar sounding strings to be easily grouped

```
public class SoundexEqualityComparer
    : IEqualityComparer<string>
{
    public bool Equals(string x, string y)
    {
        return GetHashCode(x) == GetHashCode(y);
    }

    public int GetHashCode(string obj)
    {
        // E.g. convert soundex code A123,
        // to an integer: 65123
        int result = 0;

        string s = soundex(obj);
        if (string.IsNullOrEmpty(s) == false)
            result = Convert.ToInt32(s[0]) * 1000 +
                    Convert.ToInt32(s.Substring(1, 3));

        return result;
    }

    private string soundex(string s)
    {
        // Algorithm as listed on
        //      http://en.wikipedia.org/wiki/Soundex.
        // builds a string code in the format:
        //      [A-Z][0-6][0-6][0-6]
        // based on the phonetic sound of the input.

        if (String.IsNullOrEmpty(s))
            return null;
```

```
StringBuilder result =
    new StringBuilder(s.Length);

// As long as there is at least one character,
// then we can proceed
    string source = s.ToUpper().Replace(" ", "");

// add the first character, then loop the
// string mapping as we go
result.Append(source[0]);
char previous = '0';

for (int i = 1; i < source.Length; i++)
{
    // map to the soundex numeral
    char mappedTo = '0';
    char thisChar = source[i];

    if ("BFPV".Contains(thisChar))
        mappedTo = '1';
    else if ("CGJKQSXZ".Contains(thisChar))
            mappedTo = '2';
    else if ("DT".Contains(thisChar))
            mappedTo = '3';
    else if ('L' == thisChar)
            mappedTo = '4';
    else if ("MN".Contains(thisChar))
            mappedTo = '5';
    else if ('R' == thisChar)
            mappedTo = '6';

    // ignore adjacent duplicates and
    // non-matched characters
    if (mappedTo != previous && mappedTo != '0')
    {
        result.Append(mappedTo);
        previous = mappedTo;
    }
}

while (result.Length < 4) result.Append("0");
```

```
        return result.ToString(0, 4);
    }
}
```

Listing 4-6 demonstrates using a custom equality comparer (in this case `SoundexEqualityComparer`). The Console output is shown in Output 4-3.

Listing 4-6 Calling code of the new **SoundexEqualityComparer** used for grouping phonetically similar names—see Output 4-3

```
string[] names = new string[] { "Janet", "Janette", "Joanne",
    "Jo-anne", "Johanne", "Katy", "Katie", "Ralph", "Ralphe" };

var q = names.GroupBy(s => s,
    new SoundexEqualityComparer());

foreach (var group in q)
{
    Console.WriteLine(group.Key);
    foreach (var name in group)
        Console.WriteLine(" - {0}", name);
}
```

Output 4-3

```
Janet
 - Janet
 - Janette
Joanne
 - Joanne
 - Jo-anne
 - Johanne
Katy
 - Katy
 - Katie
Ralph
 - Ralph
 - Ralphe
```

Projecting Grouped Elements into a New Type

The general `group by` function when using query expression syntax returns the same element type as the source collection elements. (The workaround is to use query continuation, which is discussed later in the chapter.) If you would like the grouped elements to be in a different form, you must use the extension method syntax and specify your own "element selector" expression. The element selector expression takes an instance of the original element and returns a new type based on the supplied expression.

Listing 4-7 demonstrates how to group `Contact` records by state and return a group of strings rather than a group of `Contact` instances for each element (`Contact` is the original element type). In this case, a string is returned by concatenating the contact's first and last name. The Console output result is shown in Output 4-4.

Listing 4-7 Group elements can be projected to any type. This sample projects group elements as a string type, rather than the default **Contact** instance—see Output 4-4

```
IList<Contact> contacts = Contact.SampleData();

var q = contacts.GroupBy(
          c => c.State,
          c => c.FirstName + " " + c.LastName);

foreach (var group in q)
{
    Console.WriteLine("State: {0}", group.Key);
    foreach (string name in group)
        Console.WriteLine("  {0}", name);
}
```

Output 4-4

```
State: CA
  Barney Gottshall
  Mandy Gottshall
  Anthony Gauwain
  Jeffery Deane
State: WA
  Bernadette Gottshall
```

```
    Armando Valdes
    Stewart Kagel
    Chance Lard
State: AK
  Adam Gauwain
  Chris Gauwain
State: FL
  Collin Zeeman
State: TX
  Blaine Reifsteck
  Mack Kamph
State: OR
  Ariel Hazelgrove
```

To demonstrate a slightly more complicated example, Listing 4-8 demonstrates projecting each group element into an anonymous type. This example also shows how to use the Null-Coalescing Operator to handle missing data in either the grouping predicate or the element projection expression. The Console output is shown in Output 4-5.

Listing 4-8 Grouping elements and projecting into an anonymous type and how to handle null values using the null-coalescing operator—see Output 4-5

```
List<Contact> contacts = Contact.SampleData();

var q = contacts.GroupBy(
          c => c.State ?? "state unknown",
          c => new
          {
              Title = c.FirstName + " " + c.LastName,
              Email = c.Email ?? "email address unknown"
          });

foreach (var group in q)
{
    Console.WriteLine("State: {0}", group.Key);
    foreach (var element in group)
        Console.WriteLine("  {0} ({1})",
            element.Title,
            element.Email);
}
```

Output 4-5

```
State: CA
  Barney Gottshall (bgottshall@aspiring-technology.com)
  Mandy Gottshall (email address unknown)
  Anthony Gauwain (email address unknown)
  Jeffery Deane (jeff.deane@aspiring-technology.com)
State: WA
  Bernadette Gottshall (email address unknown)
  Armando Valdes (val1@aspiring-technology.com)
  Stewart Kagel (kagels@aspiring-technology.com)
  Chance Lard (lard@aspiring-technology.com)
State: AK
  Adam Gauwain (adamg@aspiring-technology.com)
  Chris Gauwain (email address unknown)
State: FL
  Collin Zeeman (czeeman@aspiring-technology.com)
State: TX
  Blaine Reifsteck (blaine@aspiring-technology.com)
  Mack Kamph (mack.kamph@aspiring-technology.com)
State: OR
  Ariel Hazelgrove (arielh@aspiring-technology.com)
```

How to Use Grouping Results in the Same Query (Query Continuation)

It is possible to use grouping results as a local variable within the same query by appending the `into` clause after the group when using the query expression syntax (when using extension method syntax, you just continue your query from the result of the `GroupBy` extension method). The `into` clause projects the grouping result into a local variable that you can reference throughout the rest of the query expression, giving you access to the key values and the grouped elements.

The simplest form of query continuation using groups is for providing aggregation results within the query's select projection clause. Listing 4-9 demonstrates how to calculate various subtotals for a set of grouped data. This example aggregates the `CallLog` data introduced in Chapter 2 (Table 2-2) by first grouping by the call phone number; continuing the query with the `into` keyword; and then projecting subtotals, counts, and averages into an anonymous type. The Console results are shown in Output 4-6.

Listing 4-9 Query continuation allows you to calculate various aggregation values for each group (think subtotaling)—see Output 4-6

```
List<CallLog> calls = CallLog.SampleData();

var q = from c in calls
        group c by c.Number into g
        select new
        {
            Number = g.Key,
            InCalls = g.Count(c => c.Incoming),
            OutCalls = g.Count(c => !c.Incoming),
            TotalTime = g.Sum(c => c.Duration),
            AvgTime = g.Average(c => c.Duration)
        };

foreach (var number in q)
    Console.WriteLine(
        "{0} ({1} in, {2} out) Avg Time: {3} mins",
        number.Number,
        number.InCalls,
        number.OutCalls,
        Math.Round(number.AvgTime, 2));
```

Output 4-6

```
885 983 8858 (4 in, 2 out) Avg Time: 9.33 mins
165 737 1656 (2 in, 0 out) Avg Time: 13.5 mins
364 202 3644 (2 in, 2 out) Avg Time: 13.75 mins
603 303 6030 (0 in, 4 out) Avg Time: 12.5 mins
546 607 5462 (2 in, 4 out) Avg Time: 4.33 mins
848 553 8487 (2 in, 2 out) Avg Time: 13.75 mins
278 918 2789 (2 in, 0 out) Avg Time: 11 mins
```

Query continuation allows very complex rollup analysis to be performed on grouped data with any level of nesting. Listing 4-10 demonstrates how to group two levels deep. This query groups phone calls by year and month for each customer record in the source collection. (The sample data used can be seen in Chapter 2, Tables 2-1 and 2-2.) The groupings are captured in an anonymous type field (YearGroup and MonthGroup), and these are accessible when iterating the result sequence using nested `foreach` loops. The Console output of this code is shown in Output 4-7.

Listing 4-10 The example demonstrates grouping data multiple levels deep—see Output 4-7

```
List<Contact> contacts = Contact.SampleData();
List<CallLog> callLog = CallLog.SampleData();

var q = from contact in contacts
        select new
        {
            Name = contact.FirstName + " " +
                     contact.LastName,
            YearGroup = from call in callLog
                    where call.Number == contact.Phone
                    group call by call.When.Year
                        into groupYear
                    select new
                    {
                        Year = groupYear.Key,
                        MonthGroup =
                            from c in groupYear
                            group c by c.When.ToString("MMMM")
                    }
        };


foreach (var con in q)
{
    Console.WriteLine("Customer: {0}", con.Name);
    foreach (var year in con.YearGroup)
    {
        Console.WriteLine(" Year:{0}", year.Year);
        foreach (var month in year.MonthGroup)
        {
            Console.WriteLine("   Month:{0}", month.Key);
            foreach (var call in month)
            {
                Console.WriteLine("      {0} - for {1} minutes",
                                call.When, call.Duration);
            }
        }
    }
}
```

Output 4-7

```
Customer: Barney Gottshall
 Year:2006
    Month:August
       8/7/2006 8:12:00 AM - for 2 minutes
       8/7/2006 1:12:00 PM - for 15 minutes
       8/7/2006 1:47:00 PM - for 3 minutes
    Month:July
       7/12/2006 8:12:00 AM - for 5 minutes
       7/7/2006 1:47:00 PM - for 21 minutes
    Month:June
       6/7/2006 1:12:00 PM - for 10 minutes
Customer: Armando Valdes
 Year:2006
    Month:August
       8/8/2006 2:00:00 PM - for 3 minutes
       8/8/2006 2:37:00 PM - for 7 minutes
    Month:July
       7/8/2006 2:00:00 PM - for 32 minutes
       7/8/2006 2:37:00 PM - for 13 minutes


. . .


Customer: Ariel Hazelgrove
 Year:2006
    Month:August
       8/7/2006 9:23:00 AM - for 15 minutes
    Month:June
       6/14/2006 9:23:00 AM - for 12 minutes
```

How to Join with Data in Another Sequence

The basis of any Relational **Database Management System (DBMS)** is the ability to draw together data from multiple sources (tables generally) as the result of a query; this is called "Joining" data. In relational databases, the joins are most often between primary key and foreign key-related columns, but a join can be achieved on any data as long as both data sources share a common column value. One fundamental reason for splitting data into multiple sources is to avoid duplicating data—this process is called *normalization* by database developers.

Although the concept of joining in-memory collections isn't a common pattern today (it's more likely that you nest a collection inside another object to indicate a parent-child relationship), LINQ to Objects introduces the concept of joining multiple data sources through its powerful `Join` and `GroupJoin` operators and their equivalent query expression syntax options. LINQ also enables join-like functionality by using a subquery expression within the `Select` clause. This subquery style of coding is often simpler to read and helps you avoid having to use any specific `Join` syntax in the query at all. Both techniques are covered in the examples throughout this chapter.

There are three basic styles of Joins that are commonly used when drawing together data from multiple sources based on a shared key value:

- **Cross Join**—Every element in the first sequence (the outer) is projected with every element in the second sequence (the inner), often called the *Cartesian Product*. An example use for this type of join is when you want to systematically access each pixel in a bitmap by x and y locations.
- **One-to-One Inner Join**—This type of join allows you to access data in both sequences based on a common column value. The resulting sequence is flat (there is no subgroup). An example use for this type of join is when you want to access data from another sequence to extend the data you have on some element.
- **One-to-Many Join**—This type of join allows you to use the first sequence record as a key for a subgroup sequence where a given column value is used as the referential key. An example of this type of join is having a list of orders for a set of given customers.

There are numerous ways in LINQ to achieve each of these join types. Each technique and its relative merit are discussed next.

Cross Joins

Cross joins project every element in one sequence against every element in a second sequence. Cross joins in LINQ to Objects ironically aren't implemented using either of the Join operators, but rather a clever use of the `SelectMany` operator. The query expression syntax will be familiar (not identical) to anyone with knowledge of standard SQL joins. In LINQ query expression syntax, you simply specify multiple `from` statements, as shown in the following code:

```
var outer = Enumerable.Range(1, 3);
var inner = Enumerable.Range(1, 3);

var q = from x in outer
        from y in inner
        select new { x, y };

foreach (var element in q)
    Console.WriteLine("{0}, {1}", element.x, element.y);
```

The result from this query will be the Cartesian Product, which is a fancy term for all values in the outer range, x (with values 1, 2, and 3) against each value in the inner range, y (with values 1, 2, and 3) as shown in the following result:

```
1, 1
1, 2
1, 3
2, 1
2, 2
2, 3
3, 1
3, 2
3, 3
```

The following code, which is identical to the previous query except that it is written in extension method syntax, shows how the query expression syntax (using multiple from statements) is mapped to the SelectMany operator. The result that it yields is identical as well:

```
var q1 = outer
        .SelectMany(
            x => inner, // inner collection selector
            (x, y) => new { x, y } // select projection
        );
```

Cross joins allow you to expand the matrix of values, every combination of values between two or more sequences. There is no limit to the number of sequences that can participate in the cross-product operation. Listing 4-11 demonstrates how a binary sequence can be created by using a cross-join combination of four sequences. Output 4-8 shows the result, a sequence of every binary value for a 4-bit number. This might be useful when generating all combinations of a test case.

Listing 4-11   Any number of sequences can participate in a cross join. Every element will be projected against every element of included sequences—see Output 4-8

```
var binary = new int[] { 0, 1 };

var q = from b4 in binary
        from b3 in binary
        from b2 in binary
        from b1 in binary
        select String.Format(
            "{0}{1}{2}{3}", b4, b3, b2, b1);

foreach (var element in q)
    Console.WriteLine(element);
```

Output 4-8

```
0000
0001
0010
0011
0100
0101
0110
0111
1000
1001
1010
1011
1100
1101
1110
1111
```

Another common cross-join example is accessing every pixel in a bitmap, from 0 to the bitmap's width (x) and 0 to the height (y) index position. The following code demonstrates how to combine a cross join and the Range operator to achieve access to every pixel in a bitmap:

```
var q = from x in Enumerable.Range(0, bm.Width)
        from y in Enumerable.Range(0, bm.Height)
        select bm.GetPixel(x, y);
```

A cross join can also be used to achieve a one-to-one join by creating every permutation between two collections and then filtering all but those elements that share a key value; although as you will see, this is generally the worst performing technique for this purpose in LINQ to Objects.

One-to-One Joins

A one-to-one join allows data from two different sequences related to each other by a common key value to be accessible in the select projection of a query. One-to-one joins are very commonplace in relational database systems, where the central theme is separating data into multiple tables related by parent and child key relationships. This process is called **normalization**. Although LINQ to Objects supports most of the common join types available in a relational database, it is not always the most efficient way to work with large volumes of data.

NOTE   A relational database will out-perform LINQ to Objects in cases where data volume is large. The join features across object collections should be used for local fine-tuning of data retrieved from a database, not in place of that database engine.

There are a number of ways to achieve one-to-one joins using LINQ, which include

- Using the `join` (or `Join`) operator
- Using a subquery in the select projection
- Using the `SingleOrDefault` operator in the select projection
- Using a cross join with a `where` filter

Each technique for one-to-one joining is covered in detail in this section, including the relative performance of each (summarized in Table 4-1 and described in detail later in this chapter in the "One-to-One Join Performance Comparisons" section).

Table 4-1   One-to-One Join Techniques and Their Performance Comparisons

Technique	Many Record Performance	Single Record Performance	Comments
Using the `join` (or `Join`) operator	Best	Worst	Use the `join` syntax whenever you are working with five or more outer element records. Builds a lookup on the inner keys first, avoiding repetitive looping in subsequent outer iterations. Example: Listing 4-12
Using a subquery in the select projection	Good	Good	Use the `SingleOrDefault` syntax rather than a subquery. There is no benefit to using a subquery. Example: Listing 4-14
Using the `SingleOrDefault` operator in the select projection	Good	Best	Use `SingleOrDefault` syntax whenever you are working with a single (or minimal number of) outer records. Example: Listing 4-15
Using a cross join with a `where` filter	Worst	Good	Only use when a cross join is actually needed. Never use when there are many records—will result in very poor performance. Example: Listing 4-16

To add clarity it is necessary to depart from our running example data and use a very simple set of sample data to allow you to focus on the mechanics of the join syntax. Table 4-2 lists the sample data used throughout the rest of this chapter unless otherwise specified. The key field in this case is a string type, but any type can be used (integer values for instance if you retrieved data from primary keys in a database table).

Table 4-2 Sample Data Used for Demonstrating Joining Multiple Data Sources

Customers		Orders	
Key	Name	Key	Order Number
GOT1	Gottshall	GOT1	Order 1
VAL1	Valdes	GOT1	Order 2
GAU1	Gauwain	DEA1	Order 3
DEA1	Deane	DEA1	Order 4
ZEE1	Zeeman	ZEE1	Order 5

The join (or Join) Operator

The simplest join of this type is built using the `join` operator in the query expression syntax, or the `Join` operator in extension method syntax. The query expression syntax for a join takes the following general form:

```
from [outer sequence
join [inner sequence] on
        [outer key selector] equals [inner key selector]
select [result selector]
```

To understand the behavior of this operator, the following code shows a basic example of linking two arrays of strings:

```
string[] outer = new string[] { "a", "b", "c", "d" };
string[] inner = new string[] { "b", "c", "d", "e" };

var q = from s1 in outer
        join s2 in inner on s1 equals s2
        select string.Format(
                "Outer: {0} Inner: {1}", s1, s2);

foreach (string s in q)
    Console.WriteLine(s);
```

The output of this code is

```
Outer: b Inner: b
Outer: c Inner: c
Outer: d Inner: d
```

Notice that any outer element with a matching inner element is included in the result sequence, and the select projection has access to both strings in this case (s1 and s2). Also notice that any elements where the key values didn't match are skipped. This is called an inner join by relational database dictionaries, and you can simply think of it in these terms: Any record without a matching key value (a null key value for instance) is skipped.

To demonstrate how to use the join syntax over the data shown in Table 4-2, Listing 4-12 shows how to achieve an inner join from an order(s) to access all the customer data (in this case to retrieve the LastName property in the Select projection). The output from this code is shown in Output 4-9.

Listing 4-12 Simple join example between two collections—see Output 4-9. Notice there are no entries for Valdes or Gauwain.

```
var customers = Customer.SampleData();
var orders = Order.SampleData();

var q1 = from o in orders
         join c in customers on
             o.CustomerID equals c.CustomerID
         select new
         {
             o.OrderNumber,
             c.LastName
         };

foreach (var order in q1)
    Console.WriteLine(
        "Customer: {0}  Order Number: {1}",
        order.LastName.PadRight(9, ' '),
        order.OrderNumber);
```

Output 4-9

```
Customer: Gottshall    Order Number: Order 1
Customer: Gottshall    Order Number: Order 2
Customer: Deane        Order Number: Order 3
Customer: Deane        Order Number: Order 4
Customer: Zeeman       Order Number: Order 5
```

Simulating Outer Joins—Getting Unmatched Elements   **Outer joins** differ from inner joins in the way they handle missing and unmatched values. An outer join will return a result for outer elements that have no matching inner elements, whereas these elements would be skipped when using an inner join (as demonstrated in Listing 4-12).

To carry out an outer-join style query in LINQ to Objects, the DefaultIfEmpty standard query operator is used in the from clause of a join, and the null value generated by this operator handled in the select projection. Although this sounds difficult, Listing 4-13 demonstrates an outer join using the sample data shown in Table 4-2, which generates the Console output shown in Output 4-10. This query is a little ambiguous at first glance, but in essence it injects a null element (the default value for an instance of Order type) for any Customer element that would have been removed by the inner join. This propagates a null value for order that any subsequent code working with that result property can process. In this example the ternary operator in the Console.WriteLine statement is catching and handling the null values by replacing those results with the string "(no orders)".

Listing 4-13 Structuring the query for an outer join where all outer-sequence records are returned, even though they have no orders—see Output 4-10

```
var customers = Customer.SampleData();
var orders = Order.SampleData();

var q = from c in customers
        join o in orders on
            c.CustomerID equals o.CustomerID into j
        from order in j.DefaultIfEmpty()
        select new
        {
            LastName = c.LastName,
            Order = order
        };
```

```
foreach (var element in q)
    Console.WriteLine(
        "Customer: {0}   Order Number: {1}",
        element.LastName.PadRight(9, ' '),
        element.Order == null ?
            "(no orders)" : element.Order.OrderNumber);
```

Output 4-10

```
Customer: Gottshall   Order Number:  Order 1
Customer: Gottshall   Order Number:  Order 2
Customer: Valdes      Order Number:  (no orders)
Customer: Gauwain     Order Number:  (no orders)
Customer: Deane       Order Number:  Order 3
Customer: Deane       Order Number:  Order 4
Customer: Zeeman      Order Number:  Order 5
```

The alternative to handling the null values in all places that will process the query result, is to handle the null instances in the actual select projection of the query itself, avoiding duplication of null handling code. The following example demonstrates this technique and produces the identical result shown in Output 4-10:

```
var q1 = from c in customers
        join o in orders on
            c.CustomerID equals o.CustomerID into j
        from order in j.DefaultIfEmpty()
        select new
        {
            LastName = c.LastName,
            OrderNumber = order == null ?
                "(no order)" : order.OrderNumber
        };
```

Joining by Composite Keys (More Than One Value)   Similar in approach to how multiple values can be used to specify the key value for grouping, composite keys are supported for joins by using anonymous types (see Listing 4-3 for an example of grouping by composite key). In the case of joins, two anonymous types must be specified for the inner and outer keys as defined by the arguments on either side of the `equals` keyword.

The following example performs a one-to-one inner join between two in-memory collections. The key values used for joining are phone number and extension, combined using an anonymous type.

```
List<Contact> outer = Contact.SampleData();
List<CallLog> inner = CallLog.SampleData();

var q = from contact in outer
        join call in inner on
            new {
                phone = contact.Phone,
                contact.Extension
            }
        equals
            new {
                phone = call.Number,
                call.Extension
            }
        select new { call, contact };
```

The anonymous types must match exactly—in property names and property order. In the previous example, it was necessary to specifically name the phone property because that property wasn't the same name in both collections; Extension was the same, so the property name in the initializer could be omitted. (The compiler inferred the name to be Extension for this field.)

How Join Works   The query expression join syntax (like all the query expression keywords) map to the extension method appropriately named Join. This extension method takes two sequences (one as an extension method source outer, the other as an ordinary argument inner), two key selection functions (one for each source), and a result selection function. The Join extension method signature takes the following form:

```
public static IEnumerable<TResult>
        Join<TOuter, TInner, TKey, TResult>(
    this IEnumerable<TOuter> outer,
    IEnumerable<TInner> inner,
    Func<TOuter, TKey> outerKeySelector,
    Func<TInner, TKey> innerKeySelector,
    Func<TOuter, TInner, TResult> resultSelector,
    IEqualityComparer<TKey> comparer // optional
)
```

To understand how the `Join` operator works, the basic pseudo-code it carries out is as follows:

1. Create a grouping on the inner sequence for all elements that share the same inner key selector function value (as determined by the `innerKeySelector` argument). Call this list of groups *lookup*.
2. Iterate the outer sequence. Call each current element *item*.
    a. Create a grouping on the *lookup* sequence for all elements that share the same outer-key selector function value as this *item* (as determined by the `outerKeySelector` argument). If a `comparer` argument is supplied, use this `comparer` to calculate the equality.
    b. If there are any items in this grouping result
        i. Loop through all elements in this group
        ii. Yield the result returned by the result selector on each element (using the `resultSelector` argument)

The returned sequence will be in the order of the outer sequence elements, one record for each matching inner element, followed by the next outer element's records. Outer elements without matching inner elements will be skipped. (I think you get that point by now—this is an inner join. If you want the unmatched elements, see the "Simulating Outer Joins—Getting Unmatched Elements" section.)

The key selection expression for the outer and inner sequence can be any expression that evaluates to a comparable type. The `equals` operator (what is called when you do an `==` evaluation) will determine if the keys are equal or a custom `IEqualityComparer` can be supplied to customize this equality comparison in the same way a custom equality comparer was used in the grouping examples earlier in this chapter. (See the "Specifying Your Own Key Comparison Function" section.)

From the final query select projection, you have access to both sequences' matching elements. The range variable can be used for both the inner and outer records throughout the query and referenced within the select projection expression to create a new type or an anonymous type.

One-to-One Join Using a Subquery

A subquery in a queries Select projection can achieve a one-to-one join. In testing, this option did not perform as well as the alternatives and should only be considered for very small (less than ten-element) sequence sizes. This technique simply looks up related data from a second sequence within the first query's select projection. Listing 4-14 demonstrates the subquery technique, and the result is shown in Output 4-11.

Listing 4-14   One-to-One Join using Subquery syntax—see Output 4-11

```
var customers = Customer.SampleData();
var orders = Order.SampleData();

var q2 = from o in orders
         select new
         {
             OrderNumber = o.OrderNumber,
             LastName = (from c in customers
                         where c.CustomerID == o.CustomerID
                         select c.LastName).SingleOrDefault()
         };

foreach (var order in q2)
    Console.WriteLine(
        "Customer: {0}   Order Number: {1}",
        order.LastName.PadRight(9, ' '),
        order.OrderNumber);
```

Output 4-11

```
Customer: Gottshall   Order Number:   Order 1
Customer: Gottshall   Order Number:   Order 2
Customer: Deane       Order Number:   Order 3
Customer: Deane       Order Number:   Order 4
Customer: Zeeman      Order Number:   Order 5
```

One-to-One Join Using SingleOrDefault Operator

The SingleOrDefault standard query operator returns the single matching element from another sequence or null if a matching value cannot be found (if more than one matching element is found, an exception is thrown). This is ideal for looking up a matching record in another sequence and making that data accessible to your query—in other words, a one-to-one join. This technique is fast and clean when looking up only a single or a few related records.

Listing 4-15 demonstrates a one-to-one join using the SingleOrDefault technique, which generates the output shown in Output 4-11.

Listing 4-15   One-to-One Join using the **SingleOrDefault** operator—see Output 4-11

```
var customers = Customer.SampleData();
var orders = Order.SampleData();

var q3 = from o in orders
         let cust = customers
                    .SingleOrDefault(
                        c => c.CustomerID == o.CustomerID)
         select new
         {
             OrderNumber = o.OrderNumber,
             LastName = cust.LastName
         };

foreach (var order in q3)
    Console.WriteLine(
        "Customer: {0}   Order Number: {1}",
        order.LastName.PadRight(9, ' '),
        order.OrderNumber);
```

One-to-One Join Using Cross Join

This join type matches traditional relational database join techniques. However, because LINQ to Objects doesn't optimize the query (by maintaining indexes, building statistics, rewriting queries, and so on) like most good database server products, one-to-one joins using cross joins should be avoided because performance is poor and the alternatives previously shown are just as easy.

This technique cross joins two sequences to get the Cartesian Product (every element against every element) and then uses a where clause to keep only the matching outer and inner records. This achieves the goal of a one-to-one join, but at great expense in performance due to the number of elements enumerated and never passing the filter criteria. Use this technique sparingly and only if collection sizes are very small.

Listing 4-16 demonstrates a one-to-one join using the cross join/where technique and generates the code shown in Output 4-12.

Listing 4-16   One-to-one join using a cross join and **where** filter—see Output 4-12

```
var customers = Customer.SampleData();
var orders = Order.SampleData();
```

```
var q4 = from o in orders
         from c in customers
         where c.CustomerID == o.CustomerID
         select new
         {
             o.OrderNumber,
             c.LastName
         };

foreach (var order in q4)
    Console.WriteLine(
        "Customer: {0}   Order Number: {1}",
        order.LastName.PadRight(9, ' '),
        order.OrderNumber);
```

Output 4-12

```
Customer: Gottshall    Order Number: Order 1
Customer: Gottshall    Order Number: Order 2
Customer: Deane        Order Number: Order 3
Customer: Deane        Order Number: Order 4
Customer: Zeeman       Order Number: Order 5
```

One-to-One Join Performance Comparisons

Choosing the most appropriate join technique will yield large performance gains as collection size grows. To have some guidance on which technique makes sense, a simple experiment is necessary (results of such an analysis are summarized in Table 4-1). As mentioned earlier, a database management system (such as SQL Server, MySQL, and Oracle) should be used when joining large amounts of data, and although you can join in-memory using LINQ to Objects, you should exhaust other opportunities first if high performance on larger data sets is a requirement.

One-to-one join performance is primarily dependent on how many different elements will need to be looked up from the inner sequence and how often that is necessary. The Join operator builds a lookup list of all inner sequence keys ahead of time. If many of these keys are then used in the outer sequence, this step aids performance; if only a few of the inner elements will ever be eventually looked up (because there are only a few outer records), then this step actually harms performance. You will need to examine the likely number of records in both the inner and outer sequences. In the small set of test data used for this profiling example, it was evident that five records or more was the sweet-spot for building this lookup table in advance. Though if the number of records in the inner sequence grows, so will the sweet-spot—you must test given your own sequence sizes, and consider their likely growth over time.

The experimental approach used in this test was to simply run a large number of join iterations over some sample data and determine the total elapsed time. Each of the four different techniques were tested for all records in an outer sequence and a single record in the outer sequence (by adding a `where` clause for a single element).

To measure the elapsed time, a simple helper method was written that takes an action delegate and measures the elapsed time of calling that delegate a given number of times (`iterations`):

```
private long MeasureTime(Action action, int iterations)
{
    System.Diagnostics.Stopwatch watch =
        new System.Diagnostics.Stopwatch();

    watch.Start();

    for (int i = 0; i < iterations; i++)
        action();

    return watch.ElapsedMilliseconds;
}
```

This helper function is called by specifying an action inline, such as

```
long t = MeasureTime(delegate { q1.ToList(); }, 1000000)
```

In this example, `q1` is our LINQ to Objects query under test. The method `ToList` is called on this query to ensure that the full sequence is yielded, meaning that every result element is processed avoiding deferred execution making all queries appear instant.

Each Join technique has a different performance profile for the two most basic scenarios:

1. The outer sequence has many records, and you want all of them—An example of this scenario is when you are binding the full sequence of results to a grid or other repeater control. For example, the following code demonstrates a one-to-one join where outer collection has many records:

```
var q1 = from outer in orders
         join inner in customers on
             outer.CustomerID equals inner.CustomerID
```

2. The outer sequence has only a few records, either by count or because of a strict where clause (targeting a single record is the most common)—An example of this scenario is when you are looking up a single record for editing purposes. For example, the following code demonstrates a one-to-one join where a single record is isolated in the outer collection:

```
var q1 = from outer in orders
         where outer.OrderNumber == "Order 3"
         join inner in customers on
             outer.CustomerID equals inner.CustomerID
```

The actual code for each join type has been presented previously in this chapter (see Listings 4-12, 4-14, 4-15, and 4-16). A second set of each join type technique was tested, with the addition of a tight where clause filter to look up a single record (our second scenario).

The test data used for this experiment is small—up to 100 orders and 5 customers (for a full listing, see Table 4-2). This is an unrealistic size of data, but it does provide a stable platform for understanding relative performance characteristics. This experiment is looking at how the relationship between outer and inner sequence collection size impacts query performance. Table 4-3 shows the results of this experiment.

NOTE   The actual numbers in seconds are highly subject to hardware and available memory; they are shown here for relative purposes only. This experiment is to differentiate performance of the different join techniques.

Table 4-3   One-to-One Join Techniques and Their Performance Comparisons Using 1M Iterations

Join Technique Iterations = 1M	Scenario 1 - Many Record Performance Outer n = 100 Inner n = 5	Many Record Performance Outer n = 50 Inner n = 5	Many Record Performance. Outer n = 5 Inner n = 5	Scenario 2 - Single Record Performance Outer n = 1 Inner n = 5
Using the `join` (or `Join`) operator Listing 4-12	21793ms (1 - best)	11319ms	2432ms	1852ms (4 - worst)
Using a subquery in the select projection Listing 4-14	75897ms (3)	40464ms	4375ms	1493ms (2)
Using the `SingleOrDefault` operator in the select projection Listing 4-15	56335ms (2)	27412ms	3758ms	1320ms (1 - best)
Using a cross join with a `where` filter Listing 4-16	80829ms (4 - worst)	40424ms	5142ms	1636ms (3)

Plotting the results for 100, 50, and 1 demonstrates how linear the performance characteristic is against outer loop count. The join syntax always wins until the outer sequence size drops to below five. However, when the outer-sequence count is less than five, all syntax options are instant unless you are running one million iterations.

From this simple experiment, some conclusions can be drawn:

- Use the Join syntax for all one-to-one scenarios unless the outer sequence has less than five elements
- Use the `SingleOrDefault` syntax when the outer-sequence size is less than five elements and the number of iterations is in the hundreds of thousands.

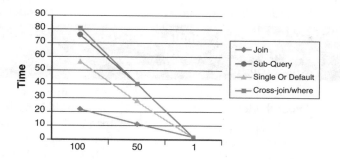

Figure 4-1   Different one-to-one Join techniques. Time taken for 1M iterations against an outer sequence of 100, 50, and 1 element count. Join syntax is faster until around an outer-sequence size of five elements.

- Never use the cross join/where syntax for one-to-one joins. Enumerating every combination of element versus element only to filter out all but a few results impacts performance in a big way.
- Use a relational database system for large volume join operations where possible.

One-to-Many Joins

A one-to-many join allows a subgroup collection of related elements to a parent element in another sequence. The most common example of a one-to-many join is a listing of Customers, each with a collection of Orders. The same caveat applies to one-to-many joins as warned in one-to-one joins. LINQ to Objects will not perform joins as well as a relational database system like SQL Server. Joining data is what DBMSs are good at, and although you can perform these joins in LINQ to Objects, it should be reserved for small data volumes. Do the heavy lifting in SQL Server and fine-tuning in LINQ to Objects.

There are a number of ways to achieve one-to-many joins using LINQ, and these include

- Using the join/into combination (or GroupJoin) operator
- Using a subquery in the select projection
- Using the ToLookup operator

Each of these approaches are covered in detail next, including their performance behavior, but Table 4-4 summarizes the different performance traits for each syntax when working with many records at one time or only joining to a single record.

Table 4-4 One-to-Many Join Techniques and Their Performance Comparisons

Technique	Many outer record performance	Single outer record performance	Comments
Using the join/into combination (or GroupJoin) operator	Generally poor; better as inner sequence size grows	Worst	When run over one million iterations, this performed slower than both other options. Unless trying to stay syntactically similar to SQL, use either a subquery or lookup technique. This technique is more effective than the subquery technique as the inner sequence size grows. Break even at around five records. Example: Listing 4-17
Using a subquery in the select projection	Good for small inner sequences only or when ordering of the inner sequence is important	Best	This technique was only marginally slower than the lookup technique. The lookup technique traverses the inner sequence only once; this technique will traverse the inner sequence multiple times. Use this technique when you need to order the inner sequence elements. Example: Listing 4-18
Using the ToLookup operator	Best	Good	If performance is a key requirement, then use this technique. Example: Listing 4-19

The identical sample data used in the previous section on one-to-one joins (Table 4-2) will continue to be used throughout this section unless otherwise specified.

The join/into (GroupJoin) Operator

A small variation of the query expression join syntax allows joined records to be captured in a subgroup. Adding an into keyword after the join is similar to query continuation as discussed earlier in this chapter in the "How to Use Grouping Results in the Same Query (Query Continuation)" section. The result yields a single element for every outer record, and within these elements, a grouping of joined (related) records.

Listing 4-17 demonstrates how to achieve a one-to-many group relationship using the `join` and `into` keyword combination. The Console output is shown in Output 4-13. The `into` keyword captures each group, and this group can be accessed in the select projection and subsequently accessed as a property of each result element.

Listing 4-17 One-to-Many Join using the **`join`/`into`** keyword combination—see Output 4-13

```
var customers = Customer.SampleData();
var orders = Order.SampleData();

var q1 = from c in customers
        join o in orders on
            c.CustomerID equals o.CustomerID
        into cust_orders
        select new
        {
            LastName = c.LastName,
            Orders = cust_orders
        };

foreach (var customer in q1)
{
    Console.WriteLine("Last name: {0}", customer.LastName);
    foreach (var order in customer.Orders)
        Console.WriteLine(" - Order number: {0}", order.OrderNumber);
}
```

Output 4-13

```
Last name: Gottshall
 - Order number: Order 1
 - Order number: Order 2
Last name: Valdes
Last name: Gauwain
Last name: Deane
 - Order number: Order 3
 - Order number: Order 4
Last name: Zeeman
 - Order number: Order 5
```

How join/into Works   The `join/into` keyword combination in query expression syntax maps to the `GroupJoin` standard query operator. The `GroupJoin` operator returns a sequence of inner elements with a matching key value for every outer element in a sequence. Unlike the pure `join` syntax, every outer-sequence element will have a represented group sequence, but those without matching inner-sequence elements will have an empty group. The `GroupJoin` extension method signature takes the following form:

```
public static IEnumerable<TResult>
    GroupJoin<TOuter, TInner, TKey, TResult>(
    this IEnumerable<TOuter> outer,
    IEnumerable<TInner> inner,
    Func<TOuter, TKey> outerKeySelector,
    Func<TInner, TKey> innerKeySelector,
    Func<TOuter, IEnumerable<TInner>, TResult> resultSelector,
    IEqualityComparer<TKey> comparer // optional
)
```

The pseudo-code for this operator is similar to the Join operator, except the groupings, rather than the individual elements in each group, are returned. The pseudo-code for `GroupJoin` is

1. Create a grouping on the inner sequence for all elements that share the same inner-key selector function value (as determined by the `innerKeySelector` argument). Call this list *lookup*.
2. Iterate the outer sequence. Call each current element *item*.
   a. Create a grouping from the key of the lookup sequence for all elements that share the same outer-key selector function result each *item* returns (as determined by the `outerKeySelector` argument, and the `comparer` equality comparer argument if specified).
   b. Yield the result by passing each *item* and the *grouping* to the `resultSelector` argument.

The returned sequence will be in the order of the outer-sequence elements, although it can be changed by any combination of `order by` clauses as required. The order of the elements in each group will be the same as the inner sequence, and if you want to change the order of the inner-sequence elements, consider using a subquery in the select projection with specific `order by` clauses instead of the `GroupJoin` syntax.

The key selection expression for the outer and inner sequence can be any expression that evaluates to a comparable type. The `equals` operator (what is called when you do an `==` evaluation) will determine if the keys are equal or a custom IEqualityComparer can be supplied to customize this equality comparison in the same way a custom equality comparer was used in the grouping examples in the "Specifying Your Own Key Comparison Function" section earlier in this chapter.

Using the extension method syntax for joins is almost never required (*almost* never—if you need a custom equality comparer, you have no choice). To demonstrate how a join/into query expression maps to the equivalent extension method syntax code, the following code is functionally equivalent to that shown in Listing 4-17:

```
var q1a = customers
        .GroupJoin(
            orders,
            c => c.CustomerID,
            o => o.CustomerID,
            (c, o) => new
            {
                LastName = c.LastName,
                Orders = o
            }
        );
```

One-to-Many Join Using a Subquery

A subquery in a query's select projection can achieve a one-to-many join. If targeting a single record (or a small number, say less than five outer records), this technique performs adequately and is easy to read. Listing 4-18 demonstrates using a subquery for a one-to-many join, and this code produces the Console output shown in Output 4-14.

Listing 4-18 One-to-Many Join using a subquery in the select projection—see Output 4-14

```
var customers = Customer.SampleData();
var orders = Order.SampleData();

var q2 = from c in customers
        select new
        {
            LastName = c.LastName,
            Orders = from o in orders
                    where o.CustomerID == c.CustomerID
                    select o
```

```
    };

foreach (var customer in q2)
{
    Console.WriteLine("Last name: {0}", customer.LastName);
    foreach (var order in customer.Orders)
        Console.WriteLine("  - Order number: {0}", order.OrderNumber);
}
```

Output 4-14

```
Last name: Gottshall
  - Order number: Order 1
  - Order number: Order 2
Last name: Valdes
Last name: Gauwain
Last name: Deane
  - Order number: Order 3
  - Order number: Order 4
Last name: Zeeman
  - Order number: Order 5
```

One-to-Many Join Using the ToLookup Operator

The ToLookup standard query operator builds an efficient lookup list based on a key selection function. The result is similar to a Hashtable, however the ToLookup operator returns a sequence for each key value rather than for a single element. Many of Microsoft's standard query operators use ToLookup internally to perform their tasks, and it is a convenient helper method in all manner of programming problems. It was surprising in testing to find that by using this operator, a major performance gain was achieved over the other one-to-many techniques. An added advantage of creating your inner-sequence grouping first is that the result can be used multiple times across multiple queries. Listing 4-19 demonstrates how to achieve a one-to-many join using the ToLookup operator; this code produces the identical output to that shown in Output 4-14.

Listing 4-19   One-to-Many Join using the **ToLookup** Operator—see Output 4-14

```
var customers = Customer.SampleData();
var orders = Order.SampleData();

// build a lookup list for the inner sequence
var orders_lookup = orders.ToLookup(o => o.CustomerID);
```

```
var q3 = from c in customers
         select new
         {
             LastName = c.LastName,
             Orders = orders_lookup[c.CustomerID]
         };

foreach (var customer in q3)
{
    Console.WriteLine("Last name: {0}", customer.LastName);
    foreach (var order in customer.Orders)
        Console.WriteLine(" - Order number: {0}", order.OrderNumber);
}
```

One-to-Many Join Performance Comparisons

As seen in one-to-one joins, choosing the correct join technique is critical when working with large collection sizes, and the same holds true for one-to-many joins. The guidance offered here is in not a substitute for running tests on your own queries and data, however the guidance offered in Tables 4-4 and 4-5 show some critical join types to avoid. A database system is the best tool for undertaking joins over larger records sets; small data sizes work fine, but if performance is a critical requirement, exhaust all options of joining the data at the source database before using LINQ to Objects.

To derive the performance guidance for one-to-many joins, do a simple experiment of using the three different join techniques over a large number of iterations and measuring the total time. (For the experiment details, see the "One-to-One Join Performance Comparisons" section earlier in this chapter.) Each join technique has a different performance profile for the two most basic scenarios:

1. The outer sequence has many records—An example of this scenario is when you are binding the full sequence of results to a grid or other repeater control and summarizing the results of a related set of records. For example, the following code demonstrates a one-to-many join where outer collection has many records:

```
var q1 = from c in customers
         join o in orders on
             c.CustomerID equals o.CustomerID
         into cust_orders
```

2. The outer sequence has only a few records, either by count or because of a strict `where` clause (targeting a single record is the most common)—An example of this scenario is when you are looking up a single record for editing purposes. For example, the following code demonstrates a one-to-many join where a single record is isolated in the outer collection:

```
var q1 = from c in customers
         where c.CustomerID == "DEA1"
         join o in orders on
             c.CustomerID equals o.CustomerID
         into cust_orders
```

Table 4-5   One-to-Many Join Techniques and Their Performance Comparisons Using 1M Iterations

Join Technique Iterations = 1Million times	Many Record Performance Outer n = 100 Inner n = 5	Many Record Performance Outer n = 50 Inner n = 5	Many Record Performance Outer n = 5 Inner n = 5	Single Record Performance Outer n = 1 Inner n = 5
Using the `join`/`into` combination (or `GroupJoin`) operator Listing 4-17	21562ms (3 - worst), although improves as inner sequence count grows larger	12284ms	2410ms	1964ms (3 - worst)
Using a subquery in the select projection Listing 4-18	20179ms (2)	9953ms	1222ms	712ms (2)
Using the `ToLookup` operator Listing 4-19	17928ms (1 - best)	9514ms	1218ms	694ms (1 - best)

The actual code for each join type has been presented previously in this chapter (see Listings 4-17, 4-18, and 4-19). A second set of each join type technique was tested, with the addition of a tight `where` clause filter to lookup a single record (our second scenario). Each join type is measured with the collection sizes ranging from 1, 5, 50, and 100 elements for each collection.

Conclusions can be drawn from these simple experiments:

- Use the `ToLookup` syntax for all one-to-many scenarios, unless the inner query is complex and easier to achieve with a subquery.
- The `join/into` syntax is slower than the other techniques and should only be used with small inner sequence counts (it gets superior as inner sequence size grows) or when aggregation operators are going to be used over the join result.
- Use a relational database system for large volume join operations where possible.

Summary

LINQ to Objects offers a variety of features that support grouping and joining multiple sources of data. Although much of the syntax is borrowed from the relational database world, it is important to understand the performance profile when working with larger sequence sizes. Whenever possible, leave grouping and joining of large datasets to a relational database (after all, that is what they are intended to be used for); however, once these results are returned in-memory, feel free to use the power of LINQ to Objects' suite of grouping and joining functionality to refine the result.

CHAPTER 5

STANDARD QUERY OPERATORS

Goals of this chapter:

- Introduce the standard query operators not covered so far.
- Show examples for each operator to help in real world application.

Up to this point, we have explored the main operators that filter, project, order, group, and join. This chapter introduces the remaining operators and demonstrates how they are used. By the end of this chapter (and Chapter 6, "Working with Set Data," which details the set-based operators), you will have seen all of the standard query operators.

The Built-In Operators

Microsoft .NET Framework 4 has 52 built-in standard query operators. These operators are in the `System.Linq` namespace and are made available in each class file by adding the following `using` clause:

```
using System.Linq;
```

Many of the operators were discussed in Chapters 3 and 4. This chapter covers the remaining operators, except set-based operators, which are covered in Chapter 6 (see Table 5-1 for a summary). These operators form the basis of most LINQ queries, and the remaining operators introduced in this chapter build on these capabilities to make more complex queries possible. Table 5-2 lists the standard query operators discussed in this chapter.

Table 5-1 LINQ Standard Query Operator Operators Introduced in Other Chapters of This Book

Operator Type	Standard Query Operator Name	Chapter
Grouping	`GroupBy`, `ToLookup`	Chapter 4
Joining	`GroupJoin`, `Join`	Chapter 4
Ordering	`OrderBy`, `ThenBy`, `OrderByDescending`, `ThenByDescending`, `Reverse`	Chapter 3
Projection	`Select`, `SelectMany`	Chapter 3
Restriction	`Distinct`, `Where`	Chapter 3
Set	`Concat`, `Except`, `Intersect`, `Union` (and `Distinct` in more detail)	Chapter 6

Table 5-2 Standard Query Operators in the .NET Framework 4 Release Discussed in This Chapter

Operator Type	Standard Query Operator Name
Aggregation	`Aggregate`, `Average`, `Count`, `LongCount`, `Max`, `Min`, `Sum`
Conversion	`AsEnumerable`, `Cast`, `OfType`, `ToArray`, `ToDictionary`, `ToList`, `ToLookup`
Element	`DefaultIfEmpty`, `ElementAt`, `ElementAtOrDefault`, `First`, `FirstOrDefault`, `Last`, `LastOrDefault`, `Single`, `SingleOrDefault`
Equality	`SequenceEqual`
Generation	`Empty`, `Range`, `Repeat`
Merging	`Zip`
Partitioning	`Skip`, `SkipWhile`, `Take`, `TakeWhile`
Quantifiers	`All`, `Any`, `Contains`

Aggregation Operators—Working with Numbers

LINQ's aggregation operators enumerate a sequence of values (normally numeric, but not mandatory), perform some operation for each element, and ultimately return a result (normally numeric, but not mandatory). In purest form, Sum, Average, Min, and Max can all be built using the Aggregate operator; however, the specifically named operators make queries cleaner in syntax by spelling out exactly the operation being performed. Each of these operators are covered in detail in the following sections, starting with the Aggregate operator.

Aggregate Operator

The Aggregate operator performs a folding pattern on each element using a given lambda expression and passing the accumulated result to the next element when processed. This operator is powerful, both in building day-to-day queries to process an entire sequence and when building other operators that carry out numeric operations on a sequence (the Aggregate operator is used as the basis for a custom operator to calculate the standard deviation and variance, as discussed in Chapter 9, "Parallel LINQ to Objects").

The Aggregate operator has three overloaded method signatures. These overloads allow you to specify a seed value and/or a selection function in addition to the aggregation function. The method signatures available are:

```
// Applies an accumulator function to each element.
public static TSource Aggregate<TSource>(
    this IEnumerable<TSource> source,
    Func<TSource, TSource, TSource> func);

// Applies an accumulator function to each element.
// The accumulator can be a different type than the elements,
// and a starting (seed) value must be specified.
public static TAccumulate Aggregate<TSource, TAccumulate>(
    this IEnumerable<TSource> source,
    TAccumulate seed,
    Func<TAccumulate, TSource, TAccumulate> func);

// Applies an accumulator function to each element.
// The accumulator can be a different type than the elements,
// and a starting (seed) value must be specified.
// The final result is computed using the
// resultSelector function.
public static TResult Aggregate<TSource, TAccumulate, TResult>(
```

```
this IEnumerable<TSource> source,
TAccumulate seed,
Func<TAccumulate, TSource, TAccumulate> func,
Func<TAccumulate, TResult> resultSelector);
```

To understand how the `Aggregate` operator works, Listing 5-1 shows an aggregation operation on an integer array. The query computes the numeric sum of all integers in an array, then adds 100 to the final result. The Console output from this example is shown in Output 5-1. The `Aggregate` operator iterates the three values in the `nums` array. At each step, it takes the running total in the accumulator, adds that value, and stores that back in the accumulator. At the completion of the loop, the accumulator value is 6, and the select function adds an additional 100. The running watch at the start of each loop on the internal variables is listed in Table 5-3.

Table 5-3 Step-by-Step Aggregation Process

Step	Accumulator (acc)	Element (i)
1	0 (initialized by seed value)	1
2	1	2
3	3	3
	6	

Listing 5-1 `Aggregate` operator example—see Output 5-1

```
var nums = new int[] { 1, 2, 3 };

var sum = nums.Aggregate(
    0, // seed value for acc (acc = 0 for first element)
    (acc, i) => acc + i, // accumulator function
    acc => acc + 100 // selector function (optional)
);

Console.WriteLine("Sum plus 100 = {0}", sum);
```

Output 5-1

```
Sum plus 100 = 106
```

Simple aggregations are easy to understand. The seed and accumulator don't have to be numeric types; they can be any type, including an array. Calculating the average for example needs two accumulated values to calculate a result in a single iteration of the source sequence. The general technique is to keep multiple values in an array and update these on each accumulation cycle. For example, to calculate the average of a sequence in a single pass, the code in Listing 5-2 can be used.

Listing 5-2 Calculating the average of an integer array; this example demonstrates how to use the **Aggregate** operator with more than a single accumulator value

```
var nums = new int[] { 1, 2, 3 };

int count = 0;

var avg = nums.Aggregate(

    0, // accumulator for sum, initially 0

    // accumulator function.
    (acc, i) =>
    {
        count += 1; // running count
        acc += i; // running sum
        return acc;
    },

    // selector function, returns 0 when no elements
    acc => count > 0 ? acc / count : 0
);

Console.WriteLine("Average  = {0}", avg);
```

Average, Max, Min, and Sum Operators

Average, Min, Max, and Sum do the expected operation given their names. Used in their simplest form, they return their numeric results when used on any numeric sequence of data as the example in Listing 5-3 shows. The Console output from this example is shown in Output 5-2.

Listing 5-3   Average, Min, Max and Sum operator examples—see Output 5-2

```
var nums = Enumerable.Range(5, 50);

var avg = nums.Average();
var max = nums.Max();
var min = nums.Min();
var sum = nums.Sum();

Console.WriteLine("{0} to {1} (Average  = {2}, Sum = {3})",
    min, max, avg, sum);
```

Output 5-2

```
5 to 54 (Average = 29.5, Sum = 1475)
```

The Aggregate, Min and Max operators don't only work on numeric types, they also can be applied to any type. For the Min and Max operators, each element is tested against each other element using the < and > operator implementation for the element type, and either the lowest or highest element being returned respectively. For example, the following code finds the lowest ('a') and highest ('x') character in a character array:

```
var letters = new char[]
    { 'v', 'e', 'x', 'a' };

var min2 = letters.Min();
var max2 = letters.Max();
```

Table 5-4 lists the various result type and element type overloads for the Average operator. Table 5-5 lists the overloads for Max, Min, and Sum. All of the built-in numeric types and their nullable counterparts are catered for.

Table 5-4 **Average** Operator Overload Element and Return Types

Result Type	Source Element Type
decimal?	decimal?
decimal	decimal
double?	double?
double	double
float?	float?
float	float
double?	int?
double	int
double?	long?
double	long

Table 5-5 **Max** / **Min** / **Sum** Operator Overload Element and Return Types

Result Type	Source Element Type
decimal?	decimal?
decimal	decimal
double?	double?
Double	double
float?	float?
float	float
int?	int?
int	int
long?	long?
long	long

NULLABLE TYPE SHORTHAND Starting with .NET Framework 2.0, it was possible to specify a value type variable declaration allowing a null value, a feature called nullable types. Earlier versions of .NET didn't support value types being null. To make it easier to define a value type as nullable, Microsoft added a shorthand way of declaring them, simply appending a question mark to the type. The following two lines both declare a nullable type of integer; the second (i2) uses the shorthand syntax:

```
Nullable<int> i1 = null;
int? i2 = null;
```

For each operator, in addition to the various overload types for different numeric element inputs, there is an overload that works on the sequence elements themselves and an overload that takes a selector function to specify the values to be aggregated. The signatures for these operators follow a repetitive pattern, and the following example shows the Sum operator that returns a decimal value:

```
public static decimal Sum<TSource>(
    this IEnumerable<TSource> source,
    Func<TSource, decimal> selector);
```

Aggregate operations using selector functions are often useful in queries that group data. Listing 5-4 demonstrates a fairly complex query that summarizes fictitious call log data. In this case, the query groups all incoming calls from the same number and then aggregates the total number of calls, call time, and average call time. This query generates the Console output shown in Output 5-3.

Listing 5-4 `Aggregate` operators are useful for generating summary data in a query that groups data—see Output 5-3

```
List<CallLog> callLog = CallLog.SampleData();

var q = from call in callLog
        where call.Incoming == true
        group call by call.Number into g
        select new {
```

```
        Number = g.Key,
        Count  = g.Count(),
        Avg    = g.Average(c => c.Duration),
        Total  = g.Sum(c => c.Duration)
    };

foreach (var call in q)
    Console.WriteLine(
        "{0} - Calls:{1}, Time:{2}mins, Avg:{3}mins",
        call.Number,
        call.Count, call.Total, Math.Round(call.Avg, 2));
```

Output 5-3

```
885 983 8858 - Calls:4, Time:31mins, Avg:7.75mins
165 737 1656 - Calls:2, Time:27mins, Avg:13.5mins
546 607 5462 - Calls:2, Time:13mins, Avg:6.5mins
848 553 8487 - Calls:2, Time:20mins, Avg:10mins
278 918 2789 - Calls:2, Time:22mins, Avg:11mins
364 202 3644 - Calls:2, Time:44mins, Avg:22mins
```

Count and LongCount Operators

Count and LongCount return the number of elements in a sequence and only differ in their return types, with Count returning an int type result and LongCount returning a long type result.

There are two overloads for each operator. The first takes no arguments and returns the total number of elements in a sequence, and the second overload takes a predicate function and returns the count of elements that passed the predicates test. The method signatures available are:

```
// Return the number of elements in the
// source sequence.
// Max value = System.Int32.MaxValue
public static int Count<TSource>(
    this IEnumerable<TSource> source);

// Return the number of elements in the
// source sequence that pass the predicate.
// Max value = System.Int32.MaxValue
public static int Count<TSource>(
```

```
        this IEnumerable<TSource> source,
        Func<TSource, bool> predicate);

// Return the number of elements in the
// source sequence.
// Max value = System.Int64.MaxValue
public static long LongCount<TSource>(
        this IEnumerable<TSource> source);

// Return the number of elements in the
// source sequence that pass the predicate.
// Max value = System.Int64.MaxValue
public static long LongCount<TSource>(
        this IEnumerable<TSource> source,
        Func<TSource, bool> predicate);
```

In its most basic use, the Count and LongCount operators return the number of elements in a sequence. Although the built-in collection classes rarely offer support for more than the int.MaxValue of elements, sources streamed from other places can exceed this limit, and LongCount should be used. Listing 5-5 demonstrates how to use the Count and LongCount operators. The Console output for this example is shown in Output 5-4.

Listing 5-5 When it is possible for the **Count** operator to be larger than an integer, use the **LongCount** operator instead—see Output 5-4

```
var nums = Enumerable.Range(1, int.MaxValue);

int c1 = nums.Count();

// the following sequence would overflow
// the Count operator, use LongCount instead.
long c2 = nums.Concat(nums).LongCount();

Console.WriteLine("{0}, {1}", c1, c2);
```

Output 5-4

```
2147483647, 4294967294
```

The second overload of `Count` and `LongCount` that takes a filter predicate as an argument allows you to count the number of elements that pass that function (return the Boolean value of true). For example, to count the number of integers divisible by ten in an integer array, the following code can be used (in case you are interested, the result is 214,748,364):

```
var nums = Enumerable.Range(1, int.MaxValue);
var q3 = nums.Count(i => i % 10 == 0);
```

The `Count` operator is optimized for sequences that implement the `ICollection<T>` interface. Collections implementing this interface support the `Count` property of their own and often avoid an iteration of their underlying collection to return their counts. For these collections, `Count` returns `source.Count` as the result. This optimization is not possible when the overload specifying a predicate is used; a full loop of the sequence is unavoidable to apply the predicate function.

DOES LINQ TO OBJECTS HAVE BUILT-IN PERFORMANCE OPTIMIZATIONS? An interesting blog posting by Alexandra Rusina from Microsoft details the performance optimizations built into the standard query operators and LINQ to Objects provider. It details how IList and ICollection tests allow for faster execution for certain operators.

This information can be found at http://blogs.msdn.com/csharpfaq/archive/2009/01/26/does-the-linq-to-objects-provider-have-built-in-performance-optimization.aspx.

Conversion Operators—Changing Types

LINQ to Objects has many operators that facilitate casting elements in a sequence and the sequence itself. This is often necessary to access specific instance methods that occur in one collection type from another or to access an instance property of an element.

AsEnumerable Operator

The `AsEnumerable` operator changes the compile time type of the source sequence, casting a sequence or collection back to `System.Collections.Generic.IEnumerable<T>`. This allows control over what LINQ provider will be called and used extensively when choosing between LINQ providers—most commonly at this time when choosing to execute part of a LINQ to SQL query in-memory rather than at the database. This technique is demonstrated in Chapter 9, where it is used to segment queries into sequential and parallel implementations.

`AsEnumerable` has a single overload with the following method signature:

```
// Returns the sequence as an IEnumerable<T> sequence.
public static IEnumerable<TSource> AsEnumerable<TSource>(
    this IEnumerable<TSource> source);
```

To demonstrate this operator, the following sample code creates a `List<int>` called `list` and then using the `AsEnumerable` operator, turns this collection into an `IEnumerable<int>`. Figure 5-1 shows the Intellisense pop-up in Visual Studio 2010. All instance and extension methods are available on the `list` instance. Figure 5-2 shows that once this collection has an `AsEnumerable` operation applied, it is type-cast down to an `IEnumerable<T>` type, and only the extension methods are available (the instance property of `List<T>`, `Count` can no longer be seen unless it is cast back into an `ICollection<int>` or `List<int>`).

```
List<int> list = new List<int> { 1, 2, 3, 4, 5 };
// enumerable will be compile-time typed
// as an IEnumerable<T>
IEnumerable<int> enumerable = list.AsEnumerable();
```

Casting a fuller-featured collection type back to a vanilla `IEnumerable<T>` can be useful when testing custom operators' handling of nonindexed collections. For example, when testing an operator begin by testing using a collection in a `List<T>` (which supports index access to element access) to

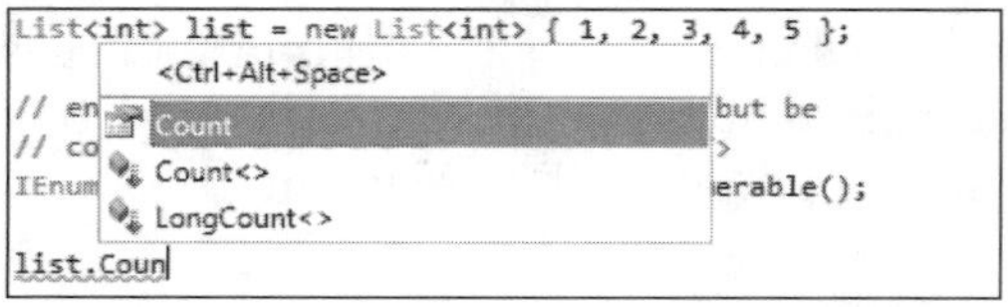

FIGURE 5-1   Visual Studio 2010 Intellisense for **List<T>**. Notice the **Count** instance property in addition to the extension method **Count()**.

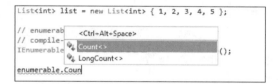

FIGURE 5-2 Visual Studio 2010 Intellisense for **IEnumerable<T>**, created by calling the **AsEnumerable()** operator. Notice the **Count** instance property is no longer accessible.

prove the IList<T> indexible path and then call AsEnumerable() on the collection to allow writing tests that exercise the vanilla IEnumerable<T> path, which cannot benefit from element access via index.

Cast Operator

The Cast operator yields all elements in a nongeneric IEnumerable collection as a given type. This is mainly to cater to the .NET 1.0 style of collections, which pre-date the generic type features of .NET Framework 2.0, such as the ArrayList collection, which holds references as Object types. If the type of the elements cannot be cast to the new type, a System.InvalidCastException is thrown.

Cast has a single overload with the following method signature:

```
// Casts an IEnumerable collection into an
// IEnumerable<T> collection.
// If the elements cannot be cast to the new type an
// InvalidCastException is thrown.
public static IEnumerable<TResult> Cast<TResult>(
    this IEnumerable source);
```

To demonstrate using the Cast<T> operator, the following code initializes a nongeneric ArrayList collection (introduced in .NET Framework 1.0). This collection only has access to a few operators (namely Cast, OfType), and to gain access to all the LINQ standard query operators, you need to use the Cast operator as shown in Listing 5-6.

Listing 5-6 Example LINQ query over the .NET 1.0 **ArrayList** type, which doesn't implement **IEnumerable<T>**

```
ArrayList list = new ArrayList();
list.Add(1);
list.Add(2);
list.Add(3);
```

```
// ArrayList doesn't implement IEnumerable<T>
// Meaning, no access to LINQ operators on
// the collection instance 'list' until the
// collection is cast using Cast<T>.
// Cast the ArrayList to an IEnumerable<int>
var avg = (from i in list.Cast<int>()
           where i < 3
           select i).Average();
```

OfType Operator

The OfType operator filters the elements of an IEnumerable collection, returning an IEnumerable<T> with only elements of the type specified. This is similar to the Cast operator, however where the elements cannot be cast to the specified type, the OfType operator simply omits those elements; the Cast operator throws an exception.

OfType has a single overload with the following method signature:

```
// Filter elements of an IEnumerable collection
// to an IEnumerable<T> collection based on type.
// Only elements of the given type will be returned.
public static IEnumerable<TResult> OfType<TResult>(
     this IEnumerable source);
```

The OfType operator will simply skip elements that can't be safely cast to the specified type. To demonstrate how to use the OfType operator, Listing 5-7 shows how to implement a type-safe query over an ArrayList collection. The collection type ArrayList implements IEnumerable but not IEnumerable<T>, which precludes it using most of the LINQ standard query operators. The ArrayList collection holds references to System.Object types, and since all types inherit from System.Object, type safety of the elements cannot be assumed (as in this example, elements can be mixed type). Generics introduced in .NET 2.0 fixed this situation, and it's unlikely that newer code doesn't use a generic collection type.

Listing 5-7   The **OfType** operator allows working safely with nongeneric collection types like **ArrayList**

```
ArrayList list = new ArrayList();
list.Add(1);
list.Add(2);
list.Add(3);
```

```
list.Add("one");
list.Add("two");
list.Add("three");

// ArrayList doesn't implement IEnumerable<T>
// Meaning, no access to LINQ operators on
// the collection instance 'list' until the
// collection is cast using OfType<T>.
// The Cast operator would throw an exception
// because not all elements can be safely cast,
// use OfType when type safety isn't guaranteed.
var avg = (from i in list.OfType<int>()
           where i < 3
           select i).Average();
```

A more day-to-day use of the OfType operator is for filtering collections to isolate elements based on specific type. This is common in many types of applications, for example in drawing programs where each element in a collection can be of different "shape" types, which inherit from a base, as the following code demonstrates:

```
public class Shape { }
public class Rectangle : Shape { }
public class Circle : Shape { }
```

The OfType operator allows you to write queries over a collection holding all shapes and isolate based on the subtypes, Rectangle or Circle. Listing 5-8 demonstrates how to restrict collection elements to a certain type, with this example returning the number of Rectangles in the source collection.

Listing 5-8 The **OfType** operator can be used to filter collection elements based on their type

```
List<Shape> shapes = new List<Shape> {
    new Rectangle(),
    new Circle(),
    new Rectangle(),
    new Circle(),
    new Rectangle() };

var q = from rect in shapes.OfType<Rectangle>()
        select rect;
```

```
Console.WriteLine("Number of Rectangles = {0}",
    q.Count());
```

ToArray Operator

The `ToArray` operator returns an array (`<T>`) of a given type from any `IEnumerable<T>` sequence. The most common reason to use this operator is to force the immediate execution of a query in order to capture the resulting data as a snapshot (forcing the execution of the query that is waiting to be enumerated because of deferred execution).

`ToArray` has a single overload with the following method signature:

```
// Returns an array of type T from a
// System.Collections.Generic.IEnumerable<T>.
public static TSource[] ToArray<TSource>(
    this IEnumerable<TSource> source);
```

To demonstrate the use of the `ToArray` operator, Listing 5-9 executes a query over an `IEnumerable<int>` sequence and captures the results in an `int[]` array.

Listing 5-9 The **ToArray** operator enumerates an **IEnumerable<T>** sequence and returns the results in an array

```
IEnumerable<int> data = Enumerable.Range(1, 5);

int[] q = (from i in data
           where i < 3
           select i).ToArray();

Console.WriteLine("Returns {0}, {1}",
    q[0], q[1]);
```

ToDictionary Operator

The `ToDictionary` operator converts an `IEnumerable<TValue>` sequence into a `Dictionary<TKey,TValue>` collection. The `System.Collections.Generic.Dictionary<TKey,TValue>` collection type keeps a list of key value pairs and demands that each key value is unique. A `System.ArgumentException` is thrown if a duplicate key insert is attempted during the conversion process. A `Dictionary` collection allows efficient access to elements based on key value, and converting a sequence to a dictionary is a way of improving lookup performance if code frequently needs to find elements by key value.

There are four method overloads of the `ToDictionary` operator. The simplest overload takes only a delegate for determining the key selection function, and the most complex takes a delegate for key selection, element selection, and an `IEqualityComparer` that is used for determining if key values are equal. When the element selector function is not passed, the element type itself is used, and when an `IEqualityComparer` is not passed, `EqualityComparer<TSource>.Default` is used. The method signatures available are:

```
// Creates a Dictionary of elements in a sequence
// Key values returned by the key selector
// function must be unique, otherwise a
// System.ArgumentException will be thrown.
// Uses EqualityComparer<TSource>.Default
// to compare keys for uniqueness.
public static Dictionary<TKey, TSource> ToDictionary<TSource, TKey>(
          this IEnumerable<TSource> source,
          Func<TSource, TKey> keySelector);


// Creates a Dictionary of elements in a sequence
// and projects the elements to a new type.
// Key values returned by the key selector
// function must be unique, otherwise a
// System.ArgumentException will be thrown.
// Uses EqualityComparer<TSource>.Default
// to compare keys for uniqueness.
public static Dictionary<TKey, TElement> ToDictionary<TSource, TKey,
// TElement>(
          this IEnumerable<TSource> source,
          Func<TSource, TKey> keySelector,
          Func<TSource, TElement> elementSelector);


// Creates a Dictionary of elements in a sequence
// Key values returned by the key selector
// function must be unique, otherwise a
// System.ArgumentException will be thrown.
// Uses the comparer to test for key uniqueness.
```

```
public static Dictionary<TKey, TSource> ToDictionary<TSource, TKey>(
          this IEnumerable<TSource> source,
          Func<TSource, TKey> keySelector,
          IEqualityComparer<TKey> comparer);

// Creates a Dictionary of elements in a sequence
// and projects the elements to a new type.
// Key values returned by the key selector
// function must be unique, otherwise a
// System.ArgumentException will be thrown.
// Uses the comparer to test for key uniqueness.
public static Dictionary<TKey, TElement> ToDictionary<TSource, TKey,
// TElement>(
          this IEnumerable<TSource> source,
          Func<TSource, TKey> keySelector,
          Func<TSource, TElement> elementSelector,
          IEqualityComparer<TKey> comparer);
```

To demonstrate the use of the ToDictionary operator, Listing 5-10 creates a Dictionary of sample contacts based on the key of last name concatenated with first name, allowing efficient lookup of a contact by name. The sample demonstrates this by looking up a contact from the resulting Dictionary by key value.

Listing 5-10 The **ToDictionary** operator creates a dictionary of elements in a sequence

```
List<Contact> contacts = Contact.SampleData();

// materialize results into a Dictionary
Dictionary<string, Contact> conDictionary =
    contacts.ToDictionary<Contact, string>(
    c => c.LastName + c.FirstName);

// all contact records now in Dictionary
// find record by key = very efficient
Contact record = conDictionary["Kamph" + "Mack"];

Console.WriteLine("Kamph DOB = {0}", record.DateOfBirth);
```

NOTE One confusing aspect of using the ToDictionary operator is the reversal of the generic type definition between the operator (element type and then key type) and the Dictionary type (key type and then element type). You will notice in the example shown in Listing 5-10, that the Dictionary is defined as Dictionary<string, Contact> and the ToDictionary operator as ToDictionary<Contact, string>. It makes sense from the method declaration perspective (source type always comes first and then the return type), it just needs to be remembered. This is often a source of confusion when learning to use this operator.

The ToDictionary operator isn't limited to projecting the sequence elements as their own type. Passing in an element selection function allows the value held in the Dictionary against a key value to be any type. The example shown in Listing 5-11 projects the elements to an anonymous type and uses case-insensitive string comparison to ensure that keys are absolutely unique (not just different by character casing), using the built-in static string comparison instances (creating custom IEqualityComparers is covered in Chapter 4 in the "Specifying Your Own Key Comparison Function" section and in Chapter 6 under "Custom EqualityComparers When Using LINQ Set Operators").

Listing 5-11 The **ToDictionary** operator also accepts a custom equality comparer and element projection expression

```
List<Contact> contacts = Contact.SampleData();

// materialize DOB values into a Dictionary
// case-insensitive key comparison
Dictionary<string, DateTime> dictionary =
    contacts.ToDictionary<Contact, string, DateTime>(
    c => c.LastName + c.FirstName,
    e => e.DateOfBirth,
    StringComparer.CurrentCultureIgnoreCase);

// dictionary contains only DOB value in elements
DateTime dob = dictionary["Kamph" + "Mack"];

Console.WriteLine("Kamph DOB = {0}", dob);
```

ToList Operator

The `ToList` operator returns a `System.Collections.Generic.List<T>` of a given type from any `IEnumerable<T>` sequence. The most common reason to use this operator is to force the immediate execution of a query in order to capture the resulting data as a snapshot, executing the query by enumerating over all elements.

`ToList` has a single overload with the following method signature:

```
// Returns an System.Collections.Generic.List<T>
// from a System.Collections.Generic.IEnumerable<T>.
public static List<TSource> ToList<TSource>(
    this IEnumerable<TSource> source);
```

To demonstrate the `ToList` operator, Listing 5-12 executes a query over an `IEnumerable<int>` sequence and captures the results in an `List<T>` and then uses the `ForEach` method on that type to write the results to the Console window.

Listing 5-12   The **ToList** operator enumerates an **IEnumerable<T>** sequence and returns the results in a **List<T>**

```
IEnumerable<int> data = Enumerable.Range(1, 5);

// Query and capture results in List<int>
List<int> q = (from i in data
               where i < 3
               select i).ToList();

// ForEach is a method on List<T>
q.ForEach(j => Console.WriteLine(j));
```

ToLookup Operator

The `ToLookup` operator was first covered in Chapter 4, "Grouping and Joining Data," where it was used to facilitate very efficient one-to-many joins between two sequences. `ToLookup` creates subsequences based on elements that share a common key value. `ToLookup` is similar in usage and behavior to `ToDictionary`, the difference being how they handle duplicate elements with the same key value. `ToLookup` allows multiple elements for a given key value, whereas `ToDictionary` throws an exception if this ever occurs.

The method signatures available for the `ToLookup` operator are:

```
// Creates a Lookup<TKey,TElm> of elements in a sequence
// using key values returned by the key selector
// function. Uses EqualityComparer<TSource>.Default
// to compare keys for uniqueness.
public static ILookup<TKey, TSource> ToLookup<TSource, TKey>(
          this IEnumerable<TSource> source,
          Func<TSource, TKey> keySelector);


// Creates a Lookup<TKey,TElm> of elements in a sequence
// and projects the elements to a new type using
// Key values returned by the key selector
// function. Uses EqualityComparer<TSource>.Default
// to compare keys for uniqueness.
public static ILookup<TKey, TElement> ToLookup<TSource, TKey,
// TElement>(
          this IEnumerable<TSource> source,
          Func<TSource, TKey> keySelector,
          Func<TSource, TElement> elementSelector);


// Creates a Lookup<TKey,TElm> of elements in a
// sequence using key values returned by the key selector
// selector function. Uses the comparer passed in
// to compare keys for uniqueness.
public static ILookup<TKey, TSource> ToLookup<TSource, TKey>(
          this IEnumerable<TSource> source,
          Func<TSource, TKey> keySelector,
          IEqualityComparer<TKey> comparer);


// Creates a Lookup<TKey,TElm> of elements in a sequence
// and projects the elements to a new type using
// Key values returned by the key selector
// function. Uses the comparer passed in
// to compare keys for uniqueness.
public static ILookup<TKey, TElement> ToLookup<TSource, TKey, TElement>(
          this IEnumerable<TSource> source,
          Func<TSource, TKey> keySelector,
          Func<TSource, TElement> elementSelector,
          IEqualityComparer<TKey> comparer);
```

To demonstrate the ToLookup operator, the example shown in Listing 5-13 builds a look-up list of all calls made from or to the same phone number (calls_lookup). The look-up groupings are then used in a second query to project a sequence of calls against each contact. The resulting Console output is (shortened to the first three records) is shown in Output 5-5.

Listing 5-13 Sample usage of the **ToLookup** operator to achieve a one-to-many outer join—see Output 5-5

```
var contacts = Contact.SampleData();
var calls = CallLog.SampleData();

// build a lookup list for the inner sequence
var calls_lookup =
    (from c in calls
    orderby c.When descending
    select c)
    .ToLookup(c => c.Number);

// one to many join on the phone number
var q3 = from c in contacts
        orderby c.LastName
        select new
        {
            LastName = c.LastName,
            Calls = calls_lookup[c.Phone]
        };

foreach (var contact in q3)
{
    Console.WriteLine("Last name: {0}", contact.LastName);

    foreach (var call in contact.Calls)
        Console.WriteLine(" - {0} call on {1} for {2}min.",
            call.Incoming ? "Incoming" : "Outgoing",
            call.When,
            call.Duration);
}
```

Output 5-5

```
Last name: Deane
Last name: Gauwain
Last name: Gottshall
  - Incoming call on 8/7/2006 1:47:00 PM for 3min.
  - Outgoing call on 8/7/2006 1:12:00 PM for 15min.
...
```

The result of a `ToLookup` operator is a `System.Linq.ILookup<TKey, TElement>`. The definition for the `ILookup<TKey, TElement>` interface and the `IGrouping<TKey, TElement>` interface are shown in Listing 5-14.

Listing 5-14 Definition for the **ILookup** and **IGrouping** interfaces

```
// Defines an interface for data structures that map key
// values to System.Collections.Generic.IEnumerable<T>
// sequences of values.
public interface ILookup<TKey, TElement> :
    IEnumerable<IGrouping<TKey, TElement>>, IEnumerable
{
    // Gets the number of key/value collection pairs.
    int Count { get; }

    // Gets the IEnumerable<T> sequence of values indexed
    // by the specified key.
    IEnumerable<TElement> this[TKey key] { get; }

    // Returns true if the specified key, otherwise false.
    bool Contains(TKey key);
}

// Represents a collection of objects that have a common key.
public interface IGrouping<out TKey, out TElement> :
    IEnumerable<TElement>, IEnumerable
{
    // Gets the key of the System.Linq.IGrouping<TKey,TElement>.
    TKey Key { get; }
}
```

Element Operators

DefaultIfEmpty, ElementAt, ElementAtOrDefault, First, FirstOrDefault, Last, LastOrDefault, Single, and SingleOrDefault are all types of operators that return an individual element from a sequence or a default value if no element of a specific type exists.

The OrDefault variation of each of these operators (and DefaultIfEmpty) neatly handles the situation where an element cannot be found that satisfies the criteria, returning a default(T) result in these cases. The variations that don't end with OrDefault throw an exception if no element satisfies the criteria.

WHAT DOES THE DEFAULT KEYWORD RETURN?   The default keyword solves the issue of not knowing what default value to initially assign to a generic type. The default keyword returns null for reference types and zero for numeric value types. For structs, it returns each member of the struct initialized to zero or null, depending on whether they are value or reference types.

DefaultIfEmpty Operator

The DefaultIfEmpty operator allows the graceful handling of when a sequence is empty (has no elements). There are two method overloads; the first handles an empty sequence by returning a single element of default(TSource) within an IEnumerable<T>. The second overload takes an argument specifying a default value to return if the source sequence is empty. In both cases, the default value is only returned if the source sequence is empty. The method signatures available are:

```
// Returns the source sequence, or the default(TSource)
// in an IEnumerable<TSource> if the source sequence has
// no elements
public static IEnumerable<TSource> DefaultIfEmpty<TSource>(
    this IEnumerable<TSource> source);

// Returns the source sequence, or the defaultValue
// specified in an IEnumerable<T> if the source sequence
// has no elements
public static IEnumerable<TSource> DefaultIfEmpty<TSource>(
    this IEnumerable<TSource> source,
    TSource defaultValue);
```

To demonstrate the use of `DefaultIfEmpty`, Listing 5-15 defines two arrays, one empty (`empty`) and one with a sequence of data (`nums`). `DefaultIfEmpty` is called on these arrays to demonstrate the behavior. The Console output from this example is shown in Output 5-6.

Listing 5-15 The **`DefaultIfEmpty`** operator allows safe handling of potentially empty source sequences — see Output 5-6

```
var nums = new int[] { 1, 2, 3, 4, 5 };
var empty = new int[] { };

// returns 1, because the array isn't empty
Console.WriteLine("nums.DefaultIfEmpty() = {0}",
    nums.DefaultIfEmpty().First());

// returns default(int) in an IEnumerable<int>
Console.WriteLine("empty.DefaultIfEmpty() = {0}",
    empty.DefaultIfEmpty().First());

// returns 100. The array is empty, but an explicit
// default value is passed in as an argument.
Console.WriteLine("empty.DefaultIfEmpty(100) = {0}",
    empty.DefaultIfEmpty(100).First());
```

Output 5-6

```
nums.DefaultIfEmpty() = 1
empty.DefaultIfEmpty() = 0
empty.DefaultIfEmpty(100) = 100
```

ElementAt and ElementAtOrDefault Operators

The `ElementAt` operator returns the element at a given zero-based index position in a sequence. An `ArgumentOutOfRangeException` is thrown if the index position is less than zero or beyond the end of the sequence. To avoid this exception being thrown, use the `ElementAtOrDefault` operator instead, and a `default(T)` instance will be returned when the index is out of range.

The method signatures available for the ElementAt and ElementAtOrDefault operators are:

```
// Returns the element at the zero-based index position
// specified. Throws an ArgumentOutOfRangeException if
// index is less than zero, or beyond the end of the sequence.
public static TSource ElementAt<TSource>(
    this IEnumerable<TSource> source,
    int index);

// Returns the element at the zero-based index position
// specified. Returns a default(T) instance if index is
// less than zero, or beyond the end of the sequence.
public static TSource ElementAtOrDefault<TSource>(
    this IEnumerable<TSource> source,
    int index);
```

To demonstrate the ElementAt and ElementAtOrDefault operators, Listing 5-16 calls these operators on a simple array of integers. To avoid an exception being thrown where an index is out of bounds, as for the sample query called error, the ElementAtOrDefault operator is used instead. The Console output from this example is shown in Output 5-7.

Listing 5-16   The **ElementAt** operator allows elements to be accessed by zero-based index position—see Output 5-7

```
var nums = new int[] { 1, 2, 3, 4, 5 };

// get the third element (zero-based index position of 2)
var third = nums.ElementAt(2);

// ERROR: System.ArgumentOutOfRangeException, if the
// index is < 0 or beyond the end of the sequence.
// var error = nums.ElementAt(100);

// returns a default(T), 0 for a value int type.
var no_error = nums.ElementAtOrDefault(100);

Console.WriteLine("nums.ElementAt(2) = {0}",
    nums.ElementAt(2));
```

```
Console.WriteLine("nums.ElementAtOrDefault(100) = {0}",
    nums.ElementAtOrDefault(100));
```

Output 5-7

```
nums.ElementAt(2) = 3
nums.ElementAtOrDefault(100) = 0
```

First and FirstOrDefault Operators

The `First` and `FirstOrDefault` operators return the first element in a sequence. There are two overloads for each operator. The first overload takes no arguments and returns the first element from the sequence; the second takes a predicate argument and returns the first element that satisfies that predicate. If no elements are in the sequence or pass the predicate function, a `System.InvalidOperationException` is thrown, or if using the `FirstOrDefault` operator, an instance of `default(T)` is returned.

The method signatures available for the `First` and `FirstOrDefault` operators are:

```
// Returns the first element in a sequence. If the
// sequence is empty an InvalidOperationException
// is thrown.
public static TSource First<TSource>(
    this IEnumerable<TSource> source);

// Returns the first element in a sequence that
// satisfies the predicate function. If the
// sequence is empty or no elements satisfy the
// predicate, an InvalidOperationException
// is thrown.
public static TSource First<TSource>(
    this IEnumerable<TSource> source,
    Func<TSource, bool> predicate);

// Returns the first element in a sequence. If the
// sequence is empty a default(TSource) instance
// is returned.
public static TSource FirstOrDefault<TSource>(
    this IEnumerable<TSource> source);
```

```
// Returns the first element in a sequence that
// satisfies the predicate function. If the
// sequence is empty or no elements satisfy the
// predicate, a default(TSource) instance
// is returned.
public static TSource FirstOrDefault<TSource>(
    this IEnumerable<TSource> source,
    Func<TSource, bool> predicate);
```

To demonstrate the use of the First and FirstOrDefault operators, Listing 5-17 calls these operators with a simple array of integers and an empty array. To avoid an exception being thrown when there is no first element or no first element that passes the predicate function, the FirstOrDefault operator is used instead. The Console output from this example is shown in Output 5-8.

Listing 5-17   The **First** operator returns the first element in a sequence—see Output 5-8

```
var nums = new int[] { 1, 2, 3, 4, 5 };
var empty = new int[] { };

// get the first element
var first = nums.First();

// get the first element > 2
var third = nums.First(i => i > 2);

// ERROR: System.InvalidOperationException
// var error = empty.First();

// returns a default(T), 0 for a value int type.
var no_error = empty.FirstOrDefault();

// ERROR: System.InvalidOperationException.
// No value > 10 in this sequence.
// var error = nums.First(i => i > 10);

// No value > 10 in this sequence. default(T) returned.
var no_error2 = nums.FirstOrDefault(i => i > 10);
```

```
Console.WriteLine("first = {0}, third = {1}",
    first, third);

Console.WriteLine("no_error = {0}, no_error2 = {1}",
    no_error, no_error2);
```

Output 5-8

```
first = 1, third = 3
no_error = 0, no_error2 = 0
```

Last and LastOrDefault Operators

The `Last` and `LastOrDefault` operators return the last element in a sequence. There are two overloads for each operator. The first overload takes no arguments and returns the last element from the sequence; the second takes a predicate argument and returns the last element that satisfies that predicate. If no elements are in the sequence or pass the predicate function, a `System.InvalidOperationException` is thrown, or if using the `LastOrDefault` operator, an instance of `default(T)` is returned.

The method signatures available for the `Last` and `LastOrDefault` operators are:

```
// Returns the last element in a sequence. If the
// sequence is empty an InvalidOperationException
// is thrown.
public static TSource Last<TSource>(
    this IEnumerable<TSource> source);

// Returns the last element in a sequence that
// satisfies the predicate function. If the
// sequence is empty or no elements satisfy the
// predicate, an InvalidOperationException
// is thrown.
public static TSource Last<TSource>(
    this IEnumerable<TSource> source,
    Func<TSource, bool> predicate);
```

```
// Returns the last element in a sequence. If the
// sequence is empty a default(TSource) instance
// is returned.
public static TSource LastOrDefault<TSource>(
    this IEnumerable<TSource> source);


// Returns the last element in a sequence that
// satisfies the predicate function. If the
// sequence is empty or no elements satisfy the
// predicate, a default(TSource) instance
// is returned.
public static TSource LastOrDefault<TSource>(
    this IEnumerable<TSource> source,
    Func<TSource, bool> predicate);
```

To demonstrate the use of the Last and LastOrDefault operators, Listing 5-18 calls these operators with a simple array of integers and an empty array. To avoid an exception being thrown when there is no last element or no last element that passes the predicate function, the LastOrDefault operator is used instead. The Console output from this example is shown in Output 5-9.

Listing 5-18 The **Last** operator returns the last element in a sequence—see Output 5-9

```
var nums = new int[] { 1, 2, 3, 4, 5 };
var empty = new int[] { };

// get the last element
var last = nums.Last();

// get the last element < 4
var third = nums.Last(i => i < 4);

// ERROR: System.InvalidOperationException
// var error = empty.Last();

// returns a default(T), 0 for a value int type.
var no_error = empty.LastOrDefault();

// ERROR: System.InvalidOperationException.
// No value > 10 in this sequence.
// var error = nums.Last(i => i > 10);
```

```
// No value > 10 in this sequence. default(T) returned.
var no_error2 = nums.LastOrDefault(i => i > 10);

Console.WriteLine("last = {0}, third = {1}",
    last, third);

Console.WriteLine("no_error = {0}, no_error2 = {1}",
    no_error, no_error2);
```

Output 5-9

```
last = 5, third = 3
no_error = 0, no_error2 = 0
```

Single and SingleOrDefault Operators

The `Single` and `SingleOrDefault` operators return the single element from a sequence or the single element that passes a predicate function. The `Single` operator throws a `System.InvalidOperationException` if there is zero or more than one element in the sequence. The `SingleOrDefault` operator returns an instance of `default(T)` if there are zero elements in a sequence and still throws a `System.InvalidOperationException` if there is more than one element in the sequence or more than one element that passes the predicate.

If there are situations when more than one element might pass a filter or query and you want to avoid the chance of an exception being raised (considering the implications of just choosing one of the elements over another), consider using the `First` or `Last` operators instead.

The method signatures available for the `Single` and `SingleOrDefault` operators are:

```
// Returns the single element in a sequence. If the
// sequence is empty or has more than one element an
// InvalidOperationException is thrown.
public static TSource Single<TSource>(
    this IEnumerable<TSource> source);
```

```
// Returns the single element in a sequence that passes
// the predicate function. If the sequence is empty or
// more than one element passes the predicate, an
// InvalidOperationException is thrown.
public static TSource Single<TSource>(
    this IEnumerable<TSource> source,
    Func<TSource, bool> predicate);

// Returns the single element in a sequence. If the
// sequence is empty an instance of default(TSource)
// is returned. If the sequence has more than one
// element, an InvalidOperationException is thrown.
public static TSource SingleOrDefault<TSource>(
    this IEnumerable<TSource> source);

// Returns the single element in a sequence that passes
// the predicate function. If the sequence is empty or
// more than one element passes the predicate, an
// instance of default(T) is returned.
public static TSource SingleOrDefault<TSource>(
    this IEnumerable<TSource> source,
    Func<TSource, bool> predicate);
```

To demonstrate the `Single` and `SingleOrDefault` operators, Listing 5-19 calls these operators with a simple array of integers, an array with a single element, and an empty array. To avoid an exception being thrown when there is no element or no element that passes the predicate function, the `SingleOrDefault` operator is used instead. If there is ever more than a single element in the sequence or that passes the predicate function, a `System.InvalidOperationException` is thrown in all cases. The Console output from this example is shown in Output 5-10.

Listing 5-19 The **Single** operator returns a single element from a sequence—see Output 5-10

```
var single = new int[] { 5 };
var nums = new int[] { 1, 2, 3, 4, 5 };
var empty = new int[] { };

// get the single element
var five = single.Single();
```

```
// get the element equal to 3
var third = nums.Single(i => i == 3);

// ERROR: System.InvalidOperationException
// more than one element in the sequence nums.
// var error = nums.Single();
// var error = nums.SingleOrDefault();

// returns a default(T), 0 for a value int type.
var no_error = empty.SingleOrDefault();

// ERROR: System.InvalidOperationException.
// No value == 10 in this sequence.
// var error = nums.Single(i => i == 10);

// No value == 10 in this sequence. default(T) returned.
var no_error2 = nums.SingleOrDefault(i => i == 10);

Console.WriteLine("five = {0}, third = {1}",
    five, third);

Console.WriteLine(
    "no_error = {0}, no_error2 = {1}",
    no_error, no_error2);
```

Output 5-10

```
five = 5, third = 3
no_error = 0, no_error2 = 0
```

Equality Operator—SequenceEqual

There is a single operator that can be used for testing sequence equality—the SequenceEqual operator.

SequenceEqual Operator

The `SequenceEqual` operator compares one sequence with another and only returns true if the sequences are equal in element values, element order, and element count. There are two method signatures for `SequenceEqual`, one that takes the sequence to compare to as an argument, and one that also allows a custom `IEqualityComparer` to be passed to control how element equality testing is carried out. When no `IEqualityComparer` is passed in, the default equality comparer for the source element type is used.

The method signatures available for the `SequenceEqual` operator are:

```
// Return true if the two sequences are equal
// in element values, order and count.
// Uses EqualityComparer<TSource>.Default
// to compare elements for equality.
public static bool SequenceEqual<TSource>(
    this IEnumerable<TSource> first,
    IEnumerable<TSource> second);


// Return true if the two sequences are equal
// in element values, order and count.
// Uses the IEqualityComparer passed in to
// compare elements for equality.
public static bool SequenceEqual<TSource>(
    this IEnumerable<TSource> first,
    IEnumerable<TSource> second,
    IEqualityComparer<TSource> comparer);
```

To demonstrate the use of the `SequenceEqual` operator, Listing 5-20 calls this operator to compare three string array sequences. The Console output from this example is shown in Output 5-11.

Listing 5-20 The **SequenceEqual** operator compares two sequences for equal element values—see Output 5-11

```
var n1 = new string[] { "peter", "paul", "mary" };
var n2 = new string[] { "paul", "peter", "mary" };
var n3 = new string[] { "PETER", "PAUL", "MARY" };
```

```
// order dependent
bool n1n2 = n1.SequenceEqual(n2);

// case-sensitive using the default comparer
bool n1n3 = n1.SequenceEqual(n3);

// passing in a comparer - this time using the
// built-in StringComparer static instances.
bool n1n3_2 = n1.SequenceEqual(
    n3, StringComparer.CurrentCultureIgnoreCase);

Console.WriteLine("n1n2 = {0}, n1n3 = {1}, n1n3_2 = {2}",
    n1n2, n1n3, n1n3_2);
```

Output 5-11

```
n1n2 = False, n1n3 = False, n1n3_2 = True
```

Generation Operators—Generating Sequences of Data

Generating sequences of data to combine with LINQ to Object queries is often necessary when building unit tests and when working with indexible data sources, like iterating through the x and y coordinates of a bitmap image. The generation methods aren't extension methods; they are simply static method calls in the `System.Linq.Enumerable` class and are included with the LINQ operators because they fulfill the important task of creating sequences of data without using a for-loop construct.

Empty Operator

The `Empty` operator doesn't appear very useful at first sight. So why return an empty `IEnumerable<T>` sequence? The main use for this operator is for testing the empty sequence error handling behavior of other operators.

An empty sequence is not a collection type initialized to `null`; it is an array of zero elements of the specified type. Pseudo-code would be longer than the implementation of this method, and the following code example reproduces the `Empty` operator:

```
public static T[] Empty<T>()
{
    return new T[0];
}
```

The most common use I've found for this operator is for unit testing other operators. The following is an example of testing that an operator correctly throws the correct exception when called on an empty sequence of `int` types. (This sample used NUnit, but any testing framework has similar capabilities. The `RandomElement` operator is built as an example in Chapter 7, "Extending LINQ to Objects.")

```
[Test]
[ExpectedException("System.InvalidOperationException")]
public void EmptySourceTest()
{
    IEnumerable<int> empty = Enumerable.Empty<int>();
    int result = empty.RandomElement();
}
```

Range Operator

The `Range` operator builds a sequence of integers, starting for a given integer and increments of one, a given number of times. It has the following method signature:

```
public static IEnumerable<int> Range(int start, int count);
```

This is useful for quickly generating a sequence of numbers. The following example generates and writes the integer numbers 1900 through to 1904 to the Console window (`1900 1901 1902 1903 1904`):

```
var years = Enumerable.Range(1900, 5);

foreach (var item in years)
    Console.Write(item + " ");
```

Sequences of numbers can be useful for data-binding to controls. One example of this is binding a list of years to a combo-box control on a form. This can simply be achieved by assigning the Datasource property of any bindable control to a List<int> generated by Range, and in this particular case, reversing the order (so the most recent years are at the top):

Listing 5-21   The **Range** operator generates numeric sequences, in this case all years from 1900 to 2010—**Form** output is shown in Figure 5-3

```
// useful for databinding int sequences to combo-boxes
ComboBox yearsCombo = new ComboBox();
yearsCombo.DataSource =
    Enumerable.Range(1900, 111).Reverse().ToList();

Form form = new Form();
form.Controls.Add(yearsCombo);
form.ShowDialog();
```

FIGURE 5-3   Using the **Range** operator to populate years in a **ComboBox** control.

This operator shows its true practical potential for generating sequences within queries to target indexible locations. This is often the case when working with data in a bitmap. The example shown in Listing 5-22 demonstrates how to address every x and y location in a bitmap loaded from a file, and return the luminance of each pixel as shown in Output 5-12.

Listing 5-22 Using the **Range** operator to address every pixel in a bitmap image—see Output 5-12

```
// example of using range to address x,y locations in a bitmap
string filename = Path.Combine(
    Environment.CurrentDirectory, @"data\4pixeltest.bmp");

Bitmap bmp = (Bitmap)Image.FromFile(filename);

var q = from x in Enumerable.Range(0, bmp.Width)
        from y in Enumerable.Range(0, bmp.Height)
        let pixel = bmp.GetPixel(x, y)
        let lum = (byte)((0.2126 * pixel.R)
                       + (0.7152 * pixel.G)
                       + (0.0722 * pixel.B))
        select new { x, y, lum };

foreach (var item in q)
{
    Console.WriteLine("{0},{1} - {2}",
        item.x, item.y, item.lum);
}
```

Output 5-12

```
0,0 - 220
0,1 - 73
1,0 - 101
1,1 - 144
```

Repeat Operator

The Repeat operator replicates a given data value any number of times you specify. The simplest example of using the Repeat operator is to initialize an array. The following code creates an array of integer values, with each element in the array initialized to -1:

```
int[] i = Enumerable.Repeat(-1, 10).ToArray();
```

The Repeat operator isn't limited to integer value; any type can be used. For instance, the same array initialization using a string type initializing an array of string values to "No data" for three elements is

```
string[] s = Enumerable.Repeat("No data", 3).ToArray();
```

Value types work as expected, and caution must be used when the type of the repeating value argument is a reference type. It is obvious once pointed out, but the following code will initialize a bitmap array with all elements pointing to the same single bitmap instance as shown in the first example in Listing 5-23 (b1). It is likely the intention of this code is to create five separate bitmaps with dimensions five pixels by five pixels. The LINQ Repeat operator way of achieving this is to use the operator to cause a loop of five Select projections using the second example in Listing 5-23 (b2).

Listing 5-23 Be careful when using the **Repeat** operator for reference types

```
// WARNING! Reference types will all point to the same bitmap
// instance. Use care to determine if this is the desired behavior.
Bitmap[] b1 = Enumerable.Repeat(new Bitmap(5,5), 5).ToArray();

// Instead - use repeat as a looping construct,
// and project using a select operator. You will
// have 5 different Bitmap instances in the array.
Bitmap[] b2 = Enumerable.Repeat(0, 5)
   .Select(x => new Bitmap(5, 5)).ToArray();
```

Merging Operators

zip, a single merging operator, was added into .NET Framework 4.

Zip Operator

The zip operator merges the corresponding elements of two sequences using a specified selector function. The selector function takes an element from the first sequence and the corresponding element from the second sequence and projects a result using the function supplied. This process continues until one of the sequences (or both) has no more elements.

zip has a single overload with the following method signature:

```
// Merges (combines) the elements from two sequences using the
// resultSelector function until one sequence has no more elements.
public static IEnumerable<TResult> Zip<TFirst, TSecond, TResult>(
    this IEnumerable<TFirst> first,
    IEnumerable<TSecond> second,
    Func<TFirst, TSecond, TResult> resultSelector);
```

To demonstrate the use of the `zip` operator, Listing 5-24 calls this operator to merge a string array with an integer array. The first element in both sequences is passed to the result selector function, then the second elements, and then the third elements. Even though the string array has two more elements, they are skipped because the integer array has only three elements. The Console output from this example is shown in Output 5-13.

Listing 5-24   The **zip** operator merges (combines) two sequences—see Output 5-13

```
var letters = new string[] { "A", "B", "C", "D", "E" };
var numbers = new int[] { 1, 2, 3 };

var q = letters.Zip(numbers, (s, i) => s + i.ToString());

foreach (var s in q)
    Console.WriteLine(s);
```

Output 5-13

```
A1
B2
C3
```

Partitioning Operators—Skipping and Taking Elements

Paging data involves restricting the amount of data returned to segments of the entire sequence. For instance, it is common for websites to return the results of a search in groups of a certain increment to improve performance by not transferring all one million items, just the first ten, then the next ten when asked, and so on. The `Skip` and `Take` operators form the basis for achieving this using LINQ queries. `SkipWhile` and `TakeWhile` allow conditional statements to control the segmentation of data, skipping data until a predicate fails or taking data until a predicate fails.

Skip and Take Operators

Skip and Take do as their names suggest; Skip jumps over the number of elements in a sequence (or skips the entire sequence if the count of elements is less than the number to skip), and Take returns the given number of elements (or as many elements as possible until the end of the sequence is reached).

The method signatures available for the Skip and Take operators are:

```
// skips the number of elements specified from the
// start of a sequence, then returns each element
public static IEnumerable<TSource> Skip<TSource>(
    this IEnumerable<TSource> source,
    int count);

// Returns the number of elements specified from the
// start of a sequence, then skips the remaining
public static IEnumerable<TSource> Take<TSource>(
    this IEnumerable<TSource> source,
    int count);
```

Although the operators are independent, they are often combined to achieve paging a result sequence. The pattern generally used for paging is shown in Listing 5-25, which demonstrates retrieving elements 21 to 30 (the third page), where each page is ten records long (normally the page number is passed in as a variable). The Console output from this example is shown in Output 5-14.

Listing 5-25 The **Skip** and **Take** operator combine to return paged segments of a sequence—see Output 5-14

```
int[] nums = Enumerable.Range(1, 50).ToArray();

int page = 3;
int pageSize = 10;

var q = nums
        .Skip( (page-1) * pageSize )
        .Take( pageSize );

foreach (var i in q)
    Console.Write (i + " ");
```

Output 5-14

```
21  22  23  24  25  26  27  28  29  30
```

The `Take` operator also allows the topmost records (the first) to be returned similar to SQL's SELECT TOP(n) statement. This can be to protect against extreme result set sizes or to limit the result set size during development and testing to a manageable quantity. If the page size is being retrieved from user input (like the query string in a URL), then this input should be checked and limited to avoid denial of service attacks by someone setting page size to an unrealistic extreme. Listing 5-26 shows a custom extension method operator that has safeguards to avoid paging exploitation through malicious input. In this case, this operator limits page size to 100 elements, and handles the translation of page number and page size into `Skip` and `Take` operations making repetitive code like that shown in Listing 5-25 centralized in one place. When this operator is called with the following line, the identical results shown in Output 5-14 are returned.

```
var q = nums.Page(3, 10);
```

Listing 5-26 Custom paging extension method with safeguards from extreme inputs taken from untrusted sources

```
public static class PagingExtensions
{
    public static IEnumerable<T> Page<T>(
        this IEnumerable<T> source,
        int page,
        int pageSize)
    {
        const int maxPageSize = 100;

        // clip page size to maximum
        pageSize = pageSize < maxPageSize ?
            pageSize : maxPageSize;

        return source
            .Skip((page - 1) * pageSize)
            .Take(pageSize);
    }
}
```

SkipWhile and TakeWhile Operators

The SkipWhile and TakeWhile operators skip or return elements from a sequence while a predicate function passes (returns True). The first element that doesn't pass the predicate function ends the process of evaluation.

There are two overloads for each operator—one that takes a predicate to determine if an element should be skipped, and the second that takes the predicate but also provides an element index position that can be used in the predicate function for any given purpose. The method signatures available are:

```
// Skip elements while a predicate passes,
// then return all the remaining elements.
public static IEnumerable<TSource> SkipWhile<TSource>(
    this IEnumerable<TSource> source,
    Func<TSource, bool> predicate);

// Skip elements while a predicate passes,
// then return all the remaining elements.
// This overload also provides index position as an
// argument for use in the predicate function.
public static IEnumerable<TSource> SkipWhile<TSource>(
    this IEnumerable<TSource> source,
    Func<TSource, int, bool> predicate);

// Return elements while a predicate passes,
// then skip all the remaining elements.
public static IEnumerable<TSource> TakeWhile<TSource>(
    this IEnumerable<TSource> source,
    Func<TSource, bool> predicate);

// Return elements while a predicate passes,
// then skip all the remaining elements.
// This overload also provides index position as an
// argument for use in the predicate function.
public static IEnumerable<TSource> TakeWhile<TSource>(
    this IEnumerable<TSource> source,
    Func<TSource, int, bool> predicate);
```

A simple example of where these operators are useful is when parsing text files from the beginning. The example shown in Listing 5-27 skips any lines at the start of a file (in this case, this data is in string form for simplicity) and then returns all lines until an empty line is found. All lines after this blank line are ignored. The Console output from this example is shown in Output 5-15.

Listing 5-27   The `SkipWhile` and `TakeWhile` operators skip or return elements while their predicate argument returns `true`—see Output 5-15

```
string sampleString =
@"# comment line 1
# comment line 2
Data line 1
Data line 2

This line is ignored
";

var q = sampleString.Split('\n')
    .SkipWhile(line => line.StartsWith("#"))
    .TakeWhile(line => !string.IsNullOrEmpty(line.Trim()));

foreach (var s in q)
    Console.WriteLine(s);
```

Output 5-15

```
Data line 1
Data line 2
```

Quantifier Operators—All, Any, and Contains

The Quantifier operators, `All`, `Any`, and `Contains` return Boolean result values based on the presence or absence of certain data within a sequence. These operators could all be built by creating queries that filter the data using a `Where` clause and comparing the resulting sequence element count to see if it is greater than zero. But these operators are optimized for their purpose and return a result at the first possible point, avoiding iterating an entire sequence (often referred to as short-circuit evaluation).

All Operator

The `All` operator returns the Boolean result of `true` if all elements in a sequence pass the predicate function supplied.

All has a single overload with the following method signature:

```
// Returns true if all elements pass the predicate
// function, otherwise returns false.
public static bool All<TSource>(
    this IEnumerable<TSource> source,
    Func<TSource, bool> predicate);
```

To demonstrate the All operator, Listing 5-28 tests three arrays of integer values and returns the value of true if all elements are even (are divisible by two with no remainder). The Console output from this example is shown in Output 5-16.

Listing 5-28 The **All** operator returns **true** if all objects pass the predicate—see Output 5-16

```
var evens = new int[] { 2, 4, 6, 8, 10 };
var odds = new int[] { 1, 3, 5, 7, 9 };
var nums = Enumerable.Range(1, 10);

Console.WriteLine("All even? evens: {0}, odds: {1}, nums: {2}",
    evens.All(i=> i%2 == 0),
    odds.All(i => i%2 == 0),
    nums.All(i => i%2 == 0)
);
```

Output 5-16

```
All even? evens: True, odds: False, nums: False
```

The predicate can be as complex as necessary; it can contain any number of logical ands (&&) and ors (||), but it must however return a Boolean value. Listing 5-29 demonstrates querying to determine if all contacts (from the same sample data introduced in Chapter 2, "Introducing LINQ to Objects," Table 2-1) are over the age of 21 and that each contact has a phone number and an email address. The Console output from this example is shown in Output 5-17.

Listing 5-29 Example of using the `All` operator over a sample set of contact data—see Output 5-17

```
var contacts = Contact.SampleData();

bool allOver21 = contacts.All(
    c => c.DateOfBirth.AddYears(21) < DateTime.Now);

bool allContactsHaveContactData = contacts.All(
    c => string.IsNullOrEmpty(c.Phone) == false &&
        string.IsNullOrEmpty(c.Email) == false);

Console.WriteLine("Are all contacts over 21 years old? {0}",
    allOver21);

Console.WriteLine("Do all contacts have email and phone? {0}",
    allContactsHaveContactData);
```

Output 5-17

```
Are all contacts over 21 years old? True
Do all contacts have email and phone? True
```

Any Operator

The `Any` operator returns the Boolean result of `true` if there are any elements in a sequence or if there are any elements that pass a predicate function in a sequence.

The `Any` operator has two overloads. The first overload takes no arguments and tests the sequence for at least one element, while the second takes a predicate function and tests that at least one element passes that predicates logic. The method signatures are:

```
// Returns true there is at least one element
// in the sequence, otherwise returns false any.
public static bool Any<TSource>(
    this IEnumerable<TSource> source);

// Returns true if any element passes the
// predicate function, otherwise returns false.
public static bool Any<TSource>(
    this IEnumerable<TSource> source,
    Func<TSource, bool> predicate);
```

To demonstrate the Any operator, Listing 5-30 tests three sequences—one that is empty (has no elements), one that has a single element, and a third that has many elements. Calling the Any operation on these sequences returns a Boolean result. The Console output from this example is shown in Output 5-18.

Listing 5-30 The **Any** operator returns **true** if there are any elements in a sequence—see Output 5-18

```
var empty = Enumerable.Empty<int>();
var one   = new int[] { 1 };
var many  = Enumerable.Range(1,5);

Console.WriteLine("Empty: {0}, One: {1}, Many: {2}",
    empty.Any(), one.Any(), many.Any());
```

Output 5-18

```
Empty: False, One: True, Many: True
```

The Any operator is the most efficient way to test if any elements are in a sequence, and although the following code is equivalent, it is highly discouraged because it potentially requires iterating the entire sequence if the source doesn't implement ICollection<T>, which has a Count property. This is only shown here to explain the basic logic of Any:

```
bool b = one.Count() > 0;
```

The second overload of Any that takes a predicate function is equally easy to use. It takes a predicate function and returns the Boolean result of true if any element in the sequence passes (returns true). The example shown in Listing 5-31, looks for certain strings in an array of strings to determine if there are any cats or fish-like animals (albeit in a simplistic fashion). The Console output from this example is shown in Output 5-19.

Listing 5-31   The **Any** operator returns **true** if there are any elements in a sequence that pass the predicate function—see Output 5-19

```
string[] animals = new string[] { "Koala", "Kangaroo",
    "Spider", "Wombat", "Snake", "Emu", "Shark",
    "Sting-Ray", "Jellyfish" };

bool anyFish = animals.Any(a => a.Contains("fish"));
bool anyCats = animals.Any(a => a.Contains("cat"));

Console.WriteLine("Any fish? {0}, Any cats? {1}",
    anyFish, anyCats);
```

Output 5-19

```
Any fish? True, Any cats? False
```

Again, Any is the most efficient way of determining if there are any elements in a sequence that match a predicate function; however, to demonstrate the basic logic this operator employs, the following is functionally equivalent code that is highly discouraged due to its potential performance impact:

```
bool b = animals.Where(a => a.Contains("fish")).Count() > 0;
```

The predicate employed by Any can be as complex as required. Listing 5-32 demonstrates how to use Any on a set of contact records to determine if there are any people under the age of 21 and a second test to see if there are any people without an email address or a phone number (from the same sample data introduced in Chapter 2, Table 2-1). The Console output from this example is shown in Output 5-20.

Listing 5-32   Example of using the **Any** operator over a sample set of contact data—see Output 5-20

```
var contacts = Contact.SampleData();

bool anyUnder21 = contacts.Any(
    c => c.DateOfBirth.AddYears(21) > DateTime.Now);

bool anyMissingContactData = contacts.Any(
    c => string.IsNullOrEmpty(c.Phone) ||
        string.IsNullOrEmpty(c.Email));
```

```
Console.WriteLine("Are any contacts under 21 years old? {0}",
    anyUnder21);

Console.WriteLine("Are any records without email or phone? {0}",
    anyMissingContactData);
```

Output 5-20

```
Are any contacts under 21 years old? False
Are any records without email or phone? False
```

Contains Operator

The contains operator returns the Boolean value of true if the sequence contains an equivalent element as the test argument passed into this operator.

There are two overloads for this operator—one that takes a single argument of the test value and the second that takes the test value and an IEqualityComparer<T> instance that is employed for equality testing. The method signatures for the contains operator are:

```
// Returns true if the test element is in the
// sequence, otherwise returns false.
public static bool Contains<TSource>(
    this IEnumerable<TSource> source, TSource value);

// Returns true if the test element is in the
// sequence, otherwise returns false. Uses the
// Equality Comparer passed in to test equality.
public static bool Contains<TSource>(
    this IEnumerable<TSource> source,
    TSource value,
    IEqualityComparer<TSource> comparer);
```

To demonstrate the contains operator, Listing 5-33 looks to see if various versions of the name Peter are contained in the elements of a string array. The test b1 will be false because the default comparison of a string is case sensitive. Test b2 will be true because it is an exact string match, and test b3 will be true even though the string case is different because a custom IEqualityComparer<T> was used to determine string equality. (Creating custom IEqualityComparers is covered in Chapter 4 in the "Specifying Your

Own Key Comparison Function" section and in Chapter 6 under "Custom EqualityComparers When Using LINQ Set Operators.") The Console output from this example is shown in Output 5-21.

Listing 5-33   The **Contains** operator returns **true** if the test element is in the sequence—see Output 5-21

```
string[] names = new string[] { "peter", "paul", "mary" };

bool b1 = names.Contains("PETER");
bool b2 = names.Contains("peter");

// Custom comparers or the built-in comparers can be used.
bool b3 = names.Contains(
    "PETER", StringComparer.CurrentCultureIgnoreCase);

Console.WriteLine("PETER: {0}, peter: {1}, PETER: {2}",
    b1, b2, b3);
```

Output 5-21

```
PETER: False, peter: True, PETER: True
```

Some collection types that implement IEnumerable<T> and are in scope for the Contains extension method implement their own instance method called Contains (List<T> for instance). This doesn't cause any problems in most cases, but if you explicitly want to call the extension Contains, specify the generic type. Listing 5-34 demonstrates how to explicitly control what Contains gets called (instance method or extension method) when using a collection of type List<T>. The Console output from this example is shown in Output 5-22.

Listing 5-34   How to explicitly specify which **Contains** you want to call when a collection has an instance method called **Contains**—see Output 5-22

```
// List<T> already has an instance method called "Contains"
// The instance method doesn't have an overload that
// supports EqualityComparer's, and the Contains
// extension method can be used for this call.
```

```
List<string> list =
    new List<string> { "peter", "paul", "mary" };

// will use the List<T>.Contains method
bool b4 = list.Contains("PETER");

// will force use of the Contains Extension method
bool b5 = list.Contains<string>("PETER");

// or better still, just call the Extension Method
bool b5a = Enumerable.Contains(list, "PETER");

// will use the Contains Extension method because
// the List<T>.Contains has no overload taking
// an IEqualityComparer
bool b6 = list.Contains(
    "PETER", StringComparer.CurrentCultureIgnoreCase);

Console.WriteLine(
    "Instance: {0}, Extension: {1}, With Comparer: {2}",
    b4, b5, b6);
```

Output 5-22

```
Instance: False, Extension: False, With Comparer: True
```

Summary

This chapter introduced many of the remaining standard query operators that are available to you in .NET Framework 4. The next chapter covers the last few operators that specifically apply set-based functions over data sources.

CHAPTER 6

WORKING WITH SET DATA

Goals of this chapter:

- Define the two options for working with set data using LINQ.
- Introduce the HashSet type and how this relates to LINQ.
- Introduce the LINQ standard query operators that relate to working with set data.

There are two ways of applying set-based functions over data sequences using LINQ. This chapter explores the merits of both options and explains when and why to use one method over another.

Introduction

Set operations allow various functions to compare elements in collections (and in some cases, the same collection) against each other in order to determine overlapping and unique elements within a collection.

Framework libraries for set operations were missing in the .NET Framework 1, 2, and 3. The HashSet was introduced in .NET Framework 3.5, and this collection type solves most set problems often faced by developers. LINQ extended set function capability with specific operators, some of which overlap with HashSet functionality. It is important to understand the benefits of both strategies and when to choose one over another. This section looks in detail at the two main choices:

- LINQ standard query operators
- HashSet<T> class from the Systems.Collections.Generic namespace

The decision of how to approach a set-based task depends on problem specifics, but in general the strengths of each can be described in the following ways:

Use HashSet and its operators when

- Duplicate items are not allowed in the collections.
- Modifying the original collection is desired. These operators make changes to the original collection.

Use LINQ Operators when

- Duplicate items are allowed in the collections.
- When returning a new `IEnumerable<T>` is desired rather than modifying the original collection.

The LINQ Set Operators

LINQ to Objects has standard query operators for working on sets of elements within collections. These operators allow two different collections (containing the same types of elements) to be merged into a single collection using various methods.

The set operators all implement a deferred execution pattern, simply meaning that they do not evaluate the next element until they are iterated over one element at a time. Each operator is detailed in this section, including the method signatures for each operator.

Concat Operator

`Concat` combines the contents of two collections. It operates by looping over the first collection yield returning each element, then looping over the second collection yield returning each element. If returning the duplicate elements is not the desired behavior, consider using the `Union` operator instead. An `ArgumentNullException` is thrown if either collection is `null` when this operator is called.

`Concat` has a single overload with the following method signature:

```
// Combines the contents of two collections.
// Returns all elements from the first collection,
```

```
// then all elements from the second collection.
IEnumerable<TSource> Concat<TSource>(
    this IEnumerable<TSource> first,
    IEnumerable<TSource> second);
```

Listing 6-1 demonstrates the simplest use of the Concat operator and the subtle difference between Concat and Union. The Console output from this example is shown in Output 6-1.

Listing 6-1   Simple example showing the difference between **Concat** and **Union**—see Output 6-1

```
int[] first = new int[] { 1, 2, 3 };
int[] second = new int[] { 3, 4, 5 };

// concat returns elements from both collections
var q = first.Concat(second);

Console.WriteLine(
    "Concat example: 1,2,3 concatenated with 3,4,5 - ");

foreach (var item in q)
    Console.Write(item + " ");

// union returns the distinct concat of the collections
var q1 = first.Union(second);

Console.WriteLine();
Console.WriteLine(
    "Union example: 1,2,3 unioned with 3,4,5 - ");

foreach (var item in q1)
    Console.Write(item + " ");
```

Output 6-1

```
Concat example: 1,2,3 concatenated with 3,4,5 -
1 2 3 3 4 5

Union example: 1,2,3 unioned with 3,4,5 -
1 2 3 4 5
```

A useful application of the `Concat` operator when binding a sequence to a control is its ability to add an additional entry at the start or end as a placeholder. For example, to make the first entry in a bound sequence the text "— none chosen —", the code in Listing 6-2 can be used, with the result shown in Figure 6-1.

FIGURE 6-1 The **Concat** operator is useful for adding prompt text to bound sequences.

Listing 6-2 Using the **Concat** operator to add values to a sequence—see Figure 6-1

```
// the actual list of status
string[] status = new string[] {
    "Not Started", "Started", "Complete" };

// the desired first entry
string[] prompt = new string[] {
    "-- none chosen --"};

ComboBox combo = new ComboBox();

// this is the where the two sequences get
// combined and bound to the combobox
combo.DataSource = prompt.Concat(status).ToList();

// display resulting combo in test form.
Form form = new Form();
form.Controls.Add(combo);
form.ShowDialog();
```

Distinct Operator

The `Distinct` operator removes duplicate elements from a sequence using either the default `EqualityComparer` or a supplied `EqualityComparer`.

It operates by iterating the source sequence and returning each element of equal value once, effectively skipping duplicates. An `ArgumentNullException` is thrown if the source collection is `null` when this operator is called.

The method signatures available for the `Distinct` operator are:

```
// Returns unique elements from the source collection
// Uses EqualityComparer<TSource>.Default
// to compare elements for uniqueness.
IEnumerable<TSource> Distinct<TSource>(
    this IEnumerable<TSource> source);

// Returns unique elements from the source collection
// Uses the supplied comparer to compare
// elements for uniqueness.
IEnumerable<TSource> Distinct<TSource>(
    this IEnumerable<TSource> source,
    IEqualityComparer<TSource> comparer);
```

Listing 6-3 demonstrates how to use the `Distinct` operator to remove duplicate entries from a collection. This example also demonstrates how to use the built-in string comparison types in order to perform various cultural case-sensitive and insensitive comparisons. The Console output from this example is shown in Output 6-2.

Listing 6-3   Example showing how to use the **Distinct** operator—this example also shows the various built-in string comparer statics—see Output 6-2

```
int[] source = new int[] { 1, 2, 3, 1, 2, 3, 4, 5 };

// Distinct de-duplicates a collection
var q = source.Distinct();

Console.WriteLine(
    "Distinct example: 1, 2, 3, 1, 2, 3, 4, 5 - ");

foreach (var item in q)
    Console.Write(item + " ");

// distinct on string using comparer
string[] names = new string[]
    { "one", "ONE", "One", "Two", "Two" };
```

```
/* built-in string comparer statics are helpful.
 * See the topic heading later in this chapter -
 * Custom EqualityComparers When Using LINQ Set Operators,
 * Built-in String Comparers
 */

var q1 = names.Distinct(
    StringComparer.CurrentCultureIgnoreCase);

Console.WriteLine();
Console.WriteLine(
    "Distinct example: one, ONE, One, Two, Two - ");

foreach (var item in q1)
    Console.Write(item + " ");
```

Output 6-2

```
Distinct example: 1, 2, 3, 1, 2, 3, 4, 5 -
1 2 3 4 5

Distinct example: one, ONE, One, Two, Two -
one Two
```

Except Operator

The Except operator produces the set difference between two sequences. It will only return elements in the first sequence that don't appear in the second sequence using either the default EqualityComparer or a supplied EqualityComparer. It operates by first obtaining a distinct list of elements in the second sequence and then iterating the first sequence and only returns elements that do not appear in the second sequence's distinct list. An ArgumentNullException is thrown if either collection is null when this operator is called.

The method signatures available for the Except operator are:

```
// Returns the elements from the source sequence
// that are NOT in the second collection using the
// EqualityComparer<TSource>.Default comparer to
// to compare elements.
IEnumerable<TSource> Except<TSource>(
```

```
    this IEnumerable<TSource> first,
    IEnumerable<TSource> second);

// Returns the elements from the source sequence
// that are NOT in the second collection using the
// supplied comparer to compare elements.
IEnumerable<TSource> Except<TSource>(
    this IEnumerable<TSource> first,
    IEnumerable<TSource> second,
    IEqualityComparer<TSource> comparer);
```

Listing 6-4 shows the most basic example of using the Except operator. The Console output from this example is shown in Output 6-3.

Listing 6-4   The **Except** operator returns all elements in the first sequence, not in the
second sequence—see Output 6-3

```
int[] first = new int[] { 1, 2, 3 };
int[] second = new int[] { 3, 4, 5 };

// Except returns all elements from the first
// collection that are not in the second collection.
var q = first.Except(second);

Console.WriteLine(
    "Except example: 1,2,3 Except with 3,4,5 - ");

foreach (var item in q)
    Console.Write(item + " ");
```

Output 6-3

```
Except example: 1,2,3 Except with 3,4,5 -
1 2
```

Intersect Operator

The Intersect operator produces a sequence of elements that appear in
both collections. It operates by skipping any element in the first collection that cannot be found in the second collection using either the

default `EqualityComparer` or a supplied `EqualityComparer`. An `ArgumentNullException` is thrown if either collection is `null` when this operator is called.

The method signatures available for the `Intersect` operator are:

```
// Returns the elements from the source collection
// that ARE ALSO in the second collection using the
// EqualityComparer<TSource>.Default comparer to
// to compare elements.
IEnumerable<TSource> Intersect<TSource>(
    this IEnumerable<TSource> first,
    IEnumerable<TSource> second);

// Returns the elements from the source collection
// that ARE ALSO in the second collection using the
// supplied comparer to compare elements.
IEnumerable<TSource> Intersect<TSource>(
    this IEnumerable<TSource> first,
    IEnumerable<TSource> second,
    IEqualityComparer<TSource> comparer);
```

Listing 6-5 shows the most basic use of the `Intersect` operator. The Console output from this example is shown in Output 6-4.

Listing 6-5 `Intersect` operator example—see Output 6-4

```
int[] first = new int[] { 1, 2, 3 };
int[] second = new int[] { 3, 4, 5 };

// intersect returns only elements from the first collection
// collection that are ALSO in the second collection.
var q = first.Intersect(second);

Console.WriteLine(
    "Intersect example: 1,2,3 Intersect with 3,4,5 - ");

foreach (var item in q)
    Console.Write(item + " ");
```

Output 6-4

```
Intersect example: 1,2,3 Intersect with 3,4,5 -
3
```

Union Operator

The Union operator returns the distinct elements from both collections. The result is similar to the Concat operator, except the Union operator will only return an equal element once, rather than the number of times that element appears in both collections. Duplicate elements are determined using either the default EqualityComparer or a supplied EqualityComparer. An ArgumentNullException is thrown if either collection is null when this operator is called.

The method signatures available for the Union operator are:

```
// Combines the contents of two collections.
// Returns all elements from the first collection,
// then all elements from the second collection.
// Duplicate elements are removed (only the first
// occurrence is returned).
// Uses EqualityComparer<TSource>.Default
// to compare elements for uniqueness.
IEnumerable<TSource> Union<TSource>(
    this IEnumerable<TSource> first,
    IEnumerable<TSource> second);

// Combines the contents of two collections.
// Returns all elements from the first collection,
// then all elements from the second collection.
// Duplicate elements are removed (only the first
// occurrence is returned).
// Uses the supplied comparer to compare elements
// for uniqueness.
IEnumerable<TSource> Union<TSource>(
    this IEnumerable<TSource> first,
    IEnumerable<TSource> second,
    IEqualityComparer<TSource> comparer);
```

Listing 6-1 demonstrated the subtle difference between Union and Concat operators. Use the Union operator when you want each unique element only returned once (duplicates removed) and Concat when you want every element from both collection sequences.

Listing 6-6 demonstrates a useful technique of combining data from multiple source types by unioning (or concatenating, excepting, intersecting, or distincting for that matter) data from either a collection of Contact elements or CallLog elements based on a user's partial input. This feature is similar to the incremental lookup features offered by many smart-phones, in which the user inputs either a name or phone number, and a drop-down displays recent numbers and searches the contacts held in storage for likely candidates. This technique works because of how .NET manages equality for anonymous types that are projected. The key to this technique working as expected is to ensure that the projected names for each field in the anonymous types are identical in name, case, and order. If these conditions are satisfied, the anonymous types can be operated on by any of the set-based operators.

Listing 6-6 uses the sample data of Contact and CallLog types introduced earlier in this book in Table 2-1 and Table 2-2 with sample partial user-entered data of Ka and 7. The Console output from this example is shown in Output 6-5.

Listing 6-6 Anonymous types with the same members can be unioned and concatenated—see Output 6-5

```
// lookup recent  phone number OR contact first and last
// names to incrementally build a convenient picklist on
// partial user entry (narrow the list as data is typed).
string userEntry = "Ka";

var q = (

        // userEntry is contact name
        from contact in Contact.SampleData()
        where contact.FirstName.StartsWith(userEntry)
           || contact.LastName.StartsWith(userEntry)
        select new { Display = contact.FirstName + " " +
                                contact.LastName }).Distinct()


     .Union(

        // userEntry is partial phone number
        (from call in CallLog.SampleData()
         where call.Number.Contains(userEntry)
            && call.Incoming == false
         select new { Display = call.Number }).Distinct()

     );

Console.WriteLine(
     "User Entry - " + userEntry);

foreach (var item in q)
     Console.WriteLine(item.Display);
```

Output 6-5

```
User Entry - Ka
   Stewart Kagel
   Mack Kamph

User Entry - 7
   165 737 1656
   546 607 5462
   848 553 8487
   278 918 2789
```

Custom EqualityComparers When Using LINQ Set Operators

LINQ's set operators rely on instances of EqualityComparer<T> to determine if two elements are equal. When no equality comparer is specified, the default equality comparer is used for the element type by calling the static property Default on the generic EqualityComparer type. For example, the following two statements are identical for the Distinct operator (and all of the set operators):

```
first.Distinct();
first.Distinct(EqualityComparer<string>.Default);
```

For programming situations where more control is needed for assessing equality, a custom comparer can be written, or one of the built-in string comparisons can be used.

Built-in String Comparers

Listing 6-3 introduced an example that showed case-insensitive matching of strings using the distinct operator. It simply passed in a static instance of a built-in comparer type using the following code:

```
var q1 = names.Distinct(
    StringComparer.CurrentCultureIgnoreCase);
```

In addition to the string comparer used in this example, there are a number of others that can be used for a particular circumstance. Table 6-1 lists the available built-in static properties that can be called on the StringComparer type to get an instance of that comparer.

Table 6-1 Built-in String Comparers

CurrentCulture	Case-sensitive string comparison using the word comparison rules of the current culture. Current culture is determined by the System.Threading.Thread.CurrentThread.CurrentCulture property.
CurrentCultureIgnoreCase	Case-insensitive string comparison using the word comparison rules of the current culture. Current culture is determined by the System.Threading.Thread.CurrentThread.CurrentCulture property.
InvariantCulture	Case-sensitive string comparison using the word comparison rules of the invariant culture.
InvariantCultureIgnore-Case	Case-insensitive string comparison using the word comparison rules of the invariant culture.
Ordinal	Case-sensitive ordinal string comparison.
OrdinalIgnoreCase	Case-insensitive ordinal string comparison.

WHEN TO USE CURRENTCULTURE AND INVARIANTCULTURE In addition to worrying about case-sensitive and case-insensitive string comparison, it is important to consider the culture sensitivity of the strings being compared and how the results of this comparison are displayed to the user.

Microsoft has recommended guidelines documented on MSDN (see http://msdn.microsoft.com/en-us/library/kzwcbskc.aspx), and these generally state that if the result of a sort is going to be displayed to an end user, culture-sensitive sorting (the built-in comparers starting with CurrentCulture) should be used (sorting items in a listbox for example). Culture-insensitive comparison (the built-in comparers starting with InvariantCulture) should be used when comparing strings internally, and the result of string comparison should not depend on the end user's culture settings, for example when comparing XML tokens in a file with those needed for processing in an application.

Building and Using a Custom EqualityComparer Type

In Chapter 4 in the "Specifying Your Own Key Comparison Function" section, you first saw the ability to customize how LINQ evaluates equality between objects by writing a custom equality comparer type. As an example we wrote a custom comparison type that resolved equality based on the age-old phonetic comparison algorithm, Soundex. The code for the `SoundexEqualityComparer` is shown in Listing 4-5, and in addition to being useful for grouping extension methods, the same equality comparer can be used for the LINQ set operators. For example, Listing 6-7 shows how to use the Soundex algorithm to determine how many distinct phonetic names are present in a list of names. The following code will correctly return the Console window text, `Number of unique phonetic names = 4`.

Listing 6-7   Using a custom equality comparer with the **Distinct** operator

```
// find number of phonetic common names in list
string[] names = new string[] { "Janet", "Janette", "Joanne",
    "Jo-anne", "Johanne", "Katy", "Katie", "Ralph", "Ralphe" };

var q = names.Distinct(
    new SoundexEqualityComparer());

Console.WriteLine("Number of unique phonetic names = {0}",
    q.Count());
```

The HashSet<T> Class

`HashSet<T>` was introduced in .NET Framework 3.5 as part of the `System.Collections.Generic` namespace. HashSet is an unordered collection containing unique elements and provides a set of standard set operators such as intersection and union (plus many more). It has the standard collection operations `Add` (although this method returns a Boolean indicating whether or not that element already existed in the collection), `Remove`, and `Contains`, but because it uses a hash-based implementation for object identity, these operations are immediately accessible without looping the entire list as occurs with the `List<T>` collection for example (O(1) rather than O(n)).

Although the operators on HashSet would appear to overlap with the LINQ set operators, `Intersect` and `Union`, these HashSet implementations modify the set they were called on, rather than return a new `IEnumerable<T>` collection, as is the behavior of the LINQ operators.

For this reason, the names on the HashSet operators are differentiated as `IntersectWith` and `UnionWith`, and the LINQ operators are also available with a HashSet collection as `Intersect` and `Union`. This naming distinction avoids naming clashes and also allows the desired behavior to be chosen in a specific case.

HashSet implements the `IEnumerable<T>` pattern and therefore can be used in a LINQ query. Listing 6-8 demonstrates a LINQ query to find even numbers in a `HashSet` made by unioning two collections. The Console output from this example is shown in Output 6-6.

Listing 6-8 LINQ query over a HashSet collection—see Output 6-6

```
int[] first = new int[] { 1, 2, 3 };
int[] second = new int[] { 3, 4, 5 };

// modify the current set by unioning with second.
HashSet<int> set = new HashSet<int>(first);
set.UnionWith(second);

// return only the even values from the set.
// the values in the HashSet are IEnumerable<T>.
var q = from i in set
        where i % 2 == 0
        select i;

foreach (var item in q)
    Console.WriteLine(item);
```

Output 6-6

```
2
4
```

The differences between the `HashSet` and LINQ operator support are listed here (as documented in the Visual Studio documentation), although LINQ-equivalent approximations are easy to construct as documented in Table 6-2 and implemented in Listing 6-9.

Table 6-2 Comparison of the LINQ Set Operators and the HashTable Type Methods

HashSet<T> operator	LINQ equivalent operator	Description
UnionWith	Union	All distinct elements in both collections.
IntersectWith	Intersect	Only elements that are in both collections.
ExceptWith	Except	Elements from the first collection, except those listed in the second collection.
Unnecessary because only unique elements can be added to a HashSet<T>	Distinct	Removes duplicate elements from a collection. HashSet doesn't allow duplicates to be added to the collection, making it unnecessary for it to have a Distinct operator equivalent.
SymmetricExcept-With	Not provided. To approximate the same result with LINQ, combine two reciprocal Except operators in the following fashion: `a.Except(b).Concat(b.Except(a));`	Returns elements that appear in either of the collections, but not both. This is an exclusive-or operation on two collections.
Overlaps	Not provided. To approximate the same result with LINQ, determine the intersect with the second collection and return true if there are any results in the following fashion: `b.Intersect(a).Distinct().Any();`	Returns the Boolean value true if any element in the given collection appears in the second collection.

Table 6-2 Comparison of the LINQ Set Operators and the HashTable Type Methods

HashSet<T> operator	LINQ equivalent operator	Description

IsSubsetOf	Not provided. To approximate the same result using LINQ, return the Boolean of true if the intersect count with the second collection equals the count of the distinct elements in the collection in the following fashion:
	
	`var aCount =`
	`    a.Distinct().Count();`
	
	`var intersectCount =`
	`    a.Intersect(b)`
	`    .Distinct()`
	`    .Count();`
	
	`return`
	`    intersectCount == aCount;`
		Returns the Boolean value of true if all of the elements in the given collection are present in the second collection. Will return the Boolean value of true if the collections share the same elements.

IsProperSubsetOf	Not provided. To approximate the same result with LINQ, return the Boolean of true if the intersect count with the second collection is less than the count of the distinct elements in the second collection, and the intersect count equals the count of the distinct elements in the collection in the following fashion:
	
	`var aCount =`
	`    a.Distinct().Count();`
	
	`var bCount =`
	`    b.Distinct().Count();`
	
	`var intersectCount =`
	`    a.Intersect(b)`
	`    .Distinct()`
	`    .Count();`
	
	`return`
	`    (intersectCount < bCount) &&`
	`    (intersectCount == aCount);`
		Returns the Boolean value of true if all of the elements in the given collection are present in the second collection. Will return the Boolean value of false if the collections share exactly the same elements; the collection must be an actual subset with at least one element less than that in the second collection.

Table 6-2   Comparison of the LINQ Set Operators and the HashTable Type Methods

HashSet<T> operator	LINQ equivalent operator	Description

IsSupersetOf	Not provided. To approximate the same result using LINQ, return the Boolean of true if the intersect count equals the count of the distinct elements in the second collection in the following fashion:
	
	```var bCount =```
	``` b.Distinct().Count();```
	
	```var intersectCount =```
	``` b.Intersect(a)```
	``` .Distinct()```
	``` .Count();```
	
	```return```
	``` intersectCount == bCount;```
		Returns the Boolean value of true if all of the elements in the second collection are present in the given collection. Will return the Boolean value of true if the collections share the same elements.

IsProperSuperset-Of	Not provided. To approximate the same result with LINQ, return the Boolean of true if the intersect count is less than the count of the distinct elements in the collection and the intersect count equals the count of the distinct elements in the second collection in the following fashion:
	
	```var aCount =```
	``` a.Distinct().Count();```
	
	```var bCount =```
	``` b.Distinct().Count();```
	
	```var intersectCount =```
	``` b.Intersect(a)```
	``` .Distinct()```
	``` .Count();```
	
	```return```
	``` (intersectCount < aCount) &&```
	``` (intersectCount == bCount);```
		Returns the Boolean value of true if all of the elements in the second collection are present in the given collection. Will return the Boolean value of false if the collections share exactly the same elements. The collection must be an actual superset with at least one element more than that in the second collection.

Table 6-2 Comparison of the LINQ Set Operators and the HashTable Type Methods

HashSet\<T\> operator	LINQ equivalent operator	Description

SetEquals	Not provided. To approximate the same result with LINQ, compare the distinct, ordered collections in the following fashion:
	
	`a.Distinct().OrderBy(x => x)`
	`.SequenceEqual(`
	`b.Distinct().OrderBy(y => y));`
		Returns the Boolean value of true if both collections share the same distinct element values.

Listing 6-9 Approximate LINQ implementations of the operators in the HashSet type

```
public static IEnumerable<T> SymmetricExcept<T>(
    this IEnumerable<T> first,
    IEnumerable<T> second)
{
    if (first == null)
        throw new ArgumentNullException("first");

    if (second == null)
        throw new ArgumentNullException("second");

    return  first.Except(second)
            .Concat(
            second.Except(first));
}


public static bool Overlaps<T>(
    this IEnumerable<T> first,
    IEnumerable<T> second)
{
    if (first == null)
        throw new ArgumentNullException("first");

    if (second == null)
        throw new ArgumentNullException("second");

    return second.Intersect(first).Distinct().Any();
}
```

```csharp
public static bool IsSupersetOf<T>(
    this IEnumerable<T> first,
    IEnumerable<T> second)
{
    if (first == null)
        throw new ArgumentNullException("first");

    if (second == null)
        throw new ArgumentNullException("second");

    var secondCount = second.Distinct().Count();

    var intersectCount = second
        .Intersect(first)
        .Distinct()
        .Count();

    return intersectCount == secondCount;
}

public static bool IsProperSupersetOf<T>(
    this IEnumerable<T> first,
    IEnumerable<T> second)
{
    if (first == null)
        throw new ArgumentNullException("first");

    if (second == null)
        throw new ArgumentNullException("second");

    var firstCount = first.Distinct().Count();
    var secondCount = second.Distinct().Count();

    var intersectCount =
        second
        .Intersect(first)
        .Distinct()
        .Count();

    return (intersectCount < firstCount) &&
           (intersectCount == secondCount);
}
```

```
public static bool IsSubsetOf<T>(
    this IEnumerable<T> first,
    IEnumerable<T> second)
{
    // call the Superset operator and reverse the arguments
    return IsSupersetOf(second, first);
}

public static bool IsProperSubsetOf<T>(
    this IEnumerable<T> first,
    IEnumerable<T> second)
{
    // call the Superset operator and reverse the arguments
    return IsProperSupersetOf(second, first);
}

public static bool SetEquals<T>(
    this IEnumerable<T> first,
    IEnumerable<T> second)
{
    return first.Distinct().OrderBy(x => x)
        .SequenceEqual(
            second.Distinct().OrderBy(y => y));
}
```

Summary

Working with set data using LINQ is no harder than choosing the correct standard query operator. The existing `HashSet<T>` collection type can also be used, and the decision on which set approach suits your problem boils down to the following factors:

Use `HashSet` and its operators when
- Duplicate items are not allowed in the collections.
- Modifying the original collection is desired. These operators make changes to the original collection.

Use LINQ Operators when
- Duplicate items are allowed in the collections.
- When returning a new `IEnumerable<T>` is desired instead of modifying the original collection.

Having explained all of the built-in standard query operators in this and previous chapters, the next chapter looks at how to extend LINQ by building custom operators that extend the LINQ story and integrate into the language just like the Microsoft-supplied operators.

CHAPTER 7

EXTENDING LINQ TO OBJECTS

Goals of this chapter:

- Define the different types of operators and what makes them unique.
- Define the common patterns used in building each type of operator.
- Understand the best practices and patterns used for error handling.

LINQ to Objects is designed to be extended. This chapter discusses how new operators can be written to perform any custom requirement and then be used in exactly the same way as the standard query operators Microsoft has provided.

Writing a New Query Operator

Although the standard query operators supplied are comprehensive, there is often the need to build more operators to satisfy a programming problem at hand. LINQ to Object operators are in their purest form, extension methods that add functionality to any `IEnumerable<T>` collection type. Although writing new operators might seem ambitious at first, the implementation code for the standard query operators supplied by Microsoft rarely span more than a few lines, and it is unlikely your custom operators will be any more complex.

Query operators for LINQ to Objects fall into four categories based on their return type and action. The basic operator categories are

- **Single element operator**—Those that return a single element from a sequence (for example, `First`, `Last`, `ElementAt`).
- **Sequence operator**—Those that return a sequence of elements (`Where`, `Select`).
- **Aggregate operator**—Those that return an aggregate result value (`Count`, `Min`, `Max`, `Average`).

■ **Grouping operator**—Those that return groupings of elements from a sequence (GroupBy, GroupJoin).

This chapter looks at each type of operator in detail and constructs (and tests) a sample operator for each operator type.

Writing a Single Element Operator

The role of a single element operator is to add an extension method to any type that implements IEnumerable<T> and return a single element from that collection. The built-in standard query operators First, Last and ElementAt are examples of this category of operator, returning the first element, the last element, or the element at a given index position, respectively.

Understanding how Microsoft constructed the standard query operators is the first step to understanding how to write custom operators. To explore Microsoft's approach to operator construction, let's build our own version of the Last operator before moving onto building a more complex operator.

Building Our Own Last Operator

To learn how to build an operator that returns a single element, let's first look at how the built-in standard query operator Last is implemented. The shortest compilable implementation for the Last operator is shown in Listing 7-1.

Listing 7-1 Shortest compilable **Last** operator implementation

```
public static T Last<T>(
    this IEnumerable<T> source)
{
    using (IEnumerator<T> enumerator = source.GetEnumerator())
    {
        if (enumerator.MoveNext())
        {
            T current;
            do
            {
                current = enumerator.Current;
            }
            while (enumerator.MoveNext());
```

```
        return current;
    }
}

throw new InvalidOperationException("No elements");
}
```

WHETHER TO USE FOREACH OR GETENUMERATOR LOOPING

SYNTAX   In the `Last` example, I chose to manually create and use the enumerator based on the `IEnumerable` interface pattern. Using a `foreach` loop in this example would also have worked and may have made the code easier to read. There is some (not much, but some) performance improvement when using the pure enumerator pattern over the `foreach` style of looping. Here is an implementation using the `foreach` syntax:

```
public static T Last<T>(
    this IEnumerable<T> source)
{
    bool hasElements = false;
    T lastElement = default(T);

    foreach (T item in source)
    {
        hasElements = true;
        lastElement = item;
    }

    // if there are no elements
    if (!hasElements) throw new
       InvalidOperationException("No elements");

    // return the last element.
    return lastElement;
}
```

Operators are often used in loops, and attention to performance should be a goal. Other developers will assume that these operators are optimized, and we shouldn't disappoint.

The code in Listing 7-1 satisfies the compiler and is completely functional. It simply takes an IEnumerable<T> collection as its source, iterates to the last element, and returns that element as its result. The one error condition trapped by this implementation is the case where there are no elements in the source collection. Throwing an InvalidOperationException is the standard pattern used by Microsoft's operator implementations, and custom operators should follow this pattern for consistency (omitting the InvalidOperationException in the previous code would cause an error in compilation because not all code paths return a value, so it is not really optional).

Another error condition to be handled is when the source collection is itself null (not empty, but uninitialized). The pattern used by Microsoft in this case is to throw an ArgumentNullException and to test the source argument for this condition at the beginning of any operator, as the following code demonstrates:

```
public static T Last<T>(
    this IEnumerable<T> source)
{
    if (source == null)
        throw new ArgumentNullException("source");

    // ... same code as shown in Listing 7-1 ...
```

This implementation is fully functional and follows all of the error condition patterns that Microsoft employs in their operators. Once the error conditions are satisfied, performance improvement can be explored.

The current implementation iterates the entire source collection to get to the last element, all 100,000 of them if that is the size of the source collection. If the collection has a high element count, this could be considered a performance issue. For many collection types, the last element can be retrieved with a single statement. Many collections that implement IEnumerable<T> also implement the interface IList<T>. IList<T> collections allow access by element index position, a zero-based count from the first element. If a collection implements IList<T>, then custom operators should first exhaust that avenue of processing before using the slower IEnumerable<T> enumeration algorithm approach. The code shown in Listing 7-2 demonstrates how to use index position if possible (otherwise using the enumeration pattern of choice).

Listing 7-2 `Last` operator implementation with recommended error handling and performance optimizations

```
public static T Last<T>(
    this IEnumerable<T> source)
{
    if (source == null)
        throw new ArgumentNullException("source");

    IList<T> list = source as IList<T>;
    if (list != null)
    {
        int count = list.Count;
        if (count > 0)
            return list[count - 1];
    }
    else
    {
        using (IEnumerator<T> enumerator =
            source.GetEnumerator())
        {
            if (enumerator.MoveNext())
            {
                T current;
                do
                {
                    current = enumerator.Current;
                }
                while (enumerator.MoveNext());

                return current;
            }
        }
    }

    throw new InvalidOperationException("No elements");
}
```

This implementation first tries to cast the source collection to the `IList<T>` interface; if it is successful, it uses that interface to resolve the last element in a single statement. If the collection does not implement

ILIst<T>, the do-while enumeration pattern using the IEnumerable<T> interface is employed. The same error-handling patterns are followed, and this implementation is equivalent to the patterns used by Microsoft in its operator implementations.

DOES THE LINQ TO OBJECTS PROVIDER HAVE BUILT-IN PERFORMANCE OPTIMIZATIONS?   Alexandra Rusina, a Microsoft programming writer, added a FAQ entry on this topic, which can be viewed at http://blogs.msdn.com/csharpfaq/archive/2009/01/26/does-the-linq-to-objects-provider-have-built-in-performance-optimization.aspx.

More detail is available in the blog posting, but Table 7-1 covers the main points.

Table 7-1   LINQ to Objects Built-in Performance Optimizations

LINQ method	Optimization
Cast	If the data source already implements IEnumerable<T>for the given T, then the sequence of data is returned without a cast.
Contains Count	If the data source implements the ICollection or ICollection<T> interface, the corresponding method of the interface is used.
ElementAt ElementAtOrDefault First FirstOrDefault Last LastOrDefault Single SingleOrDefault	If the data source implements the IList or IList<T> interface, the interface's Count method and indexing operations are used.

Throwing an exception when there are no source collection elements (an empty sequence) may not be desirable behavior when using single element return operators. It is difficult dealing with exceptions from within a query expression (nowhere to put the try-catch statement). Many operators implement a variant of these operators that return a null value or a default value you specify. The operators `FirstOrDefault` and `LastOrDefault` are examples that carry out the basic function of their partners, but instead of throwing an exception when the source sequence is empty, they return the default value of the type by calling the `default` keyword on the specific underlying generic type. For our `Last` implementation, we would add an operator called `LastOrDefault`, and the code for this operator would be (the only alteration from the code for the final `Last` operator is the operator's name and the last line):

```
public static T LastOrDefault<T>(
    this IEnumerable<T> source)
{
    // ... Same code as shown in Listing 7-2 except ...
    //
    // throw new InvalidOperationException("No elements");
    //
    // BECOMES -

    return default(T);
}
```

WHAT DOES THE DEFAULT KEYWORD RETURN? The `default` keyword solves the issue of not knowing what default value to initially assign to a generic type and returns null for reference types and zero for numeric value types. For structs, it will return each member of the struct initialized to zero or null, depending on whether they are value or reference types.

Building the RandomElement Operator

To demonstrate how to build a custom operator that returns a single element from a source sequence, let's look at an operator that returns an element at random. There are often times when picking a candidate at random from a collection is necessary, either for test data or deriving a random sample from a customer list to provide specific advertising or business offers. This new operator will be called `RandomElement` and will return one element at random from a given sequence (pseudo-random to be exact—it can be difficult to get the randomness you need for a small collection or when retrieving more than one in a tight loop).

The `RandomElement` operator has the following requirements:

- Take an input source `IEnumerable<T>` sequence and return one element at random.
- Allow control over the random number generator by optionally accepting a seed value.
- Throw an `ArgumentNullException` if the source sequence is null.
- Throw an `InvalidOperationException` if the source sequence is empty.

As seen when implementing the `Last` operator, although it is certain that sequences you extend implement the `IEnumerable<T>` interface, many sequences also implement the `IList<T>` and `ICollection<T>` interfaces, which can be used to improve performance. Any collection type that implements `IList` allows elements to be accessed by index position (for example, `list[2]` will return the third element), and any collection implementing `ICollection` exposes a `Count` property that immediately retrieves element count. These performance enhancements should be used if possible.

The code shown in Listing 7-3 uses the built-in .NET Framework random number generator to find an index position that is within a sequence's bounds and returns that element. It first tries to use the `IList` indexer to retrieve the element (because it is faster), and if that interface isn't supported by the collection, this operator uses a slower enumeration looping pattern (completely valid code, just slower).

OPTIONAL PARAMETERS IN C# 4.0   Listing 7-3 demonstrates the use of optional parameters in the method declaration. This is covered in Chapter 8, "C# 4.0 Features," in detail but is shown here to demonstrate that the value for `seed` is optional. If this method is called by omitting a value for `seed`, its value will be 0 in the method.

Listing 7-3   Sample **RandomElement** operator returns an element at random from a source sequence and takes an optional seed value for the random number generator

```
public static T RandomElement<T>(
    this IEnumerable<T> source,
    int seed = 0 /* optional param, new to C# 4.0(see Chapter 8) */)
{
    // check for invalid source conditions
    if (source == null)
        throw new ArgumentNullException("source");
```

```
// the Count() extension method already has this
// optimization built-in. I'm showing it here to
// make the point it is being considered!
int count = 0;
if (source is ICollection)
    count = ((ICollection)source).Count;
else
    count = source.Count();

if (count == 0)
    throw new InvalidOperationException("No elements");

// use the passed in seed value, or use time-based seed
Random random;
if (seed == 0)
    random = new Random();
else
    random = new Random(seed);

// IList implementers, access by indexer. It's faster.
IList<T> list = source as IList<T>;
if (list != null)
{
    int index = random.Next(0, count);
    return list[index];
}
else
{
    // Other collection types must be
    // enumerated (eg. Dictionary, IEnumerable)
    int index = random.Next(0, count);
    using (IEnumerator<T> e = source.GetEnumerator())
    {
        // move to the first element (the initial
        // position is BEFORE the first element.
        e.MoveNext();

        // iterate and move until we hit our index
        while (index > 0)
        {
            e.MoveNext();
            index--;
        }
    }
```

```
        return e.Current;
    }
  }
}
```

Although it is completely up to the implementer to decide behavior for empty and null source collections, following the same pattern used for the standard query operators is highly recommended, as it makes consuming your custom operators the same as the other LINQ operators. The general conventions are as follows:

1. If the source collection being extended is null, throw an `ArgumentNullException`.
2. If the source collection is empty, throw an `InvalidOperation-Exception`.
3. Provide a variation of the operator with the suffix of "OrDefault" that doesn't raise the `InvalidOperationException`, but returns the value `default(T)` instead.

Listing 7-4 shows the basic unit tests written to confirm correct behavior of the `RandomElement` operator. (I used NUnit—see www.nunit.org—but any unit testing framework would have worked.) The basic test cases for specific input sequence types that should be confirmed at a minimum are as follows:

- The source sequence is `null`.
- The source sequence has no elements (is empty).
- The source sequence implements `IList`.
- The source sequence implements `IEnumerable<T>`.

These tests, shown in Listing 7-4, are the minimum required for the `RandomElement` operator, and lightly confirm both the `IList<T>` and `IEnumerable` implementations with a single element source and a two-element source. Pay attention to boundary conditions when writing these tests; my first attempt at coding this operator never returned the last element—the unit tests allowed me to find and correct this error quickly.

ITERATING OVER INPUT SEQUENCES MULTIPLE TIMES The unit tests shown here, in some cases, iterate over the same input sequence multiple times. This should be avoided unless you have no choice but to avoid some operators failing. In this case, we know the operator and the tests we are writing, but it is generally a poor pattern.

Listing 7-4   Basic set of unit tests for the **RandomElement** operator—these tests are written for the NUnit testing framework (www.nunit.org); more tests are included in the sample code.

```
[Test]
[ExpectedException("System.ArgumentNullException")]
public void NullSourceTest()
{
    int[] values = null;
    int result = values.RandomElement();
}


[Test]
[ExpectedException("System.InvalidOperationException")]
public void EmptySourceTest()
{
    var values = Enumerable.Empty<int>();
    int result = values.RandomElement();
}


[Test]
public void IEnumerableTest()
{
    // create a test enumerable of int's 0-999
    var values = Enumerable.Range(0, 1000);
    int result1 = values.RandomElement(1);

    // Random class seed is different
    int result2 = values.RandomElement(2);

    // ensure a different result is returned
    // it is OK for this operator to return the same
    // element. However, we only have a 1 in 1000 chance.
    Assert.AreNotSame(result1, result2);
}


[Test]
public void IListTest()
{
    // create a test array of int's 0-999
    var values = Enumerable.Range(0, 1000).ToArray();
    int result1 = values.RandomElement(1);
```

```csharp
    // use a different random seed
    int result2 = values.RandomElement(2);

    // it is OK for this operator to return the same
    // element. However, we only have a 1 in 1000 chance.
    Assert.AreNotSame(result1, result2);
}


[Test]
public void SingleElementTest()
{
    // for a single element source,
    // it should be returned every time

    // IEnumerable<T>
    var values = Enumerable.Range(10, 1);
    int result1 = values.RandomElement(1);
    Assert.AreEqual(10, result1);

    // IList<T>
    var values2 = values.ToArray();
    int result2 = values.RandomElement(2);
    Assert.AreEqual(10, result2);
}


[Test]
public void BoundaryEnumerableTest()
{
    // for a two element source, we want
    // to check the boundaries can be returned
    var values = Enumerable.Range(10, 2);

    // check both results are returned at
    // least once in 25 attempts using
    // different random number generator seeds.
    int result1 = values.RandomElement();
    bool foundDifferent = false;
    for (int i = 0; i < 25; i++)
    {
        int result2 = values.RandomElement(i+100);

        if (result1 != result2)
        {
            foundDifferent = true;
```

```
            break;
        }
    }
    Assert.IsTrue(foundDifferent);
}


[Test]
public void BoundaryIListTest()
{
    // for a two element source, we want
    // to check the boundaries can be returned
    var values = Enumerable.Range(10, 2).ToArray();

    // check both results are returned at
    // least once in 25 attempts using
    // different random number generator seeds.
    int result1 = values.RandomElement();
    bool foundDifferent = false;
    for (int i = 0; i < 25; i++)
    {
        int result2 = values.RandomElement(i+100);

        if (result1 != result2)
        {
            foundDifferent = true;
            break;
        }
    }
    Assert.IsTrue(foundDifferent);
}
```

The code for our `RandomElement` operator in Listing 7-3 satisfies the requirements listed earlier; however, there is one more requirement that will make this single element operator conform to the patterns common in the standard query operators. We need to add a variation called `RandomElementOrDefault` to cater to empty source sequences without throwing an exception. This is necessary to allow the single element operators to be used on sequences that might ordinarily be empty, and rather than throwing an exception, the operator should return null for reference types or zero for numeric value types.

To add this variation of our new operator, I simply cut and pasted the code from Listing 7-3, changed its name to `RandomElementOrDefault`, and then altered the empty source check to `return default(T);` rather than `throw new InvalidOperationException`. The remaining part of the operator is unchanged (although good coding practice would have you refactor out the common code into a separate method). The additional operator begins with the following code:

```
public static T RandomElementOrDefault<T>(
    this IEnumerable<T> source)
{
    // check for invalid source conditions
    if (source == null)
        throw new ArgumentNullException("source");

    if (source.Count() == 0)
        return default(T);

    //... same code as shown in Listing 7-3 ...
}
```

Following are a few tips for developing new single element operators:

- Remember to test and make use of any performance efficiencies offered by collections that implement `IList<T>` and `ICollection` interfaces in addition to `IEnumerable<T>` if present on the source collection. Make certain to support the `IEnumerable<T>` sequences first before looking for performance optimizations.
- Implement an additional variation of these operators (suffixed with `OrDefault`) that returns a legal default value for a given type, rather than throw an `InvalidOperationException` (change the `throw new InvalidOperationException` to `return default(T);`)
- Keep your extension methods in a consistent namespace so that consumers of your operators only need to add a single namespace `using` clause to get access to your custom operators.

Writing a Sequence Operator

The role of a sequence operator is to return an `IEnumerable<T>` sequence based on the elements of a source sequence that have been reordered, filtered, or transformed in some way. The `Where` and `Select` standard query operators are examples of sequence operators.

Sequence operators make use of the `yield return` and `yield break` keywords introduced in C# 2.0. They enable you to write code that implements an `iterator` pattern, which allows consumers to use the familiar `foreach` pattern (the `foreach` uses the `IEnumerable` interface methods, `GetEnumerator` and `MoveNext`, behind the scenes; you can call these methods directly to gain a small performance improvement if necessary).

Enumerators implemented using the `yield return` keyword can be thought of as suspending execution after each `yield return` until the next element is requested. When the next element is requested, execution begins at the point and in the exact state the loop was previously suspended in. The simplest example of this is shown in Listing 7-5, which simply writes out 1, 2, and 3 in the Console window as shown in Output 7-1.

Listing 7-5   Simple yield return example—execution begins at the point after each yield return each time around the loop—see Output 7-1

```
public static IEnumerable<int> MyIterator() {
    yield return 1;
    yield return 2;
    yield return 3;
}

public static void Main() {
    foreach(int i in MyIterator())
        Console.WriteLine(i);
}
```

Output 7-1

```
1
2
3
```

The job of any sequence operator is to return elements using the `yield return` keyword, until there are no more candidates in a sequence. The classic sequence operator to look to for guidance is the `Where` operator included with the standard query operators.

The `Where` operator extends any collection that implements `IEnumerable<T>` and loops through the elements in the source sequence, testing each element as it goes. If an element passes the predicate function (predicate is a function that takes a single argument and returns true or false based on the value of the parameter), that element is returned. Otherwise, that element is skipped. The `yield return` statement will only ever return one element and then suspend execution until the next element is requested, either manually (calling the `MoveNext` method) or by using a `foreach` loop.

The `Where` operator (with the argument error checking code removed for clarity) is implemented in the following general form:

```
public static IEnumerable<T> Where<T>(
    this IEnumerable<T> source,
    Func<T, bool> predicate)
{
    foreach (T element in source)
    {
        if (predicate(element))
            yield return element;
    }
}
```

Building the TakeRange Operator

To demonstrate how to write a sequence operator, we can write an operator called `TakeRange`, which will return elements in a sequence after an element satisfies the `start` predicate in a sequence until an element satisfies the `end` predicate in the same sequence.

The `TakeRange` operator has the following requirements:

- Take an input source and return elements that fall between the first element that passes a "start" predicate until the first element that passes the "end" predicate.
- Allow the start predicate to be optional. In this case all elements in the sequence are returned until the end predicate is satisfied.
- Not fail if the start or end predicate is never satisfied; just return an empty sequence.
- Throw an `ArgumentNullException` if the source sequence is null.
- Throw an `ArgumentNullException` if either the start or end predicate is null in the appropriate overloads.

The `TakeRange` operator will extend any collection that implements `IEnumerable<T>`, as the LINQ to Objects standard query operators always do. Due to this knowledge, the only certainty we have about the source collections is that it can be enumerated using the enumerator pattern. (Call members defined in the IEnumerable<T> interface or use the foreach statement.) Listing 7-6 shows the functional part of the TakeRange operator, the code that creates the iterator and carries out the predicate tests.

Listing 7-6 The iterator implementation for the **TakeRange** operator—see Listing 7-7 for the actual extension method operator implementation

```
private static IEnumerable<T> TakeRangeIterator<T>(
    this IEnumerable<T> source,
    Func<T, bool> startPredicate,
    Func<T, bool> endPredicate)
{
    // check for invalid input argument conditions
    if (source == null)
        throw new ArgumentNullException("source");

    if (startPredicate == null)
        throw new ArgumentNullException("startPredicate");

    if (endPredicate == null)
        throw new ArgumentNullException("endPredicate");

    // begin the iteration ...
    bool foundStart = false;

    foreach (T element in source)
    {
        if (startPredicate(element))
            foundStart = true;

        if (foundStart)
            if (endPredicate(element))
                yield break;
            else
                yield return element;
    }
}
```

The convention when writing sequence operators is to separate the iterator code from the extension method implementation. This allows the same functional iterator to be called from multiple extension methods that have different overload signatures. The requirements described earlier for the TakeRange operator will require two extension method signatures—one that takes a start and end predicate and one that takes only an end predicate (it will always start from the first element).

The actual extension methods that expose the TakeRange operator to our collections are shown in Listing 7-7. When only one predicate is passed, it is assumed to be the end predicate, and all elements from the start of the source sequence until this end predicate passes are returned—this is just the way we have specified the operator to work.

Listing 7-7   The **TakeRange** extension method declarations—both extension methods call the same iterator method as shown in Listing 7-6

```
public static IEnumerable<T> TakeRange<T>(
    this IEnumerable<T> source,
    Func<T, bool> endPredicate)
{

    return TakeRangeIterator<T>(source, b => true, endPredicate);
}

public static IEnumerable<T> TakeRange<T>(
    this IEnumerable<T> source,
    Func<T, bool> startPredicate,
    Func<T, bool> endPredicate)
{

    return TakeRangeIterator<T>(source, startPredicate, endPredicate);
}
```

Although optional, it is highly recommended to stay consistent with the error handling patterns followed by the standard query operators. The general conventions for sequence type operators are as follows:

1. If the source collection being extended is null, throw an ArgumentNullException.
2. If the source collection is empty, throw an InvalidOperation-Exception.
3. If either predicate is null, throw an ArgumentNullException.

Listing 7-8 shows the final code that makes up the TakeRange operator. It follows the accepted practices for input argument errors, demonstrates how to factor out duplicate code into a separate iterator method, and demonstrates how to expose multiple overloaded operators.

Listing 7-8 The **TakeRange** operator extension methods showing the error handling following the traditional pattern used in the Microsoft standard query operators

```
private static IEnumerable<T> TakeRangeIterator<T>(
    this IEnumerable<T> source,
    Func<T, bool> startPredicate,
    Func<T, bool> endPredicate)
{
    // check for invalid input argument conditions
    if (source == null)
        throw new ArgumentNullException("source");

    if (startPredicate == null)
        throw new ArgumentNullException("startPredicate");

    if (endPredicate == null)
        throw new ArgumentNullException("endPredicate");

    // begin the iteration ...
    bool foundStart = false;

    foreach (T element in source)
    {
        if (startPredicate(element))
            foundStart = true;

        if (foundStart)
            if (endPredicate(element))
                yield break;
            else
                yield return element;
    }
}

public static IEnumerable<T> TakeRange<T>(
    this IEnumerable<T> source,
    Func<T, bool> endPredicate)
{
```

```
    return TakeRangeIterator<T>(
        source, b => true, endPredicate);
}

public static IEnumerable<T> TakeRange<T>(
    this IEnumerable<T> source,
    Func<T, bool> startPredicate,
    Func<T, bool> endPredicate)
{

    return TakeRangeIterator<T>(
        source, startPredicate, endPredicate);
}
```

To ensure a custom operator works as expected and stays that way in future releases, a solid set of unit tests should be written. To test the TakeRange operator and to demonstrate its basic usage, Listing 7-9 shows the minimum set of unit tests to prove the operator is functional. These tests confirm the following conditions when calling this operator:

- The operator works consistently with normal inputs. (It actually works!)
- The operator works consistently at the boundaries. (How does it handle the first or last element in the source?)
- The operator throws an exception when called from a null source sequence.
- The operator throws an exception if called with null predicates.

Listing 7-9 The following unit tests are a starting point for testing the `TakeRange` operator

```
[Test]
[ExpectedException("System.ArgumentNullException")]
public void NullSourceTest()
{
    int[] values = null;
    var result = values.TakeRange(
        start => true, end => true).ToArray<int>();
}

[Test]
[ExpectedException("System.ArgumentNullException")]
```

```
public void NullStartPredicateTest()
{
    int[] values = null;
    int[] result = values.TakeRange(
        null, b => true).ToArray<int>();
}

[Test]
[ExpectedException("System.ArgumentNullException")]
public void NullEndPredicateTest()
{
    int[] values = null;
    int[] result = values.TakeRange(
        a => true, null).ToArray<int>();
}

[Test]
public void IntArrayTest()
{
    var values = Enumerable.Range(0, 20);

    int[] result = values.TakeRange(
            start => start > 4,
            end => end > 9).ToArray<int>();

    Assert.AreEqual(
        5, result.Count(), "incorrect count returned");

    // expecting 5,6,7,8,9 to be returned
    for (int i = 0; i < result.Count(); i++)
        Assert.AreEqual(i + 5, result[i]);
}

[Test]
public void IntArrayEndPredicateOnlyTest()
{
    var values = Enumerable.Range(0, 20);

    int[] result = values.TakeRange(
            end => end > 9).ToArray<int>();

    Assert.AreEqual(
        10, result.Count(), "incorrect count returned");

    // expecting 10-19 to be returned
```

```
    for (int i = 10; i < result.Count(); i++)
        Assert.AreEqual(i, result[i]);
}
```

Following are a few tips for developing new sequence operators:

- Separate the iterator code from the extension method functions so you can provide many overloads that allow optional input arguments all calling the same main method implementation
- Test input arguments for null values and throw an `ArgumentNullException("arg");` if these input arguments are essential for correct operation.
- Follow the same patterns and error handling that Microsoft used in their operators. (I've followed as many as possible throughout this book.)

Writing an Aggregate Operator

The role of an aggregate operator is to traverse a source sequence and carry out a function (often arithmetic) on the elements. Example aggregate standard query operators are `Sum`, `Min`, and `Max`, which return the sum of values, the smallest value, and the largest value, respectively.

The Min Operator

To understand the basics of an aggregate style operator, let's look at the implementation of the `Min` standard query operator. Listing 7-10 shows the error handling and functional code to find the minimum integer in a sequence.

Listing 7-10 Implementation of the **Min** standard query operator

```
public static int Min(
    this IEnumerable<int> source)
{
    if (source == null)
        throw new ArgumentNullException("source");
```

```
int num = 0;
bool flag = false;
foreach (int num2 in source)
{
    if (flag)
    {
        if (num2 < num)
            num = num2;
    }
    else
    {
        num = num2;
        flag = true;
    }
}

if (!flag)
    throw new
        InvalidOperationException("No elements");

return num;
}
```

Listing 7-10 first checks the source sequence for a null condition and throws an exception if that is the case. If the source sequence is not null, each element is compared to the current minimum element found so far (by value), except the first element. When flag is false, the first element hasn't yet been evaluated, and if the sequence is empty (no first element ever found), an InvalidOperationException is thrown; otherwise, the first element's value is assigned to the current minimum variable on the first iteration step. After iterating and testing each element's value against the current minimum found, the lowest value is returned.

The code shown previously for the Min operator is just one of the many overloads declared for this operator in the standard query operator (there are 22 total). Of the full set of Min operators provided, 11 are similar to the Min operator just described, and 11 also take a selector expression. The full set declared in the standard query operators is shown in Listing 7-11.

Listing 7-11 The full set of operator overloads for the **Min** operator, showing the argument types and return types supported by aggregate operators

```
decimal Min(this IEnumerable<decimal> source);
double Min(this IEnumerable<double> source);
decimal? Min(this IEnumerable<decimal?> source);
double? Min(this IEnumerable<double?> source);
int? Min(this IEnumerable<int?> source);
long? Min(this IEnumerable<long?> source);
float? Min(this IEnumerable<float?> source);
int Min(this IEnumerable<int> source);
long Min(this IEnumerable<long> source);
float Min(this IEnumerable<float> source);
TSource Min<TSource>(this IEnumerable<TSource> source);

decimal Min<TSource>(this IEnumerable<TSource> source,
    Func<TSource, decimal> selector);
double Min<TSource>(this IEnumerable<TSource> source,
    Func<TSource, double> selector);
long? Min<TSource>(this IEnumerable<TSource> source,
    Func<TSource, long?> selector);
int Min<TSource>(this IEnumerable<TSource> source,
    Func<TSource, int> selector);
double? Min<TSource>(this IEnumerable<TSource> source,
    Func<TSource, double?> selector);
float? Min<TSource>(this IEnumerable<TSource> source,
    Func<TSource, float?> selector);
long Min<TSource>(this IEnumerable<TSource> source,
    Func<TSource, long> selector);
decimal? Min<TSource>(this IEnumerable<TSource> source,
    Func<TSource, decimal?> selector);
int? Min<TSource>(this IEnumerable<TSource> source,
    Func<TSource, int?> selector);
float Min<TSource>(this IEnumerable<TSource> source,
    Func<TSource, float> selector);
TResult Min<TSource, TResult>(this IEnumerable<TSource> source,
    Func<TSource, TResult> selector);
```

When building your own aggregate operators, you should consider a similar set of overloads, as laborious and clipboard-intensive as it is initially writing them. My approach is to start with the int32 variation and fully unit-test that implementation before duplicating the code with the rest of the numeric and nullable numeric types. Even with this set of overloads, some of the standard query operators still don't fulfill every need—I found this out when using the Sum operator, as is described in the next section.

Building the LongSum Operator

Early on when working with LINQ to Objects I found the built-in Sum operator that sums the values for a set of integer values returned the result as an integer type. This didn't suit my requirements, and my sequences quickly overflowed the integer maximum boundary of the return type. A custom operator was needed to return the arithmetic sum of integer values with a result type of long (overloading the built-in Min operators didn't solve the issue. Because I was only changing the return type and not an argument type, C# compiler's overload resolution wasn't satisfied—hence the name LongSum).

The LongSum operator has the following requirements:

1. Take an input IEnumerable<int> collection as a source and return the arithmetic sum as type long.
2. Follow the signature pattern of the existing Sum operators. Create two extension method overloaded signatures, one that takes a selector expression and one that doesn't.
3. Throw an ArgumentNullException if the source sequence is null.
4. If the source sequence is empty, return a result of zero.

The obvious goal is to make using the new LongSum extension method identical to using the Sum extension methods. Listing 7-12 shows the full code for implementing the LongSum operator. The code iterates the source collection using a foreach loop and simply sums the element values as it goes. If a Selector expression argument is passed into the operator, that Selector expression is first evaluated before calling the other LongSum overload with simply a source sequence of integer values.

Listing 7-12 The code for the LongSum operator, which takes a sequence of **int** values and returns the mathematical sum up to the maximum value allowed in a **Long** type

```
public static long LongSum(
    this IEnumerable<int> source)
{
    if (source == null)
        throw new ArgumentNullException("source");

    long sum = 0;
```

```
    checked
    {
        foreach (int v in source)
            sum += v;
    }

    return sum;
}

public static long LongSum<T>(
    this IEnumerable<T> source,
    Func<T, int> selector)
{
    return source
            .Select(selector)
            .LongSum();
}
```

To test the LongSum operator, Listing 7-13 shows the basic set of unit tests written to confirm correct behavior and demonstrate its usage. The basic set of unit tests you should consider for any custom aggregate style operators are:

- The operator works with normal inputs; positive and negative numbers, and all method overloads.
- The operator throws an exception when called on a null sequence (this is the standard error-handling pattern).
- The operator returns a safe value when called on an empty sequence. Return zero or an exception? The choice is up to the implementer.

Listing 7-13 Basic set of unit tests for the **LongSum** operator

```
[Test]
public void LongSumIntTest()
{
    int[] values = new int[] { 5, 4, 3, 2, 1, 6, 7, 8, 9, 0 };
    long result = values.LongSum();
    Assert.AreEqual(45, result, "LongSum incorrect result.");
}

[Test]
public void LongSumNegativeIntTest()
{
```

```
    int[] values = new int[] { int.MinValue, int.MaxValue, 1 };
    long result = values.LongSum();
    Assert.AreEqual(0, result, "Negative values incorrect result.");
}

[Test]
public void LongSumIntBigTest()
{
    int[] values = new int[] { int.MaxValue, 1, int.MaxValue };
    long result = values.LongSum();
    long correct = (long)int.MaxValue + (long)int.MaxValue + 1;
    Assert.AreEqual(correct, result);
}

[Test]
[ExpectedException(typeof(ArgumentNullException))]
public void LongSumIntNullSourceTest()
{
    int[] values = null;
    long result = values.LongSum();
}

[Test]
public void LongSumIntEmptySourceTest()
{
    var values = Enumerable.Empty<int>();
    long result = values.LongSum();
    Assert.AreEqual(0, result);
}

[Test]
public void LongSumIntWithSelectorTest()
{
    int[] values = new int[] { 5, 4, 3, 2, 1, 6, 7, 8, 9, 0 };
    long result = values.LongSum(i => i + 1);
    Assert.AreEqual(55, result);
}
```

The following provides some tips for developing new aggregate style operators:

- For completeness, you should create the full set of numeric overloads when you create your own operators. Refer to the set shown in

Listing 7-11 for the `Min` operator as a good starting list for your operators.

■ Provide an overload for each operator that takes a selector expression. Aggregate functions are often used in the select project of a grouped query result, where you want to define the numeric sequence you want aggregated. To implement these overloads, call the `Select` standard query operator passing in the select argument before calling your custom operator, for example:

```
return source
        .Select(selector)
        .LongSum();
```

■ Test input arguments for null values and throw an `ArgumentNullException("arg");` if these input arguments are essential for correct operation.

■ Look at the source code for the standard query operators by using Red Gate Reflector (http://www.red-gate.com/products/reflector/). Follow the same patterns and error handling that Microsoft uses in their operators.

Writing a Grouping Operator

Grouping operators return collections of the source elements (or variations thereof) grouped by some algorithm. Examples of grouping category operators from the standard query operators are `GroupBy` and `ToLookup`.

The general steps for building a new grouping operator are:

1. Write an `IGrouping<TKey, TElement>` list implementation to hold your groups. In a perfect world we could reuse Microsoft's `Grouping` type implementation, however it is marked as internal. I recommend copying it as a template for your own grouping list implementation (which is what I did in this example, and provided in Listing 7-14).

2. Write an enumeration method that builds the groups and yields the grouped results using instances of the `IGrouping<TKey, TElement>` types.

3. Write an extension method signature(s) and implement each method by calling the enumeration method with the appropriate arguments.

4. Write unit tests and ensure they pass (avoiding the religious debate as to whether tests should be written before the code or vice versa).

The ToLookup standard query operator almost universally caters to any grouping requirement (for instance, it is the basis for the GroupBy operator). If you can find an implementation by using the ToLookup operator, you can save a lot of time. For educational purposes, we are going to build a grouping operator from scratch.

Grouping Collection Implementation

Each group result from a grouping operator should follow the IGrouping<TKey,TElement> interface. This collection implementation should be read-only from the consuming application code and only populated by our grouping operator code. Listing 7-14 shows a basic implementation for a suitable grouping collection class. This implementation is a close facsimile of the Grouping type used by Microsoft in the standard query operator's; however, we need to duplicate that code because that class is marked internal. You will notice that any property setter or method call that can alter the contents of the collection throws a NotSupportedException (the collection is read-only). You can iterate, access elements by index, and retrieve the key property for the group—but that is essentially all.

Listing 7-14   Example grouping element collection implementation—predominately read-only

```
public class Grouping<TKey, TElement> :
        IGrouping<TKey, TElement>, IList<TElement>
{
    internal TKey key;
    internal TElement[] elements;
    internal int count;

    public Grouping(int count)
    {
        elements = new TElement[count];
    }

    internal void Add(TElement element)
```

```csharp
    {
        if (elements.Length == count)
            Array.Resize(ref elements, count * 2);

        elements[count++] = element;
    }

    public IEnumerator<TElement> GetEnumerator()
    {
        for (int i = 0; i < count; i++)
            yield return elements[i];
    }

    IEnumerator IEnumerable.GetEnumerator()
    {
        return GetEnumerator();
    }

    TKey IGrouping<TKey, TElement>.Key
    {
        get { return key; }
    }

    int ICollection<TElement>.Count
    {
        get { return count; }
    }

    bool ICollection<TElement>.IsReadOnly
    {
        get { return true; }
    }

    void ICollection<TElement>.Add(TElement item)
    {
        throw new NotSupportedException();
    }

    void ICollection<TElement>.Clear()
    {
        throw new NotSupportedException();
    }

    bool ICollection<TElement>.Contains(TElement item)
    {
```

```
        return
            Array.IndexOf(elements, item, 0, count) >= 0;
}

void ICollection<TElement>.CopyTo(
        TElement[] array, int arrayIndex)
{
    Array.Copy(elements, 0, array, arrayIndex, count);
}

bool ICollection<TElement>.Remove(TElement item)
{
    throw new NotSupportedException();
}

int IList<TElement>.IndexOf(TElement item)
{
    return
        Array.IndexOf(elements, item, 0, count);
}

void IList<TElement>.Insert(int index, TElement item)
{
    throw new NotSupportedException();
}

void IList<TElement>.RemoveAt(int index)
{
    throw new NotSupportedException();
}

TElement IList<TElement>.this[int index]
{
    get
    {
        if (index < 0 || index >= count)
            throw new
                ArgumentOutOfRangeException("index");

        return elements[index];
    }
    set
    {
        throw new NotSupportedException();
    }
```

```
    }
}
```

Building the Segment Operator

To demonstrate writing a grouping operator, we will write an example operator called Segment. The Segment operator divides the elements in a source sequence into equal-sized groups (equal element count) where it can, except the last group if the elements can't be distributed equally.

The Segment operator has the following requirements:

- To take any collection implementing IEnumerable<T> as an input source and divide it into multiple groups with the same number of elements.
- If the number of elements doesn't allow all groups to be equally sized, the last group and all other groups of equal size should be reduced.
- If there are more segments than elements, put one element in as many as possible and return empty groups for the remaining.
- Each group should have a Key property with the sequential segment number; that is, 1 for the first group, 2 for the second, and so on.
- Throw an ArgumentNullException if the source sequence is null.
- Throw an ArgumentOutOfRangeException if the number of segments is zero or less than zero.

A quick example of how the Segment operator should work is shown in Listing 7-15. The Console output from this example is shown in Output 7-2.

Listing 7-15 Calling the **Segment** operator to divide a string array into five groups—see Output 7-2

```
string[] elements = new string[]
    { "A", "B", "C", "D", "E", "F", "G", "H", "I", "J" };

var groups = elements.Segment(5);

foreach (var g in groups)
{
    Console.WriteLine("Group key: {0}", g.Key);
    foreach (var elm in g)
        Console.WriteLine("  {0}", elm);
}
```

Output 7-2

```
Group key: 1
  A
  B
Group key: 2
  C
  D
Group key: 3
  E
  F
Group key: 4
  G
  H
Group key: 5
  I
  J
```

A real-world example (why this operator was first built) of segmenting data into groups is when generating groups for multivariate testing. For instance, imagine you wanted to send an email to all contacts in your customer list. You want to test variations in order to determine what version gets the greatest response. The Segment operator can be used to build these groups, as the code shown in Listing 7-16 demonstrates by creating two test groups. The Console output from this example is shown in Output 7-3.

Listing 7-16 Calling the **Segment** operator to divide contacts into two groups—see Output 7-3

```csharp
List<Contact> contacts = Contact.SampleData();

// split the contacts into 2 groups for A/B testing
var groups = contacts.Segment(2);

foreach (var g in groups)
{
    Console.WriteLine("Group key: {0}", g.Key);
    foreach (var elm in g)
        Console.WriteLine("  {0}, {1}",
            elm.LastName.ToUpper(), elm.FirstName);
```

Output 7-3

```
Group key: 1
   GOTTSHALL, Barney
   VALDES, Armando
   GAUWAIN, Adam
   DEANE, Jeffery
   ZEEMAN, Collin
Group key: 2
   KAGEL, Stewart
   LARD, Chance
   REIFSTECK, Blaine
   KAMPH, Mack
   HAZELGROVE, Ariel
```

The code to implement the `Segment` operator is shown in Listing 7-17. This implementation first checks the input arguments and then calls a private implementation that encapsulates the building and iteration functionality. Separating the iterator function to support reuse with multiple overloaded variations of the `Segment` operator is considered a good practice (as mentioned in the `TakeRange` operator example). The return type of this operator is an `IGrouping<TKey,TElement>` (declared publicly in the `System.Linq` namespace, so it will be in scope); instances of our grouping collections are constructed as `Grouping<int, T>[]`'s, using the collection type shown in Listing 7-14.

Listing 7-17 The **Segment** operator code, which segments the contents of the source sequence into equal-sized groups

```
public static IEnumerable<IGrouping<int, T>> Segment<T>(
    this IEnumerable<T> source,
    int segments)
{
    if (source == null)
        throw new ArgumentNullException("source");

    if (segments <= 0)
        throw new ArgumentOutOfRangeException("segments");

    return SegmentIterator<T>(source, segments);
}
```

```
private static IEnumerable<IGrouping<int, T>>
    SegmentIterator<T>(
        IEnumerable<T> source,
        int segments)
{
    // calculate the number of elements per segment
    int count = source.Count();
    int perSegment = (int)Math.Ceiling(
        (decimal)count / segments);

    // build the empty groups
    Grouping<int, T>[] groups =
        new Grouping<int, T>[segments];

    for (int i = 0; i < segments; i++)
    {
        Grouping<int, T> g =
            new Grouping<int, T>(perSegment);

        g.key = i + 1;
        groups[i] = g;
    }

    // fill the groups and yield results
    // when each group is full.
    int index = 0;
    int segment = 1;
    Grouping<int, T> group = groups[0];
    using (IEnumerator<T> e = source.GetEnumerator())
    {
        while (e.MoveNext())
        {
            group.Add(e.Current);
            index++;

            // yield return when we have filled each group
            if ((segment < segments) &&
                (index == perSegment))
            {
                yield return group;
                index = 0;
                segment++;
                group = groups[segment - 1];
            }
        }
```

```
    }

    // return the last and any remaining groups
    // (these will be empty or partially populated)
    while (segment <= segments)
    {
        yield return groups[segment - 1];
        segment++;
    }
}
```

To confirm this segment operator matches the previously stated requirements and to confirm it stays that way throughout multiple future revisions, Listing 7-18 shows some basic unit tests. In writing this operator, these tests helped me debug the boundary conditions for odd, even, and too small a quantity source sequences.

Listing 7-18   Basic unit tests for the **Segment** operator

```
[Test]
[ExpectedException("System.ArgumentNullException")]
public void NullSourceTest()
{
    int[] values = null;
    var result = values.Segment(1);
}

[Test]
public void EmptySourceTest()
{
    // expecting 4 empty groups
    int[] values = Enumerable.Empty<int>().ToArray();
    var result = values.Segment(4);
    Assert.AreEqual(4, result.Count());
}

[Test]
public void EvenSegmentTest()
{
    int[] values =
        Enumerable.Range(1, 100).ToArray<int>();

    var result = values.Segment(4);
    Assert.AreEqual(4, result.Count());
```

```
    foreach (var g in result)
        Assert.AreEqual(25, g.Count());
}


[Test]
public void MoreSegmentsThanElementsTest()
{
    int[] values = Enumerable.Range(1, 3).ToArray<int>();

    var result = values.Segment(10);

    Assert.AreEqual(10, result.Count());
    int i = 1;
    foreach (var g in result)
    {
        if (i < 4)
            Assert.AreEqual(1, g.Count());
        else
            Assert.AreEqual(0, g.Count());

        i++;
    }
}


[Test]
public void OddSegmentTest()
{
    int[] values =
        Enumerable.Range(1, 101).ToArray<int>();

    var result = values.Segment(4);
    Assert.AreEqual(4, result.Count());

    int i = 1;
    foreach (var g in result)
    {
        if (i < 4)
            Assert.AreEqual(26, g.Count());
        else
            Assert.AreEqual(23, g.Count());

        i++;
    }
}
```

The following are some tips for developing new grouping operators:

- Try and use the `ToLookup` standard query operator in your implementation if possible.
- Separate the iterator logic into its own method, so that multiple operator overloads can re-use the same iterator implementation.
- Try to build the groups in one enumeration pass through the source sequence for optimal performance.
- Try to yield return a result grouping as soon as you can build one. Avoid building all groups up-front in the case that the user never iterates past the first group (just for performance, sometimes its unavoidable, but worth looking for an algorithm that performs best with deferred execution).

Summary

This chapter introduced how to build custom operators when required. LINQ to Object operators are simply extension methods for any type implementing the `IEnumerable<T>` interface.

The general guidance for building operators is to look at the implementation of Microsoft's standard query operators and follow their patterns. This ensures that your operators are consistent in how they handle errors and how they are used when other developers begin using these extensions in query expressions.

CHAPTER 8

C# 4.0 FEATURES

Goals of this chapter:

- Define new C# 4.0 language features.
- Demonstrate the new language features in the context of LINQ to Objects.

C# is an evolving language. This chapter looks at the new features added into C# 4.0 that combine to improve code readability and extend your ability to leverage LINQ to Object queries over dynamic data sources. The examples in this chapter show how to improve the coding model for developers around reading data from various sources, including text files and how to combine data from a **COM-Interop** source into a LINQ to Objects query.

Evolution of C#

C# is still a relatively new language (circa 2000) and is benefiting from continuing investment by Microsoft's languages team. The C# language is an ECMA and ISO standard. (ECMA is an acronym for European Computer Manufacturers Association, and although it changed its name to Ecma International in 1994, it kept the name Ecma for historical reasons.[1]) The standard ECMA-334 and ISO/IEC 23270:2006 is freely available online at the Ecma International website[2] and describes the language syntax and notation. However, Microsoft's additions to the language over several versions take some time to progress through the standards process, so Microsoft's release cycle leads Ecma's acceptance by at least a version.

Each version of C# has a number of new features and generally a major theme. The major themes have been generics and nullable types in C# 2.0,

LINQ in C# 3.0, and dynamic types in C# 4.0. The major features added in each release are generally considered to be the following:

- **C# 2.0**—Generics (.NET Framework support was added, and C# benefited from this); iterator pattern (the `yield` keyword); anonymous methods (the `delegate` keyword), nullable types, and the null coalescing operator (`??`).
- **C# 3.0**—Anonymous types, extension methods, object initializers, collection initializers, implicitly typed local variables (`var` keyword), lambda expressions (`=>`), and the LINQ query expression pattern.
- **C# 4.0**—Optional Parameters and Named Arguments, Dynamic typing (`dynamic` type), improved COM-Interop, and Contra and Co-Variance.

The new features in C# 3.0 that launched language support for LINQ can be found in Chapter 2, "Introducing LINQ to Objects," and this chapter documents each of the major new features in C# 4.0 from the perspective of how they impact the LINQ story.

Optional Parameters and Named Arguments

A long-requested feature for C# was to allow for method parameters to be optional. Two closely related features in C# 4.0 fulfill this role and enable us to either omit arguments that have a defined default value when calling a method, and to pass arguments by name rather than position when calling a method.

OPTIONAL PARAMETERS OR OPTIONAL ARGUMENTS? Optional parameters and named parameters are sometimes called optional arguments and named arguments. These names are used interchangeably in this book, and in most literature, including the C# 4.0 specification that uses both, sometimes in the same section. I use "argument" when referring to a value passed in from a method call and "parameter" when referring to the method signature.

The main benefit of these features is to improve **COM-Interop** programming (which is covered shortly) and to reduce the number of method overloads created to support a wide range of parameter overloads. It is a common programming pattern to have a master method signature containing all parameters (with the actual implementation) chained to a number of overloaded methods that have a lesser parameter signature set calling the master method with hard-coded default values. This common coding pattern becomes unnecessary when optional parameters are used in the definition of the aforementioned master method signature, arguably improving code readability and debugging by reducing clutter. (See Listing 8-2 for an example of the old and new way to create multiple overloads.)

There has been fierce debate on these features on various email lists and blogs. Some C# users believe that these features are not necessary and introduce uncertainty in versioning. For example if version 2 of an assembly changes a default parameter value for a particular method, client code that was assuming a specific default might break. This is true, but the existing chained method call pattern suffers from a similar issue—default values are coded into a library or application somewhere, so thinking about when and how to handle these hard-coded defaults would be necessary using either the existing chained method pattern or the new optional parameters and named arguments. Given that optional parameters were left out of the original C# implementation (even when the .NET Runtime had support and VB.NET utilized this feature), we must speculate that although this feature is unnecessary for general programming, coding COM-Interop libraries without this feature is unpleasant and at times infuriating—hence, optional parameters and specifying arguments by name has now made its way into the language.

COM-Interop code has always suffered due to C#'s inability to handle optional parameters as a concept. Many Microsoft Office Component Object Model (**COM**) libraries, like those built to automate Excel or Word for instance, have method signatures that contain 25 optional parameters. Previously you had no choice but to pass dummy arguments until you reached the "one" you wanted and then fill in the remaining arguments until you had fulfilled all 25. Optional parameters and named arguments solve this madness, making coding against COM interfaces much easier and cleaner. The code shown in Listing 8-1 demonstrates the before and after syntax of a simple Excel COM-Interop call to open an Excel spreadsheet. It shows how much cleaner this type of code can be written when using C# 4.0 versus any of its predecessors.

Listing 8-1   Comparing the existing way to call COM-Interop and the new way using optional parameters

```
// Old way - before optional parameters
var excel = new Microsoft.Office.Interop.Excel.Application();
try
{
    Microsoft.Office.Interop.Excel.Workbook workBook =
            excel.Workbooks.Open(fileName, Type.Missing,
                Type.Missing, Type.Missing, Type.Missing,
                Type.Missing, Type.Missing, Type.Missing,
                Type.Missing, Type.Missing, Type.Missing,
                Type.Missing, Type.Missing, Type.Missing,
                Type.Missing);

    // do work with Excel...

    workBook.Close(false, fileName);
}
finally
{
    excel.Quit();
}


// New Way - Using optional parameters
var excel = new Microsoft.Office.Interop.Excel.Application();
try
{
    Microsoft.Office.Interop.Excel.Workbook workBook =
            excel.Workbooks.Open(fileName);

    // do work with Excel...

    workBook.Close(false, fileName);
}
finally
{
    excel.Quit();
}
```

The addition of object initializer functionality in C# 3.0 took over some of the workload of having numerous constructor overloads by allowing public properties to be set in line with a simpler constructor (avoiding having a constructor for every Select projection needed). Optional parameters and named arguments offer an alternative way to simplify coding a LINQ Select projection by allowing variations of a type's constructor with a lesser set of parameters. Before diving into how to use these features in LINQ queries, it is necessary to understand the syntax and limitations of these new features.

Optional Parameters

The first new feature allows default parameters to be specified in a method signature. Callers of methods defined with default values can omit those arguments without having to define a specific overload matching that lesser parameter list for convenience.

To define a default value in a method signature, you simply add a constant expression as the default value to use when omitted, similar to member initialization and constant definitions. A simple example method definition that has one mandatory parameter (p1, just like normal) and an optional parameter definition (p2) takes the following form:

```
public void MyMethod( int p1, int p2 = 5 );
```

The following invocations of method MyMethod are legal (will compile) and are functionally equivalent as far as the compiler is concerned:

```
MyMethod( 1, 5 );
MyMethod( 1 ); // the declared default for p2 (5) is used
```

The rules when defining a method signature that uses optional parameters are:

1. Required parameters cannot appear after any optional parameter.
2. The default specified must be a constant expression available at compile time or a value type constructor without parameters, or default(T) where T is a value type.
3. The constant expression must be implicitly convertible by an identity (or nullable conversion) to the type of the parameter.
4. Parameters with a ref or out modifier cannot be optional parameters.
5. Parameter arrays (params) can occur after optional parameters, but these cannot have a default value assigned. If the value is omitted by the calling invocation, an empty parameter array is used in either case, achieving the same results.

Valid optional parameter definitions take the following form:

```
public void M1(string s, int i = 1) { }
public void M2(Point p = new Point()) { }
public void M3(Point p = default(Point)) { }
public void M4(int i = 1, params string[] values) { }
```

The following method definitions using optional parameters will *not* compile:

```
//"Optional parameters must appear after all required parameters"
public void M1 (int i = 1, string s) {}

//"Default parameter value for 'p' must be a compile-time constant"
//(Can't use a constructor that has parameters)
public void M2(Point p = new Point(0,0)) {}

//"Default parameter value for 'p' must be a compile-time constant"
//(Must be a value type (struct or built-in value types only))
public void M5(StringBuilder p = new StringBuilder()) {}

//"A ref or out parameter cannot have a default value"
public void M6(int i = 1, out string s = "") {}

//"Cannot specify a default value for a parameter array"
public void M7(int i = 1, params string[] values = "test") {}
```

To understand how optional parameters reduce our code, Listing 8-2 shows a traditional overloaded method pattern and the equivalent optional parameter code.

Listing 8-2   Comparing the traditional cascaded method overload pattern to the new optional parameter syntax pattern

```
// Old way - before optional parameters
public class OldWay
{
    // multiple overloads call the one master
    // implementation of a method that handles all inputs
```

```csharp
public void DoSomething(string formatString)
{
    // passing 0 as param1 default,
    // and true as param2 default.
    DoSomething(formatString, 0, true);
}

public void DoSomething(string formatString, int param1)
{
    DoSomething(formatString, param1, true);
}

public void DoSomething(string formatString, bool param2)
{
    DoSomething(formatString, 0, param2);
}

// the actual implementation. All variations call this
// method to implement the methods function.
public void DoSomething(
    string formatString,
    int param1,
    bool param2)
{
    Console.WriteLine(
        String.Format(formatString, param1, param2));
}
}

// New Way - Using optional parameters
public class NewWay
{
    // optional parameters have a default specified.
    // optional parameters must come after normal params.
    public void DoSomething(
        string formatString,
        int param1 = 0,
        bool param2 = true)
    {
        Console.WriteLine(
            String.Format(formatString, param1, param2));
    }
}
```

Named Arguments

Traditionally, the position of the arguments passed to a method call identified which parameter that value matched. It is possible in C# 4.0 to specify arguments by name, in addition to position. This is helpful when many parameters are optional and you need to target a specific parameter without having to specify all proceeding optional parameters.

Methods can be called with any combination of positionally specified and named arguments, as long as the following rules are observed:

1. If you are going to use a combination of positional and named arguments, the positional arguments must be passed first. (They cannot come after named arguments.)
2. All non-optional parameters must be specified somewhere in the invocation, either by name or position.
3. If an argument is specified by position, it cannot then be specified by name as well.

To understand the basic syntax, the following example creates a `System.Drawing.Point` by using named arguments. It should be noted that there is no constructor for this type that takes the y-size, x-size by position—this reversal is solely because of named arguments.

```
// reversing the order of arguments.
Point p1 = new Point(y: 100, x: 10);
```

The following method invocations will not compile:

```
//"Named argument 'x' specifies a parameter for which a
// positional argument has already been given"
Point p3 = new Point(10, x: 10);

// "Named argument specifications must appear after all
// fixed arguments have been specified"
Point p4 = new Point(y: 100, 10);

// "The best overload for '.ctor' does not have a
// parameter named 'x'"
Point p5 = new Point(x: 10);
```

To demonstrate how to mix and match optional parameters and named arguments within method or constructor invocation calls, the code shown in Listing 8-3 calls the method definition for `NewWay` in Listing 8-2.

Listing 8-3 Mixing and matching positional and named arguments in a method invocation for methods that have optional and mandatory parameters

```
NewWay newWay = new NewWay();

// skipping an optional parameter
newWay.DoSomething(
    "({0},{1}) New way - param1 skipped.",
    param2: false);

// any order, but if it doesn't have a default
// it must be specified by name somewhere!
newWay.DoSomething(
    param2: false,
    formatString: "({0},{1}) New way - params specified" +
                  " by name, in any order.",
    param1: 5);
```

Using Named Arguments and Optional Parameters in LINQ Queries

Named arguments and optional parameters offer an alternative way to reduce code in LINQ queries, especially regarding flexibility in what parameters can be omitted in an object constructor.

Although anonymous types make it convenient to project the results of a query into an object with a subset of defined properties, these anonymous types are scoped to the local method. To share a type across methods, types, or assemblies, a concrete type is needed, meaning the accumulation of simple types or constructor methods just to hold variations of data shape projections. Object initializers reduce this need by allowing a concrete type to have a constructor without parameters and public properties used to assign values in the Select projection. Object-oriented purists take issue with a parameterless constructor being a requirement; it can lead to invalid objects being created by users who are unaware that certain properties must be set before an object is correctly initialized for use—an opinion I strongly agree with. (You can't compile using the object initialization syntax unless the type concerned has a parameterless constructor, even if there are other constructors defined that take arguments.)

Optional parameters and named arguments can fill this gap. Data can be projected from queries into concrete types, and the author of that concrete type can ensure that the constructor maintains integrity by defining the default values to use when an argument is omitted. Many online discussions have taken place discussing if this is a good pattern; one camp thinks it doesn't hurt code readability or maintainability to use optional parameters in a constructor definition, and the other says refactoring makes it an easy developer task to define the various constructors required in a given type, and hence of no value. I see both sides of that argument and will leave it up to you to decide where it should be employed.

To demonstrate how to use named arguments and optional parameters from a LINQ query, the example shown in Listing 8-4 creates a subset of contact records (in this case, contacts from California) but omits the email and phone details. The Console output from this example is shown in Output 8-1.

Listing 8-4 Example LINQ query showing how to use named arguments and optional parameters to assist in projecting a lighter version of a larger type—see Output 8-1

```
var q = from c in Contact.SampleData()
        where c.State == "CA"
        select new Contact(
            c.FirstName, c.LastName,
            state: c.State,
            dateOfBirth: c.DateOfBirth
            );

foreach (var c in q)
    Console.WriteLine("{0}, {1} ({2}) - {3}",
        c.LastName, c.FirstName,
        c.DateOfBirth.ToShortDateString(), c.State);

public class Contact
{
    // constructor defined with optional parameters
    public Contact(
        string firstName,
        string lastName,
```

```
        DateTime dateOfBirth,
        string email = "unknown",  // optional
        string phone = "",         // optional
        string state = "Other")    // optional
    {
        FirstName = firstName;
        LastName = lastName;
        DateOfBirth = dateOfBirth;
        Email = email;
        Phone = phone;
        State = state;
    }

    public string FirstName { get; set; }
    public string LastName { get; set; }
    public string Email { get; set; }
    public string Phone { get; set; }
    public DateTime DateOfBirth { get; set; }
    public string State { get; set; }

    public static List<Contact> SampleData() ...
    // sample data the same as used in Table 2-1.
}
```

Output 8-1

```
Gottshall, Barney (10/19/1945) - CA
Deane, Jeffery (12/16/1950) - CA
```

Dynamic Typing

The wow feature of C# 4.0 is the addition of dynamic typing. Dynamic languages such as Python and Ruby have major followings and have formed a reputation of being super-productive languages for building certain types of applications.

The main difference between these languages and C# or VB.NET is the type system and specifically when (and how) member names and method names are resolved. C# and VB.NET require (or required, as you will see) that static types be available during compile time and will fail if a member name or method name does not exist. This static typing allows for very rigorous error checking during compile time, and generally improves code performance because the compiler can make targeted optimizations based on exact member name and method name resolution. Dynamic-typed languages on the other hand enable the member and method lookups to be carried out at runtime, rather than compile time. Why is this good? The main identifiable reason is that this allows code to locate members and methods dynamically at runtime and handle additions and enhancements without requiring a recompile of one system or another.

I'm going to stay out of the religious debate as to which is better. I believe there are positives and negatives in both approaches, and C# 4.0 allows you to make the choice depending on the coding problem you need to solve. Dynamic typing allows very clean coding patterns to be realized, as you will see in an upcoming example, where we code against the column names in a CSV file without the need for generating a backing class for every different CSV file format that might need to be read.

Using Dynamic Types

When a variable is defined with the type `dynamic`, the compiler ignores the call as far as traditional error checking is concerned and instead stores away the specifics of the action for the executing runtime to process at a later time (at execution time). Essentially, you can write whatever method calls (with whatever parameters), indexers, and properties you want on a dynamic object, and the compiler won't complain. These actions are picked up at runtime and executed according to how the dynamic type's binder determines is appropriate.

A binder is the code that gets the payload for an action on a dynamic instance type at runtime and resolves it into some action. Within the C# language, there are two paths code can take at this point, depending on the binder being used (the binding is determined from the actual type of the dynamic instance):

- The dynamic type does *not* implement the `IDynamicMetaObjectProvider` interface. In this case, the runtime uses reflection and its traditional method lookup and overload resolution logic before immediately executing the actions.
- The dynamic type implements the `IDynamicMetaObjectProvider` interface, by either implementing this interface by hand or by inheriting

the new dynamic type from the `System.Dynamic.DynamicObject` type supplied to make this easier.

Any traditional type of object can be declared as type `dynamic`. For all dynamic objects that don't implement the interface `IDynamicMetaObjectProvider`, the `Microsoft.CSharp.RuntimeBinder` is used, and reflection is employed to look up property and method invocations at runtime. The example code shown in Figure 8-1 shows the Intellisense balloon in Visual Studio 2010, which demonstrates an integer type declared as `dynamic`. (The runtime resolves the type by the initialization expression, just like using the local type inference `var` keyword.) No compile error occurs at design time or compile time, even though the method call is not defined anywhere in the project. When this code is executed, the runtime uses reflection in an attempt to find and execute the fictitious method `ThisMethodIsNotDefinedAnywhere`, which of course fails with the exception:

```
Microsoft.CSharp.RuntimeBinder.RuntimeBinderException: 'int' does
not contain a definition for 'ThisMethodIsNotDefinedAnywhere'
```

```
dynamic o = 1;
o.ThisMethodIsNotDefinedAnywhere();
(dynamic expression)
This operation will be resolved at runtime
```

FIGURE 8-1   Any object declared as type dynamic is resolved at runtime. No errors will be reported at compile time.

If that method had been actually declared, it would have been simply invoked just like any traditional method or property call.

The ability to have a type that doesn't implement the `IDynamicObject` interface should be rare. The `dynamic` keyword shouldn't be used in place of a proper type definition when that type is known at compile time. It also shouldn't be used in place of the `var` keyword when working with anonymous types, as that type is known at compile time. The `dynamic` keyword should only be used to declare `IDynamicMetaObjectProvider` implementers and for interoperating with other dynamic languages and for COM-Interop.

WHEN TO USE VAR AND DYNAMIC TYPE DECLARATIONS It might seem confusing as to which type definition should be used based on circumstance. Here are my recommendations:

Concrete type—Use whenever you know the type at coding time. If you know the type when defining a field, property, or return type—use it!

The var keyword—Use this when declaring an anonymous type or when capturing the result of a LINQ query projecting to an anonymous type.

The dynamic keyword—Use only when declaring a dynamic type, generally meaning a type that implements the `IDynamicMetaObjectProvider` interface. These can be custom types or one of the run-time binders provided by Microsoft for COM-Interop that interoperate with dynamic languages like IronPython and IronRuby. Declaring types that do not implement this interface incurs the overhead of reflection at runtime.

Specific binders are written to support specific purposes. IronRuby, IronPython, and COM-Interop are just a few of the bindings available to support dynamic language behavior from within C# 4.0. However, you can write your own and consume these types in order to solve some common coding problems, as you will see shortly in an example in which text file data is exposed using a custom dynamic type and this data is used as the source of a LINQ to Objects query.

Using Dynamic Types in LINQ Queries

Initially you might be disappointed to learn that dynamic types aren't supported in LINQ. LINQ relies exclusively on extension methods to carry out each query expression operation. Extension methods cannot be resolved at runtime due to the lack of information in the compiled assembly. Extension methods are introduced into scope by adding the assembly containing the extension into scope via a `using` clause, which is available at compile time for method resolutions, but not available at runtime—hence no LINQ support. However, this only means you can't define collection types as dynamic, but you can use dynamic types at the instance level (the types in the collections being queried), as you will see in the following example.

For this example we create a type that allows comma delimited text files to be read and queried in an elegant way, often useful when importing data from another application. By "elegant" I mean not hard-coding any column name definitions into string literals in our importing code, but rather, allowing direct access to fields just like they are traditional property accessors. This type of interface is often called a *fluent interface*. Given the sample CSV file content shown in Listing 8-5, the intention is to allow coders to directly reference the data columns in each row by their relevant header names, defined in the first row—that is FirstName, LastName, and State.

Listing 8-5 Comma separated value (CSV) file content used as example content

```
FirstName,LastName,State
Troy,Magennis,TX
Janet,Doherty,WA
```

The first row contains the column names for each row of the file, and this particular implementation expects this to always be the case. When writing LINQ queries against files of this format, referring to each row value in a column by the header name makes for easily comprehensible queries. The goal is to write the code shown in Listing 8-6, and this code compiling without a specific backing class from every CSV file type to be processed. (Think of it like coding against a dynamic anonymous type for the given input file header definition.)

Listing 8-6 Query code fluently reading CSV file content without a specific backing class

```
var q = from dynamic line in new CsvParser(content)
        where line.State == "WA"
        select line.LastName;
```

Dynamic typing enables us to do just that and with remarkably little code. The tradeoff is that any property name access isn't tested for type safety or existence during compile time. (The first time you will see an error is at runtime.) To fulfill the requirement of not wanting a backing class for each specific file, the line type shown previously must be of type dynamic. This is necessary to avoid the compile-time error that would be otherwise reported when accessing the State and LastName properties, which don't exist.

To create our new dynamic type, we need our type to implement `IDynamicMetaObjectProvider`, and Microsoft has supplied a starting point in the `System.Dynamic.DynamicObject` type. This type has virtual implementations of the required methods that allow a dynamic type to be built and allows the implementer to just override the specific methods needed for a given purpose. In this case, we need to override the `TryGetMember` method, which will be called whenever code tries to read a property member on an instance of this type. We will process each of these calls by returning the correct text out of the CSV file content for this line, based on the index position of the passed-in property name and the header position we read in as the first line of the file.

Listing 8-7 shows the basic code for this dynamic type. The essential aspects to support dynamic lookup of individual CSV fields within a line as simple property access calls are shown in this code. The property name is passed to the `TryGetMember` method in the `binder` argument, and can be retrieved by `binder.Name`, and the correct value looked up accordingly.

Listing 8-7   Class to represent a dynamic type that will allow the LINQ code (or any other code) to parse a single comma-separated line and access data at runtime based on the names in the header row of the text file

```
public class CsvLine : System.Dynamic.DynamicObject
{
    string[] _lineContent;
    List<string> _headers;

    public CsvLine(string line, List<string> headers)
    {
        this._lineContent = line.Split(',');
        this._headers = headers;
    }

    public override bool TryGetMember(
        GetMemberBinder binder,
        out object result )
    {
        result = null;

        // find the index position and get the value
        int index = _headers.IndexOf(binder.Name);
```

```
        if (index >= 0 && index < _lineContent.Length)
        {
            result = _lineContent[index];
            return true;
        }

        return false;
    }
}
```

To put in the plumbing required for parsing the first row, a second type is needed to manage this process, which is shown in Listing 8-8, and is called `CsvParser`. This is in place to determine the column headers to be used for access in each line after that and also the `IEnumerable` implementation that will furnish each line to any query (except the header line that contains the column names).

The constructor of the `CsvParser` type takes the CSV file content as a string and parses it into a string array of individual lines. The first row (as is assumed in this implementation) contains the column header names, and this is parsed into a `List<string>` so that the index positions of these column names can be subsequently used in the `CsvLine` type to find the correct column index position of that value in the data line being read. The `GetEnumerator` method simply skips the first line and then constructs a dynamic type `CsvLine` for each line after that until all lines have been enumerated.

Listing 8-8   The IEnumerable class that reads the header line and returns each line in the content as an instance of our CsvLine dynamic type

```
public class CsvParser : IEnumerable
{
    List<string> _headers;
    string[] _lines;

    public CsvParser(string csvContent)
    {
        _lines = csvContent.Split('\n');

        // grab the header row and remember positions
        if (_lines.Length > 0)
            _headers = _lines[0].Split(',').ToList();
```

```
    }

    public IEnumerator GetEnumerator()
    {
        // skip the header line
        bool header = true;

        foreach (var line in _lines)
            if (header)
                header = false;
            else
                yield return new CsvLine(line, _headers);
    }
}
```

Listing 8-9 shows the LINQ query that reads data from a CSV file and
filters based on one of the column values. The important aspects of this
example are the dynamic keyword in the from clause, and the ability to
directly access the properties State, FirstName, and LastName from an
instance of our CsvLine dynamic type. Even though there is no explicit
backing type for those properties, they are mapped from the header row in
the CSV file itself. This code will only compile in C# 4.0, and its output is
all of the rows (in this case just one) that have a value of "WA" in the third
column position (State), as shown in Output 8-2.

Listing 8-9   Sample LINQ query code that demonstrates how to use dynamic types in
order to improve code readability and to avoid the need for strict backing classes—see
Output 8-2

```
string content =
    "FirstName,LastName,State\n
    Troy,Magennis,TX\n
    Janet,Doherty,WA";

var q = from dynamic c in new CsvParser(content)
        where c.State == "WA"
        select c;

foreach (var c in q)
{
```

```
Console.WriteLine("{0}, {1} ({2})",
    c.LastName,
    c.FirstName,
    c.State);
}
```

Output 8-2

```
Doherty, Janet (WA)
```

As this example has shown, it is possible to mix dynamic types with LINQ. The key point to remember is that the actual element types can be dynamic, but not the collection being queried. In this case, we built a simple enumerator that reads the CSV file and returns an instance of our dynamic type. Any CSV file, as long as the first row contains legal column names (no spaces or special characters that C# can't resolve as a property name), can be coded against just as if a backing class containing those columns names was created by code.

COM-Interop and LINQ

COM interoperability has always been possible within C# and .NET; however, it was often less than optimal in how clean and easy the code was to write (or read). Earlier in this chapter, named arguments and optional parameters were introduced, which improve coding against COM objects. And with the additional syntax improvements offered by the dynamic type, the code readability and conciseness is further improved.

To demonstrate how **COM-Interop** and LINQ might be combined, the following example shows a desirable coding pattern to read the contents of a Microsoft Excel spreadsheet, and use that data as a source for a LINQ to Objects query.

```
const int stateCol = 5;

var q = from row in GetExcelRowEnumerator(filename, 1)
        where row[stateCol] == "WA"
        select row;
```

This query returns rows where the State column equals "WA" from the spreadsheet data shown in Figure 8-2. Microsoft Excel is often used as the source for importing raw data, and although there are many ways to import this data using code, the ability to run LINQ queries over these spreadsheets directly from C# is useful.

The strategy used to implement the Microsoft Excel interoperability and allow LINQ queries over Excel data is:

1. Add a COM-Interop reference to the Microsoft Excel library in order to code against its object model in C#.
2. Return the data from a chosen spreadsheet (by its filename) into an `IEnumerable` collection (row by row) that can be used as a source for a LINQ query.

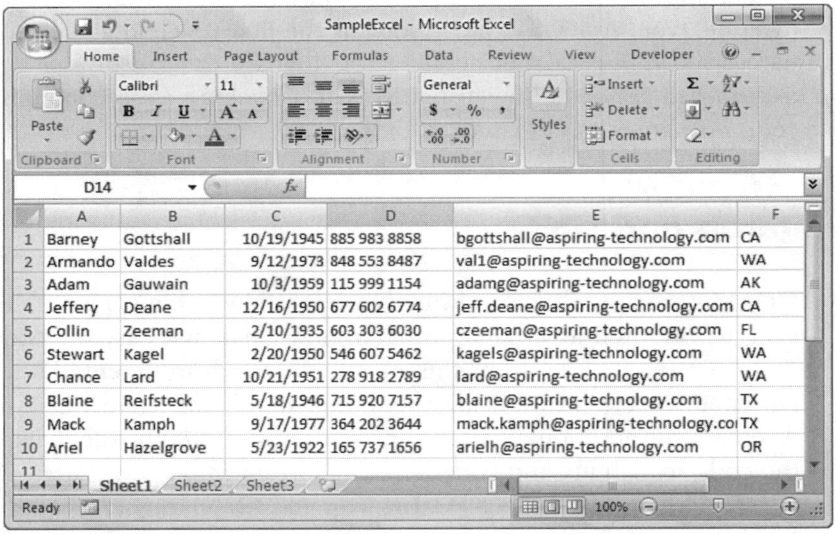

	A	B	C	D	E	F
1	Barney	Gottshall	10/19/1945	885 983 8858	bgottshall@aspiring-technology.com	CA
2	Armando	Valdes	9/12/1973	848 553 8487	val1@aspiring-technology.com	WA
3	Adam	Gauwain	10/3/1959	115 999 1154	adamg@aspiring-technology.com	AK
4	Jeffery	Deane	12/16/1950	677 602 6774	jeff.deane@aspiring-technology.com	CA
5	Collin	Zeeman	2/10/1935	603 303 6030	czeeman@aspiring-technology.com	FL
6	Stewart	Kagel	2/20/1950	546 607 5462	kagels@aspiring-technology.com	WA
7	Chance	Lard	10/21/1951	278 918 2789	lard@aspiring-technology.com	WA
8	Blaine	Reifsteck	5/18/1946	715 920 7157	blaine@aspiring-technology.com	TX
9	Mack	Kamph	9/17/1977	364 202 3644	mack.kamph@aspiring-technology.co	TX
10	Ariel	Hazelgrove	5/23/1922	165 737 1656	arielh@aspiring-technology.com	OR
11						

FIGURE 8-2 Sample Microsoft Excel spreadsheet to query using LINQ.

Adding a COM-Interop Reference

COM-Interop programming in C# 4.0 is greatly improved in one way because of a new style of interop backing class that is created when you add a COM reference to a project. The improved backing class makes use of optional parameters and named arguments and the dynamic type features that were introduced earlier this chapter. Listing 8-10 demonstrates the old code required to access an Excel spreadsheet via COM, and contrasts it with the new programming style.

Listing 8-10   Comparing the existing way to call COM-Interop and the new way using the improved COM reference libraries

```
// Old way - old COM reference and no optional parameters
var excel = new Microsoft.Office.Interop.Excel.Application();

Microsoft.Office.Interop.Excel.Workbook workBook =
    excel.Workbooks.Open(
    fileName,
    Type.Missing, Type.Missing, Type.Missing, Type.Missing,
    Type.Missing, Type.Missing, Type.Missing, Type.Missing,
    Type.Missing, Type.Missing, Type.Missing, Type.Missing,
    Type.Missing, Type.Missing);

// New Way - new COM reference and using optional parameters
var excel = new Microsoft.Office.Interop.Excel.Application();

Microsoft.Office.Interop.Excel.Workbook workBook =
    excel.Workbooks.Open(fileName);
```

When a reference is added to a COM component using Visual Studio, a backing class is generated to allow coding against that model. Listing 8-11 shows one method of the Excel COM programming model generated by Visual Studio 2008. With no optional parameters, all arguments must be passed when calling these methods.

Listing 8-11   Old style COM-Interop backing class added by Visual Studio 2008 for part of the Microsoft Excel 12 Object Library

```
Microsoft.Office.Interop.Excel.Workbook Open(
    string Filename,
    object UpdateLinks,
    object ReadOnly,
    object Format,
    object Password,
    object WriteResPassword,
    object IgnoreReadOnlyRecommended,
```

```
object Origin,
object Delimiter,
object Editable,
object Notify,
object Converter,
object AddToMru,
object Local,
object CorruptLoad)
```

Listing 8-12 shows the Visual Studio 2010 COM-Interop backing class. The addition of the default values turned all but one of the parameters (the `Filename` argument) into optional parameters; therefore, all but the filename can be omitted when this method is called, allowing the simplification shown in Listing 8-10.

Listing 8-12   New style COM-Interop backing class added by Visual Studio 2010—notice the optional parameters and the dynamic types

```
Microsoft.Office.Interop.Excel.Workbook Open(
    string Filename,
    dynamic UpdateLinks = null,
    dynamic ReadOnly = null,
    dynamic Format = null,
    dynamic Password = null,
    dynamic WriteResPassword = null,
    dynamic IgnoreReadOnlyRecommended = null,
    dynamic Origin = null,
    dynamic Delimiter = null,
    dynamic Editable = null,
    dynamic Notify = null,
    dynamic Converter = null,
    dynamic AddToMru = null,
    dynamic Local = null,
    dynamic CorruptLoad = null)
```

Adding a COM reference is painless in Visual Studio. The step-by-step process is:

1. Open the Visual Studio C# project that the COM reference is being added to.

2. Choose `Project-Add Reference...` from the main menu (or right-click the References icon in the Solution Explorer and click `Add Reference...`).
3. Click the COM tab and find the COM Object you want to reference from within your project, as seen in Figure 8-3.
4. Click the OK button for the Add Reference dialog box.

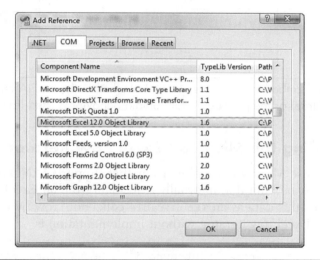

FIGURE 8-3 The Add Reference dialog box in Visual Studio 2010.

NEW FEATURE: NOT DEPLOYING PRIMARY INTEROP

ASSEMBLIES Primary Interop Assemblies are large pre-built .NET assemblies built for certain COM interfaces (like MS Excel and MS Word) to allow strongly typed coding at design time. These assemblies often were larger than the application being built (and loaded separately at runtime) and often caused version issues because they were deployed independently to the compiled application.

C# 4.0 introduces a no-PIA feature that compiles only the parts of the Primary Interop Assembly actually used into the assembly (much smaller) and avoids having to load a separate assembly at runtime (much faster).

This is the default behavior in Visual Studio 2010. To return to deploying the full PIA assembly (the default in previous versions of Visual Studio), set the Embed Interop Types property on the reference in question as shown in Figure 8-4.

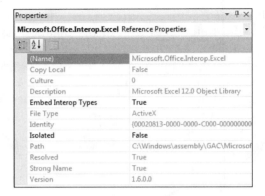

FIGURE 8-4 Set the Embed Interop Types to control whether the no-PIA feature is used (the default behavior, true) or the previous Visual Studio behavior is used (false).

Building the Microsoft Excel Row Iterator

To expose Microsoft Excel in a way that supports LINQ queries, an iterator must be built that internally reads data from an Excel spreadsheet and exposes this data as an `IEnumerable` collection, row by row. The skeleton of the Excel row iterator, without implementation is:

```
public IEnumerable<List<dynamic>> GetExcelRowEnumerator(
    string fileName,
    int sheetIndex)
{
    // Declare an array to hold our values
    // Create the COM reference to Excel
    // Open the workbook by filename
    // Get the excel worksheet, 1 for the first, etc.
    // Find the used range in the sheet
    // Read in the value array for all used rows and columns
    // Close Excel
    // Build and yield each row, one at a time
}
```

This iterator declaration takes arguments of a fully qualified filename to an Excel spreadsheet and a worksheet index as a one-based number and returns the values in each row (with each column's value as an item in a

`List<dynamic>` collection) from the chosen worksheet in the selected Excel file. The full implementation of this algorithm is shown in Listing 8-13.

This implementation isn't the strategy to be used for extremely large spreadsheets because it buffers the entire dataset into an in-memory array with a single call and then builds the row results from this array of values. This technique, however, is the fastest way to access data from Excel using COM-Interop because it avoids single cell or row access and keeps Excel open (a large executable memory footprint) for as short a time as possible. If an application is required to read a massive spreadsheet of data, experiment with alternative value access strategies supported by Excel's extensive object model, row by row perhaps, to avoid completely loading the entire array into memory upfront. This implementation is fine in performance and memory usage for most purposes.

THE USING DECLARATION FOR THE FOLLOWING EXAMPLES

To avoid having to prefix all calls to the Interop library with long namespaces, I added the following `using` declaration at the top of my class file:

```
using Excel = Microsoft.Office.Interop.Excel;
```

This simplified the code declarations and allowed me to use Excel.Application, Excel.Workbook (and others) rather than Microsoft.Office.Interop.Excel.Application, Microsoft.Office.Interop.Excel.Workbook, and so on.

Listing 8-13 Full code listing for an Excel row enumerator. Calling this method enumerates the values of a row in an Excel spreadsheet.

```csharp
public IEnumerable<List<dynamic>> GetExcelRowEnumerator(
    string fileName,
    int sheetIndex)
{
    // declare an array to hold our values
    object[,] valueArray = null;

    // create the COM reference to Excel
    var excel = new Excel.Application();
    try
    {
```

```
        // open the workbook by filename
        Excel.Workbook workBook =
                excel.Workbooks.Open(fileName);

        if ( workBook != null &&
            sheetIndex < workBook.Sheets.Count )
        {
            // get the worksheet, 1 for the first, etc.
            Excel.Worksheet sheet =
                workBook.Sheets[sheetIndex];

            // find the used range in the sheet
            Excel.Range usedRange = sheet.UsedRange;

            // read in the value array, this is the fastest
            // way to get all values in one hit.
            valueArray = usedRange.get_Value(
                Excel.XlRangeValueDataType.xlRangeValueDefault);
        }

        workBook.Close(false, fileName);
    }
    finally
    {
        // finished with Excel now, close.
        excel.Quit();
    }

    // build and yield each row at a time
    for ( int rowIndex = 1;
            rowIndex <= valueArray.GetLength(0);
            rowIndex++)
    {
        List<dynamic> row =
            new List<dynamic>(
                valueArray.GetLength(1));

        // build a list of column values for the row
        for (int colIndex = 1;
            colIndex <= valueArray.GetLength(1);
            colIndex++)
        {

            row.Add(
```

```
            valueArray[rowIndex, colIndex]);
        }

        yield return row;
    }
}
```

Writing LINQ queries against Microsoft Excel data, like that shown in Figure 8-2, can be written in the code form shown in Listing 8-14. Output 8-3 shows the three rows returned from this code, which is all rows that have a State value of 'WA.'

Listing 8-14 Example code for reading the data from an Excel spreadsheet and running a LINQ query over its contents—see Output 8-3

```
string filename = Path.Combine(
    Environment.CurrentDirectory, "Data/SampleExcel.xlsx");


const int firstNameCol = 0;
const int lastNameCol = 1;
const int stateCol = 5;

var q = from row in GetExcelRowEnumerator(filename, 1)
        where row[stateCol] == "WA"
        select row;

Console.WriteLine("Customers in WA ({0})", q.Count());

foreach (var row in q)
{
    Console.WriteLine("{0}, {1}",
        row[lastNameCol].ToUpper(), row[firstNameCol] );
}
```

Output 8-3

```
Customers in WA (3)
VALDES, Armando
KAGEL, Stewart
LARD, Chance
```

The return type of the row values is declared as type `List<dynamic>`. It easily could have been declared as type `List<object>`. The downside of declaring the values as type of `object` rather than `dynamic` comes down to the ability to treat the value members as the underlying type. For example, in Listing 8-14 the statement `row[lastNameCol].ToUpper()` would fail if the element types were declared as `object`. The `object` type doesn't have a method called `ToUpper`, even though the underlying type it is representing is a string. And to access that method a type cast needs to be added, bloating the code out to `((string)row[lastNameCol]).ToUpper()`. Declaring the element type as dynamic in the collection allows the runtime to look up method names using reflection on the underlying type at runtime, however the particular type of that column value is declared as in Excel (in this case a string, but some columns are `DateTime` and `double`). The removal of the type casting when calling methods or properties on object types simplifies and improves code readability, at the expense of performance.

The `GetExcelRowEnumerator` method could be enhanced by combining the header row reading and accessibility in a similar fashion to that used by dynamic lookup in Listing 8-7, which would eliminate the need to hardcode the column index positions and allow the row data to be accessed by column header name using simple property access syntax.

Summary

This chapter introduced the new language features of C# 4.0 and demonstrated how they can be combined to extend the LINQ to Objects story. The examples provided showed how to improve the coding model around reading data from CSV text file sources and how to combine data from Microsoft Excel using COM-Interop into LINQ to Object queries.

References

1. Ecma International History from the Ecma International website hosted at http://www.ecma-international.org/memento/history.htm.

2. Ecma-334—C# Language Specification from the Ecma International website at http://www.ecma-international.org/publications/standards/Ecma-334.htm.

CHAPTER 9

PARALLEL LINQ TO OBJECTS

Goals of this chapter:

- Discuss the drivers for parallel programming, and how Parallel LINQ fits that story.
- Demonstrate how to turn sequential queries into parallel queries using Parallel LINQ.
- Demonstrate how to create a custom parallel operator.

This chapter introduces Parallel LINQ to Objects. PLINQ introduces data parallelism into LINQ queries, giving a performance boost on multi-core and multiprocessor machines while making the results predictable and correct. This chapter also demonstrates how to build your own parallel operator.

Parallel Programming Drivers

Microsoft has invested heavily in .NET Framework 4 and Visual Studio 2010 to allow all developers to safely and easily embrace parallel programming concepts within applications. The main driver for the Parallel Programming model is simply that the era of massive doubling and redoubling of processor speed is apparently over, and therefore, the era of our code automatically doubling in speed as hardware improves is also coming an end. This breakdown in Moore's Law (proposed by an Intel executive that predicted a doubling of CPU processor speed every two years), as it is commonly known, was brought to a screeching halt due to thermal and power constraints within the heart of a PC in the silicon processor that executes programs. To counter this roadblock and to allow computing speed to continue to scale, processor manufacturers and computer hardware designers have simply added more than one processor into the hardware that runs code.

However, not all programming techniques, languages, compilers, or developers for that matter automatically scale to writing multiple core compatible code. This leaves a lot of unused processing power on the table—CPU processing power that could improve responsiveness and user experience of applications.

Microsoft's *MSDN Magazine* published an article titled "Paradigm Shift—Design Considerations for Parallel Programming" by David Callahan,[1] which offers Microsoft's insight regarding the drivers and approach Microsoft is taking in response to the need for parallel programming techniques. It begins by setting the scene:

> ...today, performance is improved by the addition of processors. So-called multicore systems are now ubiquitous. Of course, the multicore approach improves performance only when software can perform multiple activities at the same time. Functions that perform perfectly well using sequential techniques must be written to allow multiple processors to be used if they are to realize the performance gains promised by the multiprocessor machines.

And concludes with the call to action:

> The shift to parallelism is an inflection point for the software industry where new techniques must be adopted. Developers must embrace parallelism for those portions of their applications that are time sensitive today or that are expected to run on larger data sets tomorrow.

The main take-away regarding parallel programming drivers is that there is no more free application performance boost just because of a hardware CPU speed upgrade; for applications to run faster in the future, programming techniques that support multiple processors (and cores) need to be the standard approach. The techniques employed must also not be limited in how many CPU cores the code was originally authored from. The application needs to detect and automatically embrace the available cores on the executing hardware (which will likely be orders of magnitude larger in processing power) whether that be 2 cores or 64 cores. Code must be authored in a way that can scale accordingly without specifically compiled versions.

History of Processor Speed and Multicore Processors

Looking back at processor history, there was a 1GHz speed processor in 2000, which doubled in speed in 2001 to 2Ghz, and topped 3GHz in 2002; however, it has been a long hiatus from seeing processor speed increasing at that rate. In 2008 processor clock speeds were only just approaching 4Ghz. In fact, when clock speed stopped increasing, so did manufacturer marketing the speed of processors; speed was replaced by various measures of instructions per second.[2] Power consumption, heat dissipation, and memory latency are just some of the plethora of limiting factors halting pure CPU clock-speed increases. Another technique for improving CPU performance had to be found in order to keep pace with consumer demand.

The limit of pure clock-speed scaling wasn't a surprise to this industry as a whole, and Intel engineers, who first published an article in the October 1989 issue of *IEEE Spectrum* ("Microprocessors Circa 2000"[3]) predicted the use of multicore processor architecture to improve the end-user experience when using PCs. Intel delivered on their promise in 2005, as did competing processor companies, and it is almost certain that any computer bought today has multiple cores built into each microprocessor chip, and for the lucky few, multiple microprocessor chips built into the motherboard. Rather than straight improvement in processor clock speed, there are now more processor cores to do the work. Intel in their whitepaper "Intel Multi-Core Processor Architecture Development Backgrounder"[4] clearly defines in an understandable way what "multicore processors" consist of:

> Explained most simply, multi-core processor architecture entails silicon design engineers placing two or more Intel Pentium processor-based "execution cores," or computational engines, within a single processor. This multi-core processor plugs directly into a single processor socket, but the operating system perceives each of its execution cores as a discrete logical processor with all the associated execution resources.

> The idea behind this implementation of the chip's internal architecture is in essence a "divide and conquer" strategy. In other words, by divvying up the computational work performed by the single Pentium microprocessor core in traditional microprocessors and spreading it over multiple execution cores, a multi-core processor can perform more work within a given clock cycle. Thus,

it is designed to deliver a better overall user experience. To enable this improvement, the software running on the platform must be written such that it can spread its workload across multiple execution cores. This functionality is called thread-level parallelism or "threading." Applications and operating systems (such as Microsoft Windows XP) that are written to support it are referred to as "threaded" or "multi-threaded."

The final sentence of this quote is important: "Applications and operating systems...that are written to support it..." Although the operating system running code almost certainly supports multi-threading, not all applications are coded in a fashion that fully exploits that ability. In fact, the current use of multi-threading in applications is to improve the perceived performance of an application, rather than actual performance in most cases—a subtle distinction to be explored shortly.

Cores Versus Processors Versus CPUs

The operating system running on your PC (or server) exploits all processor cores in all physical processors it has available to it—aggregating these as a total number of available CPUs. An example is that if a 4-processor machine is running 4-core processors, it will show in the operating system as 16 CPUs. (Multiply the number of physical processors by the number of cores in each processor.) Sixteen CPUs is now common in server machines, and the number of CPUs is increasing due to both increased physical socket and core count growth. Expect 32, 64, or even 128+ CPU machines to be available at a commercial level now and a consumer level shortly.

Multi-Threading Versus Code Parallelism

Multi-threading is about programming a specific number of threads to deal with specific operations. Parallel programming is detecting the number of processors and splitting the work of a particular operation across those known CPUs (processor times cores). Splitting work in applications across multiple threads does introduce a form of concurrency into applications; however, multi-threading doesn't natively offer computational performance improvement (in most cases) and comes at a high price in code complexity when built using current programming paradigms.

The parallel programming goal is to make sure applications take advantage of multiple cores for improving computational performance and continue to improve performance as more cores are added over time. This doesn't simply occur by making applications multi-threaded. In fact, badly implemented threading code can hurt performance. True code parallelism offers the same benefits as multi-threading offers, but in a way that aims to improve computational performance of applications, whilst safeguarding against common concurrency defects and issues.

Pure multi-threading is most commonly used to improve the perception of performance in an application. The classic example is for common web browser applications; web browsers like Internet Explorer, Firefox, Safari all download and display the pages' HTML content first, while behind the scenes they are gathering and progressively displaying images as they download over time. Why? If it took 15 seconds to download an entire page and images, blocking the user interface from accepting a response until it is complete, end users would feel (deservedly) unsatisfied. Launching the retrieval of images on a separate background thread keeps the user-interface thread available for other user-input—"Cancel, I made a mistake" or "Changed my mind, go here instead" as examples.

Building applications with the snappiness multi-threading concepts offers is addictive, although it is often difficult to synchronize access to shared resources like the user's input or in-memory data. The permutations of what thread finishes and starts before another and the difficulty of debugging these defects leads to many abandoned attempts at improving perceived performance. Comprehending how to do even the most simple multi-threading application task without spending hours finding random crashes and application freezes is challenging and very time-consuming and mentally taxing. (These types of defects are called *race conditions*, the cause of many famous software production problems, including the North American Blackout of 2003, which was partially attributed to a software application race condition.[5])

The following are some problems with using threading alone for code parallelism:

- **Complex to write**—Race conditions are hard to envision and debug.
- **The correct number of threads is best equal to the number of CPUs**—However, this changes from machine to machine. How do I spread the work required across multiple threads? How many threads are optimal?

What Is a Race Condition?

Wikipedia has the best explanation I've found to explain what a race condition is to a "manager"[6]:

> Applications can run at different speeds on different computer systems or different situations (i.e., variations in Internet performance or processor loading), which may cause the application to crash randomly on some systems and never on others. The unpredictable nature of an intermittent bug caused by a race condition is a frequent source of frustration within the profession of software development. Example: A horse race represents the computer application. Each horse represents a specific element in the application, which are all running in parallel, such as user interface graphics versus network communications running concurrently. The software may require that a specific horse must win the race in order for the application to run properly. The application may work flawlessly if horse #5 finishes first, while the application crashes if the wrong horse finishes the race. One possible solution to this problem is to add synchronization to guarantee that horse #5 finishes before #2. Metaphorically, this is similar to jockey #2 and #5 teaming up to let #5 run ahead of #2.

- **What if not all work takes equal time to run?**—This could leave some CPUs idle when they could be taking on work overloading another CPU.
- **Threads are heavy**—Threads take memory and time to set up, manage, and teardown. Create too many of them and applications can exhaust available resources. Threads are allocated 1MB of memory by default by the CLR, not the sort of overhead you blindly want to assign. (See blog posting on the issue by Joe Duffy.[7])

The underpinnings for all parallelism features, including the parallel extensions and Parallel LINQ, are threads. However, these libraries abstract away the direct manipulation of threading and give developers an easier interface to code against. The Task Parallel Library and Parallel LINQ reusable libraries allow a lighter-weight way of scheduling work and having that work efficiently executed across multiple CPUs. Microsoft has retained all of the benefits introduced through multi-threading applications but solved the problems working at the CPU's thread level.

Application multi-threading advantages:

- Maintaining application UI responsiveness during long-running processes.
- Allows multiple requests or processes to be handled in relative isolation, that is, each input web request can be handled by a server on a different thread in isolation; if one fails, the others continue to function.
- Offload work can occur in the background—priority allows many applications to coexist sharing the available resources.

Application parallelism advantages:

- Same advantages as multi-threading offers.
- Computational performance is improved.
- Performance scales as more cores/processors are added without explicit user code to specify the hardware configuration.

Hopefully, you will see that multi-threading underpins all parallel programming techniques because it is the technology supported at a processor level. However, the perils (covered shortly) and complexity of actually utilizing threading to not only improve perceived performance, but actually reduce processing time, requires clever coding practices. Microsoft's Parallel Extensions offer an approachable on-ramp for parallelizing general application code and goes a long way to addressing the common obstacles that surface when writing parallel applications.

Parallelism Expectations, Hindrances, and Blockers

Parallel program performance isn't always a linear scaling based on the number of CPU cores, as will be shown shortly through examples. (Doubling the number of cores doesn't halve the execution time.) There are many factors that contribute to supporting and hindering performance improvements using parallel programming techniques. It is important to understand these hindrances and blockers in order to leverage the full power of the toolset provided and to know when to invoke its power.

Amdahl's Law—You Will Still Be as Slow as the Longest Sequential Part

Amdahl's Law defines the fundamental maximum performance improvement that can be expected for parallel computing. Amdahl's Law models the performance gain of a parallel implementation over its sequential counterpart. It simply states that the maximum parallel performance improvement is limited by the time needed by any sequential part of an algorithm or program.[8]

Amdahl's formula is

Overall performance gain = 1 / ((1-P) + (P/Speedup))

(P = proportion supporting parallelization, Speedup = 2 for two CPUs, etc.)

It seems reasonable to determine that if a sequential program was spread across two cores, the maximum performance gain would be 2x. However, in reality, not all of the program can run in parallel, and the actual performance gain will be lower than 2x. How much lower? That depends on how much of the algorithm supports parallelization. If a sequential algorithm implementation takes one second, and 20% of the program is written to support parallel execution on a dual-core machine (2 CPUs), the maximum performance boost from parallelization would be 1/ ((1-0.2) + (0.2/2)) = 1.11 times improvement.

Amdahl's Law is handy to put correct expectations around the benefit and time spent when optimizing an application. The more code you write to support parallelization (and therefore decrease the amount of sequential time), the closer to the theoretical maximum speedup you approach. (If you want to read more, seek out John L. Gustafson's article that looks at the shortcomings and reevaluation of Amdahl's Law with respect to massively parallel systems, like those becoming available now at http://www.scl.ameslab.gov/Publications/Gus/AmdahlsLaw/Amdahls.html.)

The key point is that to fully embrace parallelism and to achieve closer performance gains to the theoretical best possible performance (doubling for two processors, quadrupling for four, and so on), the algorithm and work partitioning should be designed to limit the sequential time required for a program.

Parallel Overhead—Finding the Ideal Work Partition Size

There is overhead in running an application across multiple CPUs. Some work is involved in forking, merging, and managing the partitioning of work that each thread (and eventually CPU) will execute. It should make sense that if the work being performed in parallel takes less time than the overhead of making that code execute in parallel, then the code will take longer to execute.

There is art in understanding what granularity work should be partitioned. Too small and you will actually harm performance; too big and you are not taking advantage of scheduling tasks across multiple CPUs. There is no substitute for testing performance tradeoffs using different granularity of work partitioning.

The key point here is that parallelism doesn't come completely free; there is a sweet-spot for work partition size, and this needs to be considered when writing parallelized code. Testing and profiling is the only way to be sure the work time is more than the overhead for parallelizing that work.

Synchronization—Parallel Partitions Working as a Team

Sometimes code running on one CPU needs to access data from another. This synchronization harms performance because the object needed has to be locked, and other parallel execution paths might need to wait for that lock to be removed before they can proceed, so it gets very hard to predict actual performance gains.

The best possible performance can be achieved when tasks being performed in parallel have no shared data; they are completely isolated, and no synchronization locks are needed. This takes careful design and sometimes means creating parallel work at a different granularity or changing your algorithm approach in such a way that the only synchronization needs to occur at the completion of the task (rather than throughout).

The key point is to keep parallel tasks as autonomous and self-contained as possible. Any external synchronization will reduce performance or introduce hard-to-debug race conditions.

Data Ordering

Ordering and parallelism have a natural tension. When a dataset order cannot be impacted, the implementation of how parallel tasks are executed and the results merged narrows considerably, causing a performance decrease. In most cases, the parallel implementation will still be superior in performance to the sequential implementation, but for the best parallelization, try and limit order dependence.

The key point is that if ordering is required to be predictable, then parallel performance is traded. This can often be minimized by increasing the granularity of the task to run order dependent code in one task, or order dependent code executed sequentially after the parallel processing has been carried out.

Exceptions—Who Stops When Something Fails?

Exception that occurs in a parallel task offers great challenges. How this exception is trapped and where that exception is marshaled is problematic to design, predict, and implement. Sounds obvious, but avoid exceptions! You have to be prudent and carry out more precondition checking to handle exception cases in an organized fashion without resorting to throwing an exception or having one raised on your behalf.

Dealing with These Constraints

Dealing with and understanding the constraints of writing operational parallel code is an important skill. Microsoft's Parallel Extensions offer solutions to the general challenges, but in order to successfully write code that performs exceptionally in a multicore environment, you often need to explicitly tell the executing framework what your requirements are for your specific case. For example, if the data order needs to be maintained, you need to tell the compiler that is the case. You will pay a performance penalty (maybe still faster than a sequential algorithm, maybe not), but for the final result to be correct, the compiler must be told to maintain the current data order.

Microsoft has addressed the issues of parallelizing data problems through a specific technology called Parallel LINQ. The technology tackles parallelizing data querying and manipulation in a coherent fashion without causing data corruption or incorrect results. It still has to abide by the constraints and limitations as listed here, but the heavy lifting and consistent programming pattern it provides reduces the variation in personal techniques.

LINQ Data Parallelism

LINQ queries are designed for working with sets of data and provide a convenient vehicle for taking the complexity out of coding data querying and manipulation tasks. Parallel LINQ to Objects is a set of standard query operators similar (almost identical) to the sequential standard query operators that are implemented using the Parallel Extensions for .NET 4, a library of data structures and thread-pool implementations that help a developer perform efficient parallelization. The implementation of these parallel standard query operator variants use the entire arsenal offered by the parallel framework extensions in order to improve the throughput of the LINQ queries; however, as will be quickly evident, it is not wise to just use these operators as direct replacements to their sequential counterparts in all cases.

To understand the benefit of Parallel LINQ queries, the following example shows the results and performance of a LINQ query before and after parallelization. The actual performance increase and CPU load during the sequential and parallel example are explored here for you to see that traditional sequential queries may not (and will not) use all of the CPU processing power natively. This CPU usage pattern will be contrasted against the CPU usage when Parallel LINQ is invoked.

Parallelizing a Query—Geonames Example

Geonames.org is an online geographic database of over eight million place names. The files are available for download under a Creative Commons license, and the website contains regional subsets of data and also a complete file of all place names (780MB when I downloaded it for this example). The files are in a specific tab-separated text structure, with over 15 columns of data, including elevation, name, and a two-letter country code. The example query will simply iterate this file and return a sorted list of all entries with an elevation greater than 8,000 meters.

NOTE   .NET 4 introduced new overloads into the `File` and `Directory` classes. `File.ReadLines` previously returned a `string[]` of all lines in a file. A new overload returns an `IEnumerable<string>`, which allows you to iterate a file (using this method, you could always iterate the file manually) without loading the entire file contents into memory. This helped a lot with our 780MB text file parsing.

Geonames Sequential LINQ

The LINQ query will iterate all the lines in a file containing all the Geonames content, looking for all places with an elevation greater than 8,000 meters and then ordering them from highest elevation to lowest elevation. Listing 9-1 shows the basic query to parse and query our target text file. (Full code and instructions for getting these samples working are available at http://hookedonlinq.com/LINQBookSamples.ashx. The Geonames AllCountries.txt text file is freely downloadable from Geonames.org at http://download.geonames.org/export/dump.) When this query is executed, the total CPU usage uneasily steadies around 55%, and 22.3 seconds later (this will of course be machine-dependent, including hard-drive speed), the results are returned. The Console output from this example is shown in Output 9-1.

Listing 9-1 Geonames parsing sequential LINQ query—CPU utilization is shown in Figure 9-1—Console output is shown in Output 9-1

```
const int nameColumn = 1;
const int countryColumn = 8;
const int elevationColumn = 15;

var lines = File.ReadLines(
      Path.Combine( Environment.CurrentDirectory,
                   "Data/AllCountries.txt"));

var q = from line in lines
        let fields = line.Split(new char[] { '\t' })
        let elevation = string.IsNullOrEmpty(
                fields[elevationColumn]) ?
                0 : int.Parse(fields[elevationColumn])
        where elevation > 8000 // elevation in m's
        orderby elevation descending
        select new
        {
            name = fields[nameColumn] ?? "",
            elevation = elevation,
            country = fields[countryColumn]
        };

foreach (var x in q)
{
    if (x != null)
        Console.WriteLine("{0} ({1}m) - located in {2}",
            x.name, x.elevation, x.country);
}
```

Output 9-1

```
Mount Everest (8850m) - located in NP
K2 (8611m) - located in PK
Kānchenjunga (8586m) - located in NP
Lo-tzu Feng (8516m) - located in NP
Qowowuyag (8201m) - located in CN
Dhaulāgiri (8167m) - located in NP
Manāslu (8156m) - located in NP
Nanga Parbat (8126m) - located in PK
Annapūrna Himāl (8091m) - located in NP
Annapurna 1 (8091m) - located in NP
Gasherbrum Shan (8068m) - located in PK
Broad Feng (8047m) - located in PK
Gasherbrum II Feng (8035m) - located in PK
Xixabangma Feng (8027m) - located in CN
...
```

During the processing of the file, a capture of the CPU utilization graph shows that one core was doing most of the processing, and although it had peaks, the average CPU usage was well below what was available with dual cores, as shown in Figure 9-1. The average displayed throughout for both CPUs was 55%. The actual time will differ from computer to computer and run from run, but for this experiment, the numbers will serve as a comparative benchmark.

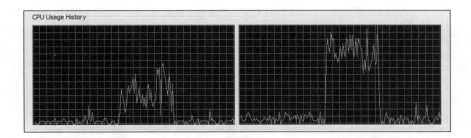

FIGURE 9-1 CPU utilization for Geoname sequential LINQ query—total time: 22.6 seconds.

Geonames Parallel LINQ

It is a very simple code change to turn a sequential query into a parallel query, although as is discussed later in this chapter, no one should blindly make all queries parallel. In most basic terms the extension `.AsParallel()` added to any `IEnumerable<T>` source will cause the parallel query operators to be invoked. Taking the query part from the code listed in Listing 9-1, the parallel-equivalent query utilizing Parallel LINQ is shown in Listing 9-2. (The only change is shown in bold.)

Listing 9-2   Geonames parsing parallel LINQ query—CPU utilization is shown in Figure 9-2 —Console output is shown in Output 9-1

```
var q = from line in lines.AsParallel()
        let fields = line.Split(new char[] { '\t' })
        let elevation = string.IsNullOrEmpty(
                fields[elevationColumn]) ?
                0 : int.Parse(fields[elevationColumn])
        where elevation > 8000 // elevation in m's
        orderby elevation descending
        select new
        {
            name = fields[nameColumn] ?? "",
            elevation = elevation,
            country = fields[countryColumn]
        };
```

When the query in Listing 9-2 is executed, the total CPU usage steadies quickly to around 95%, and 14.1 seconds later as shown in Figure 9-2 (this will of course be machine-dependent, including hard-drive speed), the identical results to the sequential query are furnished. CPU core usage

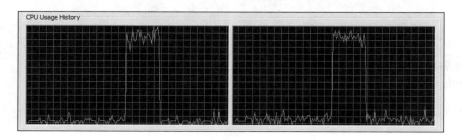

FIGURE 9-2   CPU utilization for Geoname parallel LINQ query—total time: 14.1 seconds.

is much more balanced and even throughout the query's execution, not perfectly even but far superior to the sequential version. Although the query didn't run twice as fast (as might be expected on a dual-core machine), the speed improvement is significant and was solely achieve by adding an `.AsParallel()` to the sequential query.

Falling short of the perfect doubling of performance in this case is due to the constraints spoken about earlier (Amdahl's Law, ordering, and so on); there is overhead in managing the parallelization process and sorting and is to a large degree limited by the disk access speed. It is important to also realize that if this same test had been run on a quad-core processor, the results would have been closer to a four times increase in performance with no additional code changes. (Although never exceeding, and who knows when your hard-drive access speed limits improvement, the key point is no code changes are required to take advantage of more cores.)

Having seen this example, understanding what actually occurred behind the scenes to parallelize a LINQ helps you realize what queries will substantially be improved by adding the `AsParallel` extension to a data source and what queries will actually degrade in performance.

What Happens During a Parallel LINQ Query?

The general parallelization process for a query is to partition the work, hand off the work to worker processes running on different threads, and merge the results on completion. To achieve this general process, a query marked to execute as parallel goes through the following (much simplified here for clarity) process by the Parallel LINQ runtime:

1. Query analysis (Will parallelism help?)
2. Partitioning
3. Parallel execution
4. Merging the parallel results

Each of these steps is covered briefly here in order to help you understand how queries might be structured for best parallel performance.

Query Analysis

The first step when a LINQ query is passed to the Parallel LINQ execution engine is query analysis. The query pattern is examined to determine if it is a candidate for parallelization improvement with respect to time and memory resources. If it isn't, then the query will be executed sequentially.

The runtime doesn't look at the size of the data or how much code is in the delegate functions; it simply examines (at this time, but who knows in future updates) the shape of the query and determines if it is worth the parallel overhead. The query can be forced to execute in parallel (or not) if the conservative nature of the run-time decision process isn't acceptable for a given case. To force a query to execute in parallel, add a `WithExecutionMode` extension to the `ParallelQuery` source. There are two values for the enumeration, `default` and `ForceParallelism`, which should not need further description.

```
source
  .AsParallel()
  .WithExecutionMode(
    ParallelExecutionMode.ForceParallelism)
```

There can be at most a single `WithExecutionMode` per query, even if that query is composed using the result of a previous query. Multiple `WithExecutionMode` extensions will cause a `System.InvalidOperationException` at runtime with the message:

```
The WithExecutionMode operator may be used at most once in
a query.
```

Microsoft has said that they will continue to evolve the query assessment over time and devise new algorithms for improving the parallel performance of different query patterns that currently would fall back to sequential execution. Once the framework decides that a query is a candidate for parallelization, it moves onto partitioning the data, which is simply splitting the input data for efficient execution in chunks on multiple cores.

Partitioning Data

Parallel LINQ has a number of data partitioning schemes it uses to segment the data for different worker processes. For example, if an input source has one hundred elements, when this query is run on a dual-core machine, the Parallel LINQ execution engine might break the data into two partitions of 50 elements for parallel execution. This is a simplistic case, and in practice, partitioning the data is more complex, and the actual chosen partitioning scheme depends on the operators used in the query, among other factors.

The built-in partition schemes at the time of writing are called *chunk*, *range*, *striped*, and *hash*. Each of these data partitioning schemes suits a certain set of source data types and operator scenarios; the parallel runtime chooses the appropriate one and partitions the data for execution when a worker process asks for more work.

You are not limited to the partitioners Microsoft has built-in. They have allowed for custom partitioners to be written for a specific purpose; this topic is beyond the scope of this book, but search online for `Partitioner<TSource>` for details. To understand each of the built-in partitioners and to understand their relative strengths and weaknesses, each partitioning scheme is now briefly explained.

Range Partitioning   The range partitioning scheme breaks an input source data set into equal-sized ranges optimized for the number of threads determined available (best case: equal to the number of cores available). Range partitioning is chosen when the data source is indexible (`IList<T>` and arrays, `T[]`). For indexible sources like these, the length is known without having to enumerate the data source (to determine the count), and the number of elements per partition for parallel execution is simply calculated upfront.

This partitioning scheme offers great parallel efficiency, largely from not needing any synchronization between participating threads. Threads get a range of data assigned to them and can process that data without any interaction (incoming or outgoing) with other threads. The downside of this thread isolation is that other threads cannot help out if one thread gets behind in processing due to uneven utilization; on balance though, this partitioning scheme is efficient.

Chunk Partitioning   Chunk partitioning is used when a data source isn't indexed (an `IEnumerable<T>` where the elements can't be accessed by index and the count property cannot be ascertained without an enumeration of the entire data source).

Microsoft has optimized this partitioning scheme for a wide variety of queries, and although the exact algorithm isn't known, the responsible team's blog postings[9] indicate that that the number of elements per partition is doubled after a certain number of requests and so on. This allows this partitioning scheme to be adaptable from sources with only a few elements to sources with many million elements, keeping each core filled with work, while still balancing their load to ensure the greatest chance of each core finishing close to the same time.

As mentioned previously, this partitioning algorithm can't be as exact as range partitioning, and you should strive for using an indexible collection for your parallel data sources whenever possible.

Hash Partitioning   This partitioning scheme is for queries (containing operators) that need to compare data elements. For example, the following operators compare key hash values when they execute: `Join`, `GroupJoin`, `GroupBy`, `Distinct`, `Except`, `Union`, and `Intersect`. The intention of this partitioning scheme is that elements that share the same key hash-code value will be partitioned into the same thread. The alternative options of partitioning elements would require extensive and complex inter-thread synchronization and data sharing. This partitioning scheme reduces that overhead and enhances parallel performance for queries using these operators.

The downside however is that hash partitioning is complex and has a higher overhead than the partitioning schemes listed so far. However, it is the most efficient and viable option for query operators that need to compare hash codes to do their work, such as `GroupBy` and `Join`.

HASH-CODE DISTRIBUTION CONCERNS WHEN USING HASH PARTITIONING   Stephen Toub from Microsoft's Parallel Framework team made the following note on this subject during a quick review. I couldn't have written this any better, so didn't even try:

"The system makes an assumption that hash codes for elements are equally spread out across all elements, such that the partitions will end up having similar numbers of items, resulting in a load-balanced system. If, however, too many of one hash code exist (such as if the same string appeared in a list of strings a disproportionate number of times, or if a poor hash function was used on a custom type), load balance issues can result. This is the same problem hashtables/dictionaries have, where the speed of access is expected to be O(1), but that can quickly get thrown out of whack if one bucket fills up significantly faster than other buckets."

Striped Partitioning   Striped partitioning is used for standard query operators that process and evaluate from the front of a data source. `SkipWhile` and `TakeWhile` are the operators that use this partitioning scheme. Striped partitioning is only available when the data source is indexible (`IList<T>` and arrays, `T[]`) and assumes that each element needs to be processed almost sequentially in order to avoid launching off a significant amount of work that has to be thrown away at merge time. It achieves this by taking very small ranges at a time, processing these in parallel to gain some optimization, and then merging carefully based on the result of the `while` predicate.

Striped partitioning is a sample of where a specific partitioning scheme can be written to optimize specific operators.

Parallel Execution

Once data is partitioned, it is executed in parallel using the underlying Parallel Framework extensions. Exactly how this occurs is irrelevant for our discussion, although it is safe to say that Microsoft used all of the concurrency APIs, like the Task Parallel Library, Tasks, Work Stealing Scheduler, and the co-ordination data structures that have been discussed online and demonstrated at conferences. I'm sure more information will emerge online over time as to exactly how Microsoft built the parallel versions of the standard query operators. Later in this chapter a custom parallel operator is explained by example, and this offers some insight into how many of the operators might work.

Merging the Parallel Results

After each thread has completed, its results must be merged into the final result sequence (or value). Microsoft has allowed some control over when results are made available, either immediately after a partition is processed or buffering the results until all partitions have completed. This control is provided by using the `WithMergeOptions` extension and choosing a value of `NotBuffered`, `AutoBuffered` (the default), or `FullyBuffered`.

```
source
  .AsParallel()
  .WithMergeOptions(ParallelMergeOptions.FullyBuffered)
```

Some queries (or at least the parts of the query before and up to an ordering operator) cannot honor this setting, like `Reverse` and `OrderBy`, which need the entire result set buffered in order to carry out their tasks.

Although it might seem at first glance that Microsoft should have simply made all LINQ queries just execute in parallel, the issues of data ordering, exception handling, and race conditions (all of the parallelism blockers described earlier) make the explicit decision to parallelize important for the developer to consider. The next section explores another potential pitfall of simply making all queries parallel—not enough work being carried out.

It's Not as Simple as Just Adding AsParallel

To invoke the parallel variations of the standard query operators, it can be as simple as adding an `AsParallel` extension to any `IEnumerable<T>` source collection, as shown in the following example:

```
var data =
    new int[] { 0, 1, 2, 3, 4, 5, 6, 7, 8, 9, 10 };

// sequential
var q = from i in data
        select i;

// un-ordered parallel
var q1 = from i in data.AsParallel()
        select i;
```

The addition of the `.AsParallel()` in the query `q1` invokes the parallel version of the LINQ standard query operators. If everything is working correctly, the queries should yield the same result. Here is the console output from iterating each query:

```
Sequential (q)
0 1 2 3 4 5 6 7 8 9 10

Un-ordered Parallel (q1)
0 6 1 7 2 8 3 9 4 10 5
```

Surprised? The actual order is indeterminate, and every execution of query `q1` could yield a different result (based on the partitioning scheme used and the number of cores available). Our query hasn't specified that order is important, and although the normal standard query operators retain data order unless told otherwise (more by luck than convention—it's just the way they were coded), the parallel variations do not guarantee order retention unless forced. This is to maximize parallel performance; however, the point is that improving query performance using Parallel LINQ isn't as simple as running through your code adding `AsParallel` to every query, as this may introduce unintended result changes.

Making Order Out of Chaos—AsOrdered and Sorting

Is data ordering important? If a query is simply summing a value or processing each element, then maybe order isn't important. In these cases the parallel runtime should be left alone to do its work unhindered. However, if order is in fact important during or for the final result, then control should be invoked by one of the following means:

- Add an `orderby` clause (as seen in q2 below) to force an order.
- Add an `AsOrdered` extension to tell the parallel runtime to leave the order as it is in the original source (as seen in q3 that follows).

```
// ordered parallel using sort
var q2 = from i in data.AsParallel()
         orderby i
         select i;


// ordered parallel using .AsOrdered() extension
// meaning, keep the order as it was in the source
var q3 = from i in data.AsParallel().AsOrdered()
         select i;
```

The result of both ordering schemes are the same (in this case, only because the source collection was already in the desired order) and identical to the sequential version of the query as seen in query q previously:

```
Ordered Parallel (q2)
0 1 2 3 4 5 6 7 8 9 10

.AsOrdered Parallel (q3)
0 1 2 3 4 5 6 7 8 9 10
```

These are very simple queries, and writing them for parallel execution doesn't offer great customer performance gains; however, they do allow us to understand the impact of ordering. The following data shows the length of time taken to run 100,000 iterations on my dual core laptop, and these times are only meant to be read as relative to each other—the actual time is less important in this example.

```
q=112ms - Sequential
q1=3417ms - .AsParallel()
q2=5891ms - .AsParallel() with orderby clause
q3=4087ms - .AsParallel().AsOrdered()extension
```

COMPARING Q2 AND Q3 The implementation of q2 and q3 are different. The q2 query carries out explicit sorting, whereas q3 simply honors the original source sequence ordering; this is example-specific because this example uses a pre-sorted source.

Another difference is that the C# compiler can omit outputting the `Select` call because it has no implementation, and the `OrderBy` statement is returning the same variable. However the q3 implementation has to perform the `AsOrdered` and the `Select` statement. Even a small implementation in the `Select` clause would force both q2 and q3 to perform the `Select` function.

As you can tell, parallelizing this query with only 11 elements and no `where` clause or significant element `select` processing was detrimental to performance by many times. Even increasing the number to 1,000 elements doesn't demonstrate any improvement.

DON'T PARALLELIZE VERY SIMPLE QUERIES Microsoft's Parallel LINQ engine does examine queries and will utilize a sequential algorithm if it thinks performance of the parallel algorithms will be detrimental to performance based on the query shape (operators used). However, as you saw in our simple example, you need to measure and profile your own code to make sure that your query is a candidate for parallelization. The general rule is to consider parallelization only when the function operating on each element (the `where` and `select` clause, or multiple `let` clauses) has at least a few statements with measurable impact. Resist the temptation to run through all of your code and add an `AsParallel` to every LINQ query—you will seriously destabilize your code and likely harm performance. This is one reason why Microsoft didn't just make parallelization automatic for all LINQ to Object queries (some others being ordering, exception handling, and avoiding race conditions if the query makes mutations to the data or has other side effects).

Performance improvement is most profound as query complexity and element count increases, especially in the actions that occur on each collection element. The previous example was very contrived and was introduced to demonstrate the indeterminate ordering and performance effects that just adding an `AsParallel` to a query can introduce. Listing 9-3 demonstrates how to make a simple query parallel; in this case, a function simply adds a thread sleep for 10ms for each element, but that function could carry out any type of processing per element.

Listing 9-3 Parallelizing a simple query that does "actual" work on each element

```
var data =
    new int[] { 0, 1, 2, 3, 4, 5, 6, 7, 8, 9, 10 };

// MySlowFunction(i) simply adds 10ms Sleep on
// the current thread, and returns the 'i' value

// sequential
var q = from i in data
        select MySlowFunction(i);

// un-ordered parallel
var q1 = from i in data.AsParallel()
         select MySlowFunction(i);

// ordered parallel using .orderby
var q2 = from i in data.AsParallel()
         orderby i
         select MySlowFunction(i);

// ordered parallel using .AsOrdered()
var q3 = from i in data.AsParallel().AsOrdered()
         select MySlowFunction(i);

...


public int MySlowFunction(int i)
{
    System.Threading.Thread.Sleep(10);
    return i;
}
```

The execution time of 100,000 times for each of these queries demonstrates the performance improvement on a dual-core computer in the Beta version of .NET 4, shown in Table 9-1.

Table 9-1 Query Execution Times for the Queries Shown in Listing 9-3

Query	Execution Time (100,000 loops, single dual-core processor)	Output
Sequential (q)	11,047ms	0 1 2 3 4 5 6 7 8 9 10
Parallel .AsParallel() (q1)	6,069ms	6 7 8 9 10 0 1 2 3 4 5
Parallel with orderby (q2)	6,084ms (This small difference is brought about by the data already being ordered and it being such a small set. The OrderBy extension method is expensive on large data sets and should be avoided where possible for performance-sensitive problems).	0 1 2 3 4 5 6 7 8 9 10
Parallel .AsOrdered() (q3)	6,030ms (This result is counter-intuitive because of the fake MySlowFunction and simplistic example. Forcing order will impact performance on larger data sets and complex queries.)	0 1 2 3 4 5 6 7 8 9 10

The parallel queries did operate faster, as expected. In this case, on a dual-core process, the results were generally slightly less than double. There is overhead in parallelizing, and a key advantage of this code is that with nothing more than the addition of an AsParallel extension to the sequential query, it would likely run close to (but slightly less than) four times faster on a quad-core and eight times on an eight-core processor, and so on, depending on how loaded the CPU is at runtime.

The AsParallel and AsSequential Operators

The `AsParallel` operator attached to the source of a LINQ query turns a sequential query into a parallel query. (Parallel means the overload operator extending `ParallelQuery<T>` is called rather than the overload extending `IEnumerable<T>`.) The `AsSequential` operator on the other hand, returns the query from that point forward to calling the sequential operators (the `IEnumerable<T>` overload rather than the `ParallelQuery<T>`). Put simply, these extension methods allow you to opt-in and opt-out of using the Parallel LINQ extensions from within a query expression itself.

To maximize the efficiency of LINQ queries, it is sometimes necessary for the developer to take control over what parts of a query are parallel and which parts aren't. Some operators exclude the query from seeing any parallel performance improvement, and in order to allow Parallel LINQ to operate on other parts of a query, some developer intervention is required.

When to Use the AsSequential Operator

The ability to control what parts of a query are sequential and what parts are executed parallel allows you to isolate parts of a query that run slower when executing concurrently. This is often the case when queries are composed (one query used as the source of another). When composing queries in this way, it can be useful to force one part to be sequential while another is parallel. A good strategy is to carefully consider which parts of a query benefit from parallelization, and isolate the sequential portion of any query at the end by inserting it after an `AsSequential` operator.

Remembering back to the early sections of this chapter where the Parallel LINQ process was described, the initial step in an analysis of the LINQ query is to determine if parallelization is a good fit. This process entails looking at the operators called in a query, and if certain operators are called (particularly on non-indexed collection types), then those queries are executed sequentially. You can use the `AsSequential` operator to isolate those operators and achieve a greater use of parallelization in the areas that benefit.

The exact rules about when Parallel LINQ will decide to execute a query as sequential (even though you specified an `AsParallel`) is likely to change as Microsoft adds more capabilities into their analysis and operators in the future. At the time of writing, the easiest way to see this occur is to use the `Take` operator on an `IEnumerable<T>` sequence (in our case, the anonymous projected result from a query). The following query would execute as sequential if source was an unindexed collection:

```
var q = source.AsParallel().Take(5);
```

To demonstrate this phenomenon, consider the following query, which should run parallel given it has an `AsParallel` extension. However, Listing 9-4 shows a query that due to the `Take` operator, execution will be carried out sequentially and no improvement in execution speed from the sequential version occurs (both around 30 seconds).

Listing 9-4   This query will operate sequentially without isolating the **Take** operator in this case—see Listing 9-5 for how to fix this situation

```
var lines1 = File.ReadLines(Path.Combine(
    Environment.CurrentDirectory, "Data/AllCountries.txt"));

var q1 = (from line in lines1.AsParallel()
          let fields = line.Split(new char[] { '\t' })
          where fields[countryColumn].StartsWith("A")
          orderby fields[elevationColumn] ?? "" descending
          select new
          {
              name = fields[nameColumn] ?? "",
              elevation = fields[elevationColumn] ?? "",
              country = fields[countryColumn]
          })
          .Take(5);
```

For the main part of the query in Listing 9-4 to execute as parallel, it is necessary to isolate the `Take` operator in the query by preceding it with an `AsSequential` operator. This increases the performance of this query substantially, dropping over seven seconds from the sequential time. (On a dual-core machine, these times are meant to be indicative.) The optimized version of this query is shown in Listing 9-5.

Listing 9-5   Isolating the **Take** operator with **AsSequential** shows an improvement over the sequential query

```
var lines2 = File.ReadLines(Path.Combine(
    Environment.CurrentDirectory, "Data/AllCountries.txt"));

var q2 = (from line in lines2.AsParallel()
          let fields = line.Split(new char[] { '\t' })
          where fields[countryColumn].StartsWith("A")
          orderby fields[elevationColumn] ?? "" descending
          select new
```

```
    {
        name = fields[nameColumn] ?? "",
        elevation = fields[elevationColumn] ?? "",
        country = fields[countryColumn]
    })
    .AsSequential()
    .Take(5);
```

The indicative performance of each of these queries can be measured as

```
q = 29.1 seconds    (Sequential)
q1 (Listing 9-4) = 30.7 seconds
q2 (Listing 9-5) = 23.3 seconds
```

This short example demonstrates the need to be diligent about understanding what impact some operators have on the ability to just add an `AsParallel` to a query. Developers must be diligent about profiling and measuring query performance when invoking the parallel operators.

Two-Source Operators and AsParallel

There are a number of operators in LINQ that take two data sources:

- Concat
- Except
- GroupJoin
- Intersect
- Join
- SequenceEqual
- Union
- Zip

When parallelizing queries that use any of these binary operators, both data sources must be marked with the `AsParallel` operator (and optionally with `AsOrdered`) to avoid a runtime exception being raised. Early versions of the Parallel LINQ extensions didn't enforce this dual opt-in process, and it was difficult to specifically control the ordering semantics of those queries. Forcing the developer to explicitly control the ordering semantics bridges this gap and makes queries predictable.

Failing to specify the second data source as parallel causes an obsolete warning during compilation with instructions on how to resolve the issue.

Microsoft decided to make this condition obsolete by marking the overload taking the second data source of IEnumerable<T> with an [Obsolete] attribute and by throwing a System.NotSupportedException when called; the method signatures are shown in Listing 9-6. This messaging is intended to help the developers understand what they need to do in order to parallelize these operators.

Listing 9-6 Calling binary operators with Parallel LINQ requires that both sources are **ParallelQuery<T>** types

```
[Obsolete("...")]
public static ParallelQuery<TSource> Concat<TSource>(
    this ParallelQuery<TSource> first,
    IEnumerable<TSource> second);

public static ParallelQuery<TSource> Concat<TSource>(
    this ParallelQuery<TSource> first,
    ParallelQuery<TSource> second);
```

Listing 9-7 demonstrates how to correctly call a binary operator when using ParallelQuery collections as the two input sources and shows the error message displayed when both sources aren't of ParallelQuery type.

Listing 9-7 Using binary operators with Parallel LINQ

```
var source1 = new int[] { 1,2,3,4,5 };
var source2 = new int[] { 6,7,8,9,10 };

// ERROR - Obsolete warning
// "The second data source of a binary operator must be
// of type System.Linq.ParallelQuery<T> rather than
// System.Collections.Generic.IEnumerable<T>.
// To fix this problem, use the AsParallel() extension
// method to convert the right data source to
// System.Linq.ParallelQuery<T>."
var q = source1.AsParallel().Concat(source2);

// the following queries work fine.
// remember to force ordering where appropriate.
var q1 = source1.AsParallel()
        .Concat(source2.AsParallel());

var q2 = source1.AsParallel().AsOrdered()
        .Concat(source2.AsParallel());
```

```
var q3 = source1.AsParallel().AsOrdered()
         .Concat(source2.AsParallel().AsOrdered());
```

Writing Parallel LINQ Operators

Convention would dictate that whenever a sequential LINQ operator is written, a parallel operator should be considered to support the Parallel LINQ programming pattern users will come to expect based on the support of the other standard query operators (not a definite requirement, but should be considered). Not all operators will significantly benefit from parallelization, and without an understanding of a specific operator, it's hard to capture explicit guidance in this area. The following types of operators make exceptionally good candidates for parallelization:

- Order-independent operators that iterate an entire source collection, for example, `Where`.
- Mathematical aggregate functions such as `Sum`.
- Operators that can yield partial results before the entire source collection has been processed by that operator (allowing the next operator to begin before all data is furnished by the previous operator).

Other operator types could still benefit from parallel implementations, but the overhead is high, and the linear scaling of performance versus number of CPU cores will reduce.

Parallel Operator Strategy

Implementing parallel operators in a raw form can be challenging. At the lowest level, you can use the Task Parallel Library as the basis for underlying algorithms, but you should exhaust all other avenues for operator implementation first. Here is some general guidance when attempting to build a parallel extension method operator:

- Try and compose your operator using the current Parallel LINQ operators.
- Use the aggregate extension method operator whenever possible (demonstrated shortly).

- Build the operator using the Task Parallel Library looping constructs `System.Threading.Parallel.For` and `System.Threading.Parallel.ForEach`.
- This should be rarely necessary—build your operator using the Task Parallel Library `Task` class directly.

Before going down any of these paths, however, you should optimize the sequential algorithm as much as possible. The sequential algorithm will form the basis for the parallel implementation.

To demonstrate the process for writing a new parallel operator, a statistical extension method for calculating the variance and the standard deviation of an integer data source are shown. Parallel queries are especially suited for queries over large numeric data sets, and aggregating statistical values is a common business requirement for scientific and financial software.

Building a Parallel Aggregate Operator—Sample Standard Deviation

To demonstrate making a parallel operator, we will implement a statistical function for standard deviation, which is a measure of variance for a set of data. In order to build this operator, you follow the general development steps:

1. Create and test a sequential algorithm.
2. Optimize the sequential algorithm as much as possible.
3. Create and test the parallel algorithm.
4. Add error-handling condition guard code. (This can be done at any stage.)

Creating the Sequential Algorithm

Like many computing problems nowadays, our first port of call is to search the Internet for algorithms and reference material. A quick search of Wikipedia shows that variance and standard deviation can be calculated using the following formulas:

```
Sample Standard Deviation = Square root ( Sample Variance)

Unbiased Estimate of Sample Variance = (Sum (x - mean(x))^2) / (n - 1)
```

> **NOTE** This isn't a statistics guide; I'm using the sample variance and standard deviation formula [the difference being the division of n or (n-1)]. I chose the sample variance because I get to demonstrate how to handle more error conditions later. If you use this code, check whether your situation needs the population equations or the sample equations for variance and standard deviation — Wikipedia has pages of discussion on this topic!

Focusing on building the variance operator first allows most of the mathematics to be isolated to a single function (standard deviation is simply the square-root of this value). This strategy simplifies the StandardDeviation operator to a Math.Sqrt() function on the result of the Variance function.

The most basic sequential variance operator function to start with, built using the aggregate standard query operator, is shown in Listing 9-8.

Listing 9-8 Simple sequential variance calculation

```
// sequential variance calculation
public static double Variance1(
    this IEnumerable<int> source)
{
    // traditional aggregate
    double mean = source.Average();

    return source.Aggregate(
        (double)0.0,
        (subtotal, item) =>
            subtotal + Math.Pow((item - mean), 2),
        (totalSum) => totalSum / (source.Count() - 1)
    );
}
```

After testing the operator shown in Listing 9-8 through unit tests to ensure proper mathematical results, optimizing performance can begin. A simple execution time profile of the code was undertaken by measuring the time taken to calculate the variance on a data set size of 100,000 elements 1,000 times. The results of this can be seen in Table 9-2. I also tested the data source being an indexed array and an IEnumerable<T> to isolate if there were any performance issues with both types of input

Table 9-2   Performance Refactoring on Sequential Variance Operators. Source Was an Array or an IEnumerable of 100,000 Integers—the Variance Was Calculated 1,000 Times Each Test

Algorithm	Array[int]	IEnumerable<int>
Variance1 (Listing 9-8)	17,780ms	19,564ms
Variance2 (Listing 9-9)	4,211ms	5,774ms
Variance (Listing 9-10)	2,635ms	3,169ms

data source. The results were 17 to 20 seconds, and with this baseline, optimization and refactoring can begin.

Optimize the Sequential Algorithm

The `Variance` operator functionally works and follows the most basic equation implementation possible. However, the `Math.Pow()` method is extremely expensive, as we are just squaring a single value. An easy refactoring is to use simple multiplication instead, and the resulting performance increase is dramatic (approximately four times, as shown in Table 9-2). Listing 9-9 shows the refactoring required making this optimization.

Listing 9-9   First optimization of the sequential operator—remove the **Math.Pow** function

```
public static double Variance2(
    this IEnumerable<int> source)
{
    // optimization 1 - removing the expensive Math.Pow call
    double mean = source.Average();
    return source.Aggregate(
        (double)0.0,
        (subtotal, item) => subtotal +
            ((double)item - mean) * ((double)item - mean),
        (totalSum) => totalSum / (source.Count() - 1)
    );
}
```

It should always be a goal to minimize the enumerations of the source collection whenever possible. In our current incarnation of the `Variance` operator, there are two loops through the collection. The first in the aggregate function and the second in the call to `Count` in the final aggregation argument. If the source collection is indexed, then this call might be avoided, but if it isn't, the `Count` extension method has no choice but to iterate the entire source and count as it goes. We can do better.

The `Aggregate` operator can use any type as a seed. If we use an array as that type (`double[]`), we can store multiple values in each element loop. In this case, we can keep the running total of elements (count), the running sum of the element values (sum), and also the sum of the squares (sum of squares). This enables us to do a single pass through the values and have all the required data to calculate the variance value in the final Selector function of the `Aggregate` query operator.

Listing 9-10 shows the final refactoring, although a little more complex than its predecessors, it operates much faster as seen in Table 9-2.

Listing 9-10 Optimized sequential **Variance** operator code, the basis of our parallel implementation

```
public static double Variance(
    this IEnumerable<int> source)
{
    // optimization 2 - removing count and mean calcs
    return source.Aggregate(

        // seed - array of three doubles
        new double[3] { 0.0, 0.0, 0.0 },

        // item aggregation function, run for each element
        (subtotal, item) =>
        {
            subtotal[0]++; // count
            subtotal[1] += item; // sum
            // sum of squares
            subtotal[2] += (double)item * (double)item;
            return subtotal;
        },
```

```
    // result selector function
    // (finesses the final sum into the variance)
    // mean = sum / count
    // variance = (sum_sqr - sum * mean) / (n - 1)
    result =>
        (result[2] - (result[1] * (result[1] / result[0])))
            / (result[0] - 1)
    );
}
```

As Table 9.2 shows, the performance benefits gained by optimizing the sequential algorithm are substantial—more substantial than relying on parallel optimizations alone.

Now that the Variance operator has been written, the StandardDeviation operator simply builds upon the result as shown in Listing 9-11. This example also demonstrates the generally accepted pattern of defining an overload that takes a value Selector function—this follows the pattern set forth by the supplied aggregation standard query operators and is recommended.

Listing 9-11 Sequential implementation of the **StandardDeviation** operator

```
public static double StandardDeviation(
    this IEnumerable<int> source)
{
    return Math.Sqrt(source.Variance());
}


public static double StandardDeviation<T>(
    this IEnumerable<T> source,
    Func<T, int> selector)
{
    return StandardDeviation(
        Enumerable.Select(source, selector));
}
```

Create and Test the Parallel Operator

It is a straightforward adaption from the sequential code that is built using the `Aggregate` standard query operator to derive the parallel operator using the Parallel LINQ `Aggregate` standard query operator. A Parallel LINQ operator is an extension method of the `ParallelQuery<T>` type, rather than the `IEnumerable<T>` type.

The Parallel `Aggregate` standard query operator has an extra argument not present on its sequential counterpart. You read earlier that data is partitioned and acted upon by different threads of execution during parallel query execution. This necessitates that each thread's result must be merged with the other threads' results in order for the aggregation to be mathematically sound. We need to supply this Combine Accumulator function (for each thread result), in addition to the Update Accumulator function (each element).

Listing 9-12 shows the standard query operators with no error guards or handling (we get to that in a moment). If you compare it to the optimized sequential operator in Listing 9-10, you can see the subtle changes. We continue to use our single pass aggregation function, but we update it to work in a concurrent world. The changes made were as follows:

- `IEnumerable<T>` was replaced by `ParallelQuery<T>` for this extension method. Any query that operates over a `source.AsParallel` will be routed to this extension method overload rather than the sequential overload.
- The seed array is created using a factory function; this allows each partition to create (by calling this function) and operate on its own seed array in isolation, avoiding any contention between threads during the aggregation process.
- The Combine Accumulator function can just add (sum each element with the same element by index position) the left and right side arrays.

Listing 9-12   The parallel **Variance** and **StandardDeviation** extension methods

```
public static double Variance(
    this ParallelQuery<int> source)
{
    /* based upon the blog posting by Igor Ostrovsky at -
     * http://blogs.msdn.com/pfxteam/archive/2008/06/05/8576194.aspx
     * which demonstrates how to use the factory functions in an
```

```
     * Aggregate function for efficiency
     */

  return source.Aggregate(

      // seed - array of three doubles constructed
      // using factory function, initialized to 0
      () => new double[3] { 0.0, 0.0, 0.0 },

      // item aggregation function, run for each element
      (subtotal, item) =>
      {
          subtotal[0]++; // count
          subtotal[1] += item; // sum

          // sum of squares
          subtotal[2] += (double)item * (double)item;
          return subtotal;
      },

      // combine function,
      // run on completion of each "thread"
      (total, thisThread) =>
      {
          total[0] += thisThread[0];
          total[1] += thisThread[1];
          total[2] += thisThread[2];
          return total;
      },

      // result selector function
      // finesses the final sum into the variance
      // mean = sum / count
      // variance = (sum_sqr - sum * mean) / (n - 1)
      (result) =>
          (result[2] - (result[1] * (result[1] / result[0])))
              / (result[0] - 1)
  );
}


public static double StandardDeviation(
    this ParallelQuery<int> source)
{
    return Math.Sqrt(source.Variance());
```

```
}

public static double StandardDeviation<T>(
    this ParallelQuery<T> source,
    Func<T, int> selector)
{
    return StandardDeviation(
        ParallelEnumerable.Select(source, selector));
}
```

Table 9-3 documents the simple profiling carried out over the sequential and parallel algorithms, for both a simple array and an IEnumerable<T>. These numbers will change depending on your machine—this test was carried out on a dual-core processor. You will notice that the parallel IEnumerable<T> algorithm was actually slightly slower than its sequential counterpart (even when forced parallel using the WithExecutionMode extension). There is not enough work being done here to counteract the cost of accessing the enumerable (that is, locking it, retrieving elements from it, releasing the lock, processing those elements, and going back for more).

This test was carried out on the Beta 2 version of the .NET 4 framework, and I'm interested to see how final performance tuning of the Parallel LINQ algorithms makes this number improve by release time. You can rerun these numbers at any time by downloading the sample code from the HookedOnLINQ.com website (http://www.hookedonlinq.com/LINQBookSamples.ashx).

Table 9-3 Performance Refactoring on Sequential **StandardDeviation** Operators. Source Was an Array or an IEnumerable of 100,000 Integers—the Standard Deviation Was Calculated 1,000 Times Each Test.

Algorithm	Array[int]	IEnumerable<int>
Sequential – StandardDeviation (Listings 9-10 and 9-11)	2,669ms	3,146ms
Parallel – StandardDeviation (Listing 9-12)	1,469ms (44% faster)	3,222ms

Adding Error Handling

Having written our operators, handling input and specific error cases need to be introduced. The following input source conditions need to be considered, tested, and handled accordingly:

- The source argument is null—throw an `ArgumentNullException` for the source argument.
- The source argument is an empty array—return zero.
- The source argument contains only one element—return zero.

Choosing to return zero for an empty array and an array with a single element is very specific to this operator and my particular specification. Generally, an `InvalidOperationException` is thrown, but for a statistical measure of variance, I decided to avoid an exception in this case. Microsoft Excel returns a `#DIV/0!` error for a single element sample standard deviation calculation, which I find unfriendly, albeit arguably more correct.

The null source error is easily handled with an initial check coming into the variance extension method, as we saw extensively in Chapter 7, "Extending LINQ to Objects." The error check is accomplished by adding the following code:

```
if (source == null)
    throw new ArgumentNullException("source");
```

Although the single check before the initial variance calculation for a null source is acceptable (being unavoidable), the check for zero or a single element in the source requires some thought. Adding a check before the aggregation function, similar to the following example, might cause an entire enumeration of a source array if that source is not an indexed collection, but an `IEnumerable<T>`:

```
if (source.Any() == false)
    throw new InvalidOperationException("No elements")
```

When we build parallel operators, we are doing so to improve performance, and looping over data sources should be limited to as few times as possible (one time ideally). Our algorithm using the `Aggregate` operator offers us an ideal solution. The final Selector function has access to the cumulative count determined in the aggregation loop. We can use a ternary operator to check for zero or one element at that time and return a value of zero in that case. We have avoided an extra loop and have catered to the two conditions we want to isolate with a single conditional check. That final Selector function looks like this:

```
result => result[0] > 1 ?
    (result[2] - (result[1] * (result[1] / result[0])))
        / (result[0] - 1) : 0.0
```

This code is functionally equivalent to the following `if` conditional statement:

```
if (result[0] > 1) {
    v =
      result[2] - (result[1] * (result[1] / result[0])))
      / (result[0] - 1)
}
else {
    v = 0.0;
}


return v;
```

Listing 9-13 shows the final `StandardDeviation` and `Variance` operators, including the accepted error handling code. The changes are minor (indicated in bold); an additional check for a null source and the final Selector function having logic to handle no source elements.

Listing 9-13 Final parallel **StandardDeviation** and **Variance** operators including error handling code

```
// parallel Variance aggregate extension method
// based on the optimized sequential algorithm
public static double Variance(
    this ParallelQuery<int> source)
{
    /* based upon the blog posting by Igor Ostrovsky at -
     * http://blogs.msdn.com/pfxteam/archive/2008/06/05/8576194.aspx
     * which demonstrates how to use the factory functions in an
     * Aggregate function for efficiency.
     */

    // check for invalid source conditions
    if (source == null)
        throw new ArgumentNullException("source");
```

```
    return source.Aggregate(

        // seed - array of three doubles constructed
        // using factory function, initialized to 0
        () => new double[3] { 0.0, 0.0, 0.0 },

        // item aggregation function, run for each element
        (subtotal, item) =>
        {
            subtotal[0]++; // count
            subtotal[1] += item; // sum
            // sum of squares
            subtotal[2] += (double)item * (double)item;
            return subtotal;
        },

        // combine function,
        // run on completion of each "thread"
        (total, thisThread) =>
        {
            total[0] += thisThread[0];
            total[1] += thisThread[1];
            total[2] += thisThread[2];
            return total;
        },

        // result selector function
        // finesses the final sum into the variance
        // mean = sum / count
        // variance = (sum_sqr - sum * mean) / (n - 1)

        // Sources with zero or one element return a value of 0
        (result) => (result[0] > 1) ?
            (result[2] - (result[1] * (result[1] / result[0])))
                / (result[0] - 1) : 0.0
    );
}


public static double StandardDeviation(
    this ParallelQuery<int> source)
{
    return Math.Sqrt(source.Variance());
}
```

```
public static double StandardDeviation<T>(
    this ParallelQuery<T> source,
    Func<T, int> selector)
{
    return StandardDeviation(
        ParallelEnumerable.Select(source, selector));
}
```

Summary

This chapter explained what you can expect from and how to code LINQ queries that support multi-core processors and multiple CPU machines. This has always been possible, but the complexity caused difficult-to-debug programs and hard-to-find bugs. Parallel LINQ makes coding queries that support parallelism both easier and more predictable.

Writing your own parallel operators is no more difficult than writing a good sequential operator (when building on top of existing operators), and when a programming task is going to operate on large collection sizes of data, an investment in time is worth making.

The final take-away and warning (a pattern throughout this chapter) is that an improvement in performance by using Parallel LINQ in a query should not be taken for granted. Profiling and comparing the results is always necessary in order to ensure any significant performance improvement is actually being achieved.

References

1. Callahan, David. "Paradigm Shift—Design Considerations for Parallel Programming," *MSDN Magazine:* October 2008, http://msdn.microsoft.com/en-us/magazine/cc872852.aspx.

2. http://en.wikipedia.org/wiki/Instructions_per_second.

3. Gelsinger, Patrick P., Paolo A. Gargini, Gerhard H. Parker, and Albert Y.C. Yu. "Microprocessors, Circa 2000" *IEEE Spectrum:* October 1989, http://ieeexplore.ieee.org/xpl/freeabs_all.jsp?arnumber=40684 http://mprc.pku.edu.cn/courses/architecture/autumn2007/mooreslaw-1989.pdf

4. Whitepaper: "Intel Multi-Core Processor Architecture Development Backgrounder," http://cache-www.intel.com/cd/00/00/20/57/205707_205707.pdf.

5. http://en.wikipedia.org/wiki/2003_North_America_blackout.

6. http://en.wikipedia.org/wiki/Race_condition.

7. Joe Duffy blog posting, "The CLR Commits the Whole Stack," http://www.bluebytesoftware.com/blog/2007/03/10/TheCLRCommitsTheWholeStack.aspx.

8. http://en.wikipedia.org/wiki/Amdahl's_law.

9. http://blogs.msdn.com/pfxteam/.

GLOSSARY

Chapter 1

ADO.Net   A Microsoft data-access programming interface technology shipped as part of the Microsoft .NET base class libraries. See http://en.wikipedia.org/wiki/ADO.NET for more details.

C#   Pronounced "cee sharp," C# is a managed programming language released as part of Microsoft's .NET Framework. C# is an object-oriented language and draws inspiration from C++, Delphi, and Java. See http://en.wikipedia.org/wiki/C_Sharp_(programming_language) for more details.

Delegate   Can be thought of as a typed-safe reference to a method. See http://en.wikipedia.org/wiki/Delegate_(.NET) for more details.

Domain Specific Language (DSL)   A domain-specific language is a programming language specific to an individual problem domain. Conversely, C# and VB.NET are general programming languages that can solve a range of programming tasks. Usually DSLs focus specifically on a single technique or, in this particular usage, a particular data query language. See http://en.wikipedia.org/wiki/Domain-specific_language for more details.

Microsoft .NET Framework   A managed runtime environment for Windows (Linux flavors via the Mono framework). Consists of a runtime environment for executing applications, a set of programming languages to write those applications, and a set of base-class libraries. See http://en.wikipedia.org/wiki/.NET_Framework for more details.

Microsoft SQL Server   Commonly just referred to as SQL Server, Microsoft SQL Server is a relational database system product by Microsoft. It is programmed in its own query language called Transact Structured Query Language (T-SQL). See http://en.wikipedia.org/wiki/Microsoft_SQL_Server for more details.

Transact SQL (T-SQL)   Microsoft SQL Server's built-in query language based on ANSI SQL. See http://en.wikipedia.org/wiki/Transact-SQL for more details.

Visual Basic.Net   Often referred to as VB.NET, Visual Basic.NET is an object-oriented managed language for the Microsoft .NET Framework. See http://en.wikipedia.org/wiki/VB.Net for more information.

XPath   XML Path Language is a specific domain language for selecting and navigating segments of an XML document. See http://en.wikipedia.org/wiki/XPath for more details.

XQuery   XQuery is a language designed for querying XML-based data. See http://en.wikipedia.org/wiki/XQuery for more details.

Chapter 2

Intellisense   Visual Studio has a set of features that show dynamic help tips as you type code. These tips take many forms based on the code you are editing at that time. One example is that after typing the name of an instance variable followed by a period character (.), Visual Studio will pop up a small tip balloon showing what fields, properties, or method are available on the object being typed at that time.

Chapter 4

Database Management System (DBMS)   A database management system is a (set) of software program(s) that allow the storage and retrieval of data. Although it is not a strict requirement, most DBMS systems nowadays are relational in storage structure. Some common examples of DBMSs are Microsoft's SQL Server, Sun's MySQL, and Oracle's self-named product. See http://en.wikipedia.org/wiki/Dbms for more information.

Normalization   When referring to database design, normalization aims to minimize duplicated data by spreading it across a higher number of database tables and creating relationships (accessed by joins) between these tables. Structuring a database in this way decreases inconsistencies and safeguards against some structural and logical errors. See http://en.wikipedia.org/wiki/Database_normalization for more information.

Inner join   An inner join is a join between two tables in which each table has a matching record based on a specified key value. Any record that doesn't have a matching key value as specified by the join will be omitted from the result. See http://en.wikipedia.org/wiki/Inner_join#Inner_join for more information.

Outer join   An outer join is a join between two tables in which it is not necessary that each table have a matching record based on a specific key value. More commonly, one side (left or right) is allowed to have a nonmatching record (null for instance), and this record will still be returned. See http://en.wikipedia.org/wiki/Inner_join#Outer_joins for more information.

Chapter 8

Component Object Model (COM)   COM is a binary, language neutral, interprocess communication interface standard that allows software components to communicate with each other. Many of Microsoft's software components expose a COM interface to allow other software programs to automate that software's usage (Microsoft Excel, for instance). See http://en.wikipedia.org/wiki/Component_Object_Model for more details.

COM-Interop

COM-Interop is the general name of the technology that allows .NET CLR programs to talk to COM interfaces and vice versa. See http://en.wikipedia.org/wiki/COM_Interop for more details.

INDEX

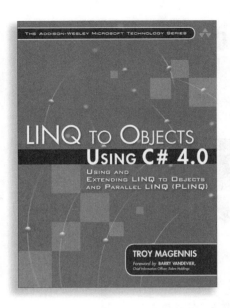

 **FREE Online Edition**

Your purchase of *LINQ to Objects Using C# 4.0* includes access to a free online edition for 45 days through the Safari Books Online subscription service. Nearly every Addison-Wesley Professional book is available online through Safari Books Online, along with more than 5,000 other technical books and videos from publishers such as Cisco Press, Exam Cram, IBM Press, O'Reilly, Prentice Hall, Que, and Sams.

SAFARI BOOKS ONLINE allows you to search for a specific answer, cut and paste code, download chapters, and stay current with emerging technologies.

Activate your FREE Online Edition at www.informit.com/safarifree

> **STEP 1:** Enter the coupon code: BDHJPXA.

> **STEP 2:** New Safari users, complete the brief registration form.
> Safari subscribers, just log in.

If you have difficulty registering on Safari or accessing the online edition, please e-mail customer-service@safaribooksonline.com